Historians and Their Craft:
A Study of the Presidential Addresses
of the American Historical Association,
1884--1945

BY

HERMAN AUSUBEL, Ph.D.

NEW YORK

RUSSELL & RUSSELL · INC

1965

STUDIES IN HISTORY, ECONOMICS AND PUBLIC LAW

Edited by the
FACULTY OF POLITICAL SCIENCE
OF COLUMBIA UNIVERSITY

Printed in the United States of America

To My Wife

ACKNOWLEDGMENTS

It is a pleasure to record my very considerable indebtedness to Professor R. L. Schuyler, of Columbia University, whose encouragement, counsel, and friendship I shall not soon forget. I also owe much to the criticisms and suggestions of Professors Dumas Malone, Richard B. Morris, and Samuel J. Hurwitz. It seems hardly necessary to add that I alone am responsible for any errors of fact, judgment, or interpretation that occur in the volume.

HERMAN AUSUBEL

Columbia University,
December, 1948

TABLE OF CONTENTS

ERRATA

Page 32, line 9—illusions should read allusions.

Page 33, line 26—Hoar may had should read may have had.

Page 44, line 17—failed more then should read failed more than.

Page 78, line 5—anecedotes should read anecdotes.

Page 121, 4th line from bottom—*The Origin of the Species* should read the *Origin of Species.*

Page 194, line 10—*Origin of the Species* should be *Origin of Species.*

Page 206, 3rd line from bottom—meditator should be mediator.

Page 235, line 11—impermanance should be impermanence.

Page 309, line 7ff—study... have been... for their... for their should be study... has been... for its... for its...,

Page 329, line 2—scholorship should be scholarship.

Page 365, Schlesinge should be Schlesinger.

Page 372—Maitland, Frederick should be Maitland, Frederic.

INTRODUCTION

ALMOST every year since the American Historical Association was founded in 1884, it has held an annual session; and at this session the president of the Association, Clio's leading American spokesman for the year, has had to meet the one inexorable demand imposed by an otherwise undemanding office. He has had to deliver a presidential message.

Free to deal with any subject whatsoever, the men and the one woman who headed the Association in its first sixty or so years preferred nevertheless to talk shop. Some of them presented the results of their recent researches. Others ventured to discuss what the manner and matter of history should be. By 1910, at the twenty-sixth annual meeting of the Association, Frederick Jackson Turner could declare that it had become something of a tradition for a president to incorporate in his message a statement of his views on the nature of history. And by 1917 Worthington C. Ford could confess that he found it difficult to make a fresh contribution to historical thought. Listing some of the subjects which his predecessors had explored in their messages, Ford noted that there were attempts to define history, to apply historical principles, to interpret events and periods, and to use knowledge of the past to forecast the future. "After such a series of treatments," he added, "the field has been so well gleaned as to leave little yet to be garnered." The fact, however, is that the need to prepare a presidential message has forced many a leader of the Association to undertake—and in some cases for the first time—a formal statement of his historical credo, the kind of statement that would take into account the common problems that faced all historians regardless of their particular specialty. As Alfred T. Mahan put it in 1902: "I have to do for myself what but for this call I probably should never have attempted, namely, to analyze and formulate to my own consciousness the various impressions . . . which have formed my mental experience as a writer of history . . . ."

As might well be expected, a list of those who have headed the Association makes quite an impressive document, one that includes many dignitaries: presidents of the United States, high government officials, descendants of distinguished American statesmen, clergymen, novelists, publicists, college presidents, librarians, non-campus historians, and professors of history. Nevertheless, the present study is not an attempt to explore the personalities and careers of these presidents. It is not an attempt to discuss the totality of their historical thought. And it is not an attempt to determine the origins of their ideas. Its object is above all to present the views of history that they set forth in their messages. What did the presidents have to say to the Association about such major subjects as the usefulness of history, history as literature, the selection and interpretation of historical facts, the philosophy and science of history, the treatment of historical persons, and the content of history?

Accordingly, when references are made to the personalities and careers of the presidents and to the origins and other phases of their thought, such references are made only to throw light on the ideas which they presented in their messages. When, moreover, a much greater amount of space is given to some of these messages than to others, the reason is that some expressed thought about the nature of history more than others; some dealt more than others with the main subjects of the present study. Yet since those portions of the messages that provided the data for this book have been divided along broad topical lines, it seemed advisable to avoid as much further fragmentation as possible. The treatment within major topics, therefore, has been chronological.

Two further points should be made concerning the manner in which this study has been prepared. For one thing, since individual presidents keep reappearing in different chapters, some repetition of both background and foreground material has been unavoidable. What Andrew D. White, for example, thought about the usefulness of history was closely connected with what he thought about the selection of historical facts, the philosophy of history, and the content of history. Secondly, though all of the addresses were published with titles, these titles have often not been indicated in the text when they have failed to throw light on the material to be found in the addresses themselves.

All members of the historical gild are certain to react favorably to at least some of the points of view that were expressed in the addresses. The scholar who believes that historical study should serve above all to explain the present and its problems; the scholar who believes that history should be literature; that facts are impotent when taken by themselves; that the study of the science and the philosophy of history is essentially fruitless; that the study of the science and the philosophy of history can be fruitful; that individuals should be viewed not as independent agents but as products of their setting; that the content of history should be as rich as the past itself—all such scholars will find much to applaud in the presidential addresses.

On the other hand, some members of the historical fraternity will be displeased that some points of view have rarely been defended in the messages. The gildsman who believes that the past should be studied above all for the sake of the past and only incidentally for the sake of the present; the gildsman who believes that content, not form, should matter in historical writing; that the historian's chief function is to unearth new facts; that the study of the science and the philosophy of history should be emphasized; that the great man approach to history is a valid one; that history should be confined for all practical purposes to subjects like politics and constitutions—all such gildsmen will find much less and sometimes even nothing to applaud in the messages.

There can be no question, at all events, that the high quality of the messages in general has been due in part to that feeling of humility which Andrew C. McLaughlin suspected would seize any gildsman who sought "to speak with some show of assurance to a body of historical scholars, of whose learning and depth of interest he is fully aware." Nevertheless, when, in the ensuing pages, there appear thoughts on the nature of history which by present-day standards show no great thinking, it would be well as a rule to err on the side of charity and remember James Ford Rhodes' defense of Tacitus against those detractors who found some of the Roman's historical meditations nothing more than commonplaces. "True enough," Rhodes argued, "but they might not have been commonplaces if Tacitus had not uttered them and his works had not been read and reread until they have become a common possession of historical students." It is clear, in any case, that the discussion of the form and content of history will continue as long as the effort to keep the present in touch with the past continues. It is equally clear that Clio's will remain a house of many mansions as long as historians keep insisting on a multiplicity of specifications.

THE PRESIDENTS OF THE AMERICAN HISTORICAL ASSOCIATION

The date indicates the year when a presidential message was delivered or scheduled to be delivered. Several presidents, it will be noted, delivered or were scheduled to deliver two messages.

Andrew D. White, 1884, 1885
George Bancroft, 1886
Justin Winsor, 1887
William F. Poole, 1888
Charles Kendall Adams, 1889
John Jay, 1890
William Wirt Henry, 1891
James Burrill Angell, 1893
Henry Adams, 1894
George F. Hoar, 1895
Richard S. Storrs, 1896
James Schouler, 1897
George Park Fisher, 1898
James Ford Rhodes, 1899
Edward Eggleston, 1900
Charles Francis Adams, 1901
Alfred T. Mahan, 1902
Henry C. Lea, 1903
Goldwin Smith, 1904
John Bach McMaster, 1905
Simeon E. Baldwin, 1906
J. Franklin Jameson, 1907
George Burton Adams, 1908
Albert Bushnell Hart, 1909
Frederick J. Turner, 1910
William M. Sloane, 1911
Theodore Roosevelt, 1912
William A. Dunning, 1913
Andrew C. McLaughlin, 1914

H. Morse Stephens, 1915
George L. Burr, 1916
Worthington C. Ford, 1917
William R. Thayer, 1918, 1919
Edward Channing, 1920
Jean Jusserand, 1921
Charles H. Haskins, 1922
Edward P. Cheyney, 1923
Woodrow Wilson, 1924
Charles M. Andrews, 1924, 1925
Dana C. Munro, 1926
Henry Osborn Taylor, 1927
James H. Breasted, 1928
James Harvey Robinson, 1929
Evarts B. Greene, 1930
Carl L. Becker, 1931
Herbert E. Bolton, 1932
Charles A. Beard, 1933
William E. Dodd, 1934
Michael I. Rostovtzeff, 1935
Charles H. McIlwain, 1936
Guy Stanton Ford, 1937
Frederic L. Paxson, 1938
William S. Ferguson, 1939
Max Farrand, 1940
James W. Thompson, 1941
Arthur M. Schlesinger, 1942
Nellie Neilson, 1943
William L. Westermann, 1944
Carlton J. H. Hayes, 1945

CHAPTER I
THE IMMEDIATE USEFULNESS OF HISTORY: EARLY YEARS

JUDGED by their presidential messages, many leaders of the American Historical Association were less concerned with the past than with the present. Though the past gave them their occupation, the present was their preoccupation; and if one theme figured more prominently than any other in their messages, it was that of the immediate usefulness of history. Many presidents went out of their way to insist that knowledge of the past had a direct bearing on the problems of their own times. Proclaiming their social consciousness, their obsession with large public issues, and their contempt for the ivory tower, they contended that the historian should justify his existence by immersing himself in those historical problems that would throw light on the problems of the here and now. Armed with this faith in the power of history to drive home urgent lessons and to provide answers to burning questions, many presidents made it clear that they prized history chiefly for its practical applications, for its immediate social utility. Strikingly few gloried in it for its own sake. Few, too, emphasized that it could be useful in other than an immediate· sense: in enriching life, building character, broadening experience, developing understanding and tolerance, and liberating the mind.

Take, for example, Andrew D. White, the first president of the Association.[1] As professor of history at the University of Michigan, White had successfully agitated for the introduction of what he considered to be European standards of historical scholarship. As the first president of Cornell, he had probably exercised a greater influence on American higher education than

1 To save space, footnote references to the presidential addresses have been eliminated. A list of these addresses, with indications of where they can be found, appears in the first part of the bibliography.

any other individual in the nineteenth century.[2] Yet White was not simply an academician. He was a man of action, too—a diplomat, a civil service reformer, and a sound-money advocate. In part, no doubt, it was these non-academic activities that went to explain the dearth of scholarly publications that he had to his credit when he was elected to head the Association in 1884. Nevertheless, in what he had written, White had frequently pointed up the practical uses to which history could be put. In the published outlines of his lectures to undergraduates at Michigan and Cornell—and in the lectures themselves—he had made it clear that his approach to the past was not an antiquarian one.[3] In his booklet on *The Warfare of Science* (1876), a product of the science-religion controversy of the late nineteenth century, he had developed the thesis that "in all modern history, interference with science in the supposed interest of religion, no matter how conscientious such interference may have been, has resulted in the direst evils both to religion and to science—and invariably."[4] In his booklet on *Paper-Money Inflation in France* (1876), he had informed Americans of the disasters that the *assignats* had brought to the French of the Revolutionary period; and he cautioned that the French experience provided a lesson that every thoughtful American would do well to ponder.[5]

It was not surprising, then, that White used his address of 1884, "On Studies in General History and the History of Civilization," to emphasize once more the need to exploit the immediate usefulness of history. He pointed out, for instance, as he

2 *Autobiography of Andrew Dickson White* (2 vols., New York, 1905), I, 257-64; Wilfred Shaw, *The University of Michigan* (New York, 1920), p. 99; Carl Lotus Becker, *Cornell University: Founders and the Founding* (Ithaca, 1943), p. 213.

3 *Outlines of a Course of Lectures on History, Addressed to the Senior Class, in the Cornell University* (Ithaca, 1870), p. 7; Walter P. Rogers, *Andrew D. White and the Modern University* (Ithaca, 1942), pp. 137-38.

4 *The Warfare of Science* (New York, 1876), p. 8. White italicized this passage in the original.

5 *Paper-Money Inflation in France: How It Came, What It Brought, and How It Ended* (New York, 1876), p. 69.

was again to do in his *Autobiography,* that knowledge of the past had served to lift Northern morale during the trying Civil War years. But White did not support historical study simply for the consolation that knowledge of the past could give the present. He was convinced that history could play a major role in the improvement of man as man and of man as a member of society. And since a new association of historians was being established, he thought it most desirable to make a survey of the historical field. If the historian was to meet "the highest necessities of men," he should know the direction in which he could most effectively pursue his investigations.

In one respect White was far from optimistic. As things stood on the academic front in 1884, he saw little hope for the American scholar who wanted to specialize in the history of a country other than the United States or Britain. There were too many difficulties involved. The fact of distance meant that the American outsider would lack access to many documentary materials. In all likelihood, too, he would lack the appreciation of native ways of thinking that the insider probably had, so that as a rule he could bring himself less readily than the native into the "historical current" that flowed through a nation. Yet White was too familiar with the history of historical writing to push his generalization too far. After all, Ranke, Buckle, Sybel, and Parkman were foreigners who had written French history; Guizot had written English history; Motley, Dutch history; Prescott, Spanish history; Robertson, Bryce, and Carlyle, German history; and Von Holst, United States history. Such impressive exceptions White did not hesitate to acknowledge; he even added a "subordinate rule" to the effect that the non-native historian could sometimes outdistance the native in scholarly performance, because he was less likely to be handicapped by religious and patriotic prepossessions. But despite these qualifying remarks White saw no escape from the conclusion that the chief investigations of a country's past would have to be done by the native historian. The foreigner could generally not compete on "equal terms and with equal chances of success."

White's advice, therefore, was that the American gildsman should generally steer clear of specialized research into the history of countries other than the United States and Britain. But above all he urged the gildman—not in so many words—to do essentially what he himself had been doing in his undergraduate courses at Michigan and Cornell and in his investigations of the warfare of science and theology: to explore general history and trace human and societal evolution through "large reaches of time and space." As White saw it, the great advantage that the investigator of general history had was equality of opportunity. Regardless of his nationality, any thinking scholar could make valuable contributions to the field—provided, of course, that he lived in a country where thought was not restrained and where love of truth took precedence over all other loyalties, "governmental, ecclesiastical, philosophical, or scientific," said White, showing something of the same hatred of intolerance that he had so often shown at Cornell.[6] In other words, White believed that the American gildsman should aim not only for a specialized knowledge of the history of his own country or of Britain but for a "philosophical synthesis of human affairs," one that would embody the conclusions of specialized research in "a large, truthloving, justice-loving spirit." As far as he was concerned, Buckle had the right idea when he declared in his *History of Civilization in England* that without genuine synthesis special research was barren and often worthless.

White did not deny that in the history of historical writing there were intimate connections between general and special studies. He even pictured general history as a trunk from which special studies and biographies emerged as branches. Just the same, when he searched for signs of "healthful growth" in historical writing, he looked not to special studies but to general works. He believed, in fact, that general history could provide special history with a valuable measuring rod, for any piece of historical information that contributed to an understanding of

6 Lois O. Gibbons, ed., *George Lincoln Burr: Selections from His Writings* (Ithaca, 1943), p. 416.

"the great lines of historical evolution" and served a didactic purpose was to that extent important. Turning to a subject that he had often exploited in his undergraduate classes,[7] White pointed out that the growth of French absolutism taught fundamental moral lessons to subsequent ages. So, too, did the Battle of Saratoga, with its demonstration of "the force of a love of freedom against the service of despotism." White did not mean to imply that the importance of a historical lesson was fixed for all times. The lesson of the early routing of French Revolutionary armies and the lesson of incompetent military leadership during the Great Rebellion took on additional significance at the time of the first Battle of Bull Run. In much the same way, White added, drawing on the booklet that he had published in 1876, the ideas of eighteenth-century Frenchmen who advocated the unlimited issuance of paper money ceased to be "dried up and withered" in the years after the American Civil War.

Convinced that the past could throw much light on the present and that a multitude of lessons could be learned from the past, White recommended that the American gildsman rewrite all history from the American point of view. "For," he asked, "is it not true that we, in this republic, called upon to help build up a new civilization, with a political and social history developing before us of which the consequences for good or evil are to rank with those which have flowed from the life of Rome and the British Empire—is it not true that, for us, the perspective of a vast deal of history is changed; that the history which, for the use of various European populations, has been written with minute attention to details, must be written for us in a larger and more philosophical way?" Yet it was not only that the past threw light on the present; what also justified the rewriting of history from the American point of view was the fact that the present threw light on the past, said White, setting forth an idea that was later to be associated especially with the name of Frederick Jackson Turner.

7 *Outlines*, pp. 50-59.

There were, then, great opportunities for the American historian who would rewrite the past from the American standpoint; but the sad truth remained that he seldom availed himself of these opportunities, and the teachings of history all too frequently went unlearned. Congress, the state legislatures, and the newspapers, all exhibited their ignorance of the past; all showed their lack of the historical insight that was required for any intelligent handling of current problems, said White, speaking at the time of the presidential campaign between Blaine and Cleveland, to which he was later to refer as perhaps the "vilest" ever waged.[8] White, who had recently served as a delegate to the National Republican Convention,[9] suspected that "never was this want of broad historical views in leaders of American opinion more keenly felt than now." And to justify his suspicion he pointed to the failure to lift duties on works of art, the failure to prepare against a possible *coup d' état* by the electoral college, and the failure to combat illiteracy in the South. Yes, he said, the disregard of the lessons of history was "never" so glaring in American legislative activities as in recent years. Gone were the statesmen who, like John Adams, Jefferson, Calhoun, John Quincy Adams, Webster, Seward, and Sumner, could take advantage of their familiarity with history. In the ascendant were public figures whose historical knowledge could stand considerable improvement.

White's concrete recommendations were designed to spread the kind of useful historical knowledge that would "contribute powerfully to the healthful development on the one hand of man as man, and on the other to the opening up of a better political and social future for the nation at large." Favoring the combination of specialization and synthesis, he suggested that the American gildsman become a specialist preferably in English or United States history; but at the same time he should work toward "something like a conspectus of human history—if not of all hu-

8 *Autobiography,* I, 209.

9 *Ibid.,* p. 201.

man history, at least of some great part of it." This combination of specialization and synthesis would serve as the surest antidote against both vagueness and triviality and would at the same time best equip the historian to teach practical lessons to his contemporaries.

Strictly speaking, White's address, "On Studies in General History and the History of Civilization," was not his presidential address, since he was not officially chosen to head the Association until the day after he read his paper.[10] This, to be sure, was only a technicality, for it had been determined in advance by those who organized the Asociation that White would be elected president.[11] But since the Association did not choose its next president until it met again in 1885, White had another opportunity to deliver a presidential message and to assert his faith in the immediate usefulness of history. Nevertheless, he had invited to this second meeting of the Association a guest speaker in the person of Goldwin Smith, the former regius professor of history at Oxford, whom he had brought to the faculty of Cornell. Owing to the presence of Smith, White cut his own remarks short. Instead of reading his address on "The Influence of American Ideas upon the French Revolution," he merely commented on an outline of it; and this outline was almost exactly the same as the one that he had been using for years in his undergraduate classes.[12] He had obviously been too busy to take time out to work up some new material.

After tracing the influence of the thought of individuals like Franklin, Jefferson, and Paine, and after indicating the influence of Frenchmen who travelled in America and of French soldiers who took part in the American Revolution, White proceeded to draw some pointed lessons for the United States of

10 American Historical Association (referred to hereafter as A.H.A.), *Papers* (New York, 1886), I, 21.

11 W. Stull Holt, ed., *Historical Scholarship in the United States, 1876-1901: As Revealed in the Correspondence of Herbert B. Adams* (Baltimore, 1938), p. 72.

12 *Outlines,* pp. 61-62.

1885. He was proud of the influence of the American "ideal of republican manhood" on the thought of the French Revolutionaries; he was proud that Americans like Washington and Franklin had rivalled even Plutarch's ancients as models of virtue. But the important point that he wished to drive home was that the one-time beneficent American influence on Europe had been lost—lost by reason of American misgovernment, especially in the big metropolitan areas. He thus returned to a subject with which he had been much occupied in recent years—civil service reform. For in the early eighties, White, running the risk of being viewed as a crank, had agitated against the spoils system in the pages of the *North American Review;*[13] and, as he was later to record in his *Autobiography,*he had tried to sell the idea of civil service reform to politicians like Thomas C. Platt, Thurlow Weed, and James G. Blaine.[14] Once more, then, in his presidential message of 1885, White complained that dishonesty had assumed such prominence in American public affairs that some Europeans were pointing to republican government as something to be avoided—definitely not something to be imitated. But had the United States come all the way for this? Certainly not; yet if the United States was to regain and retain its lost esteem, it was necessary for Americans to undertake a number of changes. Civil service reform must be considerably extended; and American cities must institute administrative systems in which honesty and efficiency figured much more conspicuously, said White, whose name was soon to appear in the list of those to whom James Bryce acknowledged his indebtedness in the preface to *The American Commonwealth* (1888).

White's conviction that history should serve current needs was shared by his most prominent student, Charles Kendall Adams. President of the Association in 1889, Adams had been

13 "Do the Spoils Belong to the Victor?", *North American Review,* CXXXIV (1882), 111-33.

14 Autobiography, I, 194-97, 208-9.

following in White's footsteps for years. His appointment as instructor in history at the University of Michigan came as the result of White's recommendations;[15] and when White resigned from the presidency of Cornell in 1885, he named Adams as his successor. Yet Adams was not indebted to White merely for reasons of job placement. He also owed much to him in the way of ideas. This was apparent in his first book, *Democracy and Monarchy in France* (1874), a study in which Adams looked to history for lessons, so that he might throw light on the political weakness of the Second Empire in the recent past.[16] White's influence was apparent, too, in the comments that Adams had to make "On the Study of History" in his most important publication, his *Manual of Historical Literature* (1882), a work that had originally been undertaken at White's suggestion.

Like White, Adams was intent on benefiting from the immediate usefulness of history. Like White, he believed that knowledge of the past should supply "the present needs of the nation." Unhappily, however, Adams, who had himself studied briefly in Europe, found that a survey of "Recent Historical Work in the Colleges and Universities of Europe and America" revealed the relative backwardness of American schools in historical study and proved that the "sluggish peoples" of Europe had a much greater appreciation of the practical value of history than Americans had.

Adams did not deny that considerable advances in historical study had been made in the United States in recent years; and reviewing in 1889 much the same material that Herbert Baxter Adams had covered in *The Study of History in American Colleges and Universities* (1887), he pointed proudly to the work of historians like Henry Adams at Harvard, George Park Fisher and George Burton Adams at Yale, and Burgess at Columbia.

15 Charles Forster Smith, *Charles Kendall Adams: A Life-Sketch* (Madison, 1925), p. 11.

16 *Democracy and Monarchy in France from the Inception of the Great Revolution to the Overthrow of the Second Empire* (New York, 1882), pp. ix-x.

He pointed even more proudly to what Andrew D. White had done at the University of Michigan to stimulate interest in history. As White's successor at Michigan, Adams did not neglect to point to his own work in introducing seminars on the model of those at Leipzig and Berlin. Nor, as White's successor at Cornell, did he neglect to praise the work of faculty members like Moses Coit Tyler, the literary historian, Herbert Tuttle, the historian of Prussia, and George Lincoln Burr, the medievalist. Adams, to be sure, did not overlook Johns Hopkins in his survey. He was, in fact, pleased to announce in 1889 that, despite all the rumors of financial difficulties, the History Department at Johns Hopkins was training forty doctoral candidates, among them, it might be added, Frederick Jackson Turner, Charles H. Haskins, and Charles M. Andrews. Indeed, once having injected a financial note, Adams could not resist suggesting that as things historical stood in the United States the chief need was for the establishment at all major universities of a special fund, such as existed at Johns Hopkins, which would be used for the publication of research findings.

Although Adams recognized the recent advances made in American higher historical education, he insisted that in the presence of English, Belgian, Italian, German, and French achievements in the same period American scholarship found "far more encouragement for its modesty than for its pride." Impressed by the influence of a scholar like Ranke, the first honorary member of the Association, Adams thought it would be of interest to determine the extent to which the development of modern Germany was affected by the training that students had received in Ranke's seminar. "How many thousands of Germans now in places of official responsibility have had their ideas shaped by the instruction thus provided!" But much as Adams admired the historical work of the German universities, he was one of the few American scholars of his generation who managed not to apotheosize German scholarship.[17] He believed that it was

17 See W. Stull Holt, ed., *op. cit.,* pp. 99-100, 281.

in France that "greater progress has been made recently in historical work than in any other nation." Schools like *l'École des chartes*, *l'École normale supérieure*, and *l'École pratique des Hautes Études*, he thought, were in a class by themselves: in organization and methods of instruction they surpassed any institutions in Germany.[18]

It was in this flourishing state of higher historical education that Adams found incontestable proof that the French appreciated—in a way that Americans did not—the potential usefulness of history; they knew that history could supply "the present needs of the nation." And Americans would do well to follow the French example; they should establish schools for advanced historical training on the French model. A college president himself, Adams found it unpleasant "to reflect that until some such facilities are afforded on this side of the Atlantic, large numbers, not only of the brightest but also of the wisest of our youth, will annually flock to the better opportunities provided by the institutions of the old world."

John Jay, who succeeded Adams, had no less faith in the immediate usefulness of history. Jay, however, had done little in the way of historical research; it was as a lawyer, diplomat, Republican reformer, and grandson of Chief Justice Jay that he had made his reputation.[19] Yet the fact that his own historical work was slight did not keep him from holding strong views about history.

That Jay used his presidential message of 1890 to stress the defects of historical education in elementary and high schools was certainly understandable. He had long been actively interested in conditions in the public schools; and in pamphlets like *Rome in America* (1869) and *Rome, the Bible and the Republic*

18 For brief descriptions of these French schools, see Charles V. Langlois and Charles Seignobos, *Introduction to the Study of History* (New York, 1898), pp. 335-46; and *Histoire et historiens depuis cinquante ans* (2 vols., Paris, 1927-28), I, 149-51.

19 A.H.A., *Annual Report, 1894* (Washington, 1895), pp. 57-58.

(1879) he had denounced the Catholic Church for what he considered to be its attempts to undermine the American school system.[20] Jay wanted young Americans to understand "aright" their country's past. Especially now that American influence in the world was growing, Jay, who had himself served as Minister to Austria, found that "The Demand for Education in American History" became all the more pressing.

Naturally, good education presupposed good educators. Whether formal education was to end with the academy or continue through the highest stages of the university, there was always need for effective teaching; but those whose formal education in history would end below the college level were most in need of first-rate instruction. Therefore, Jay thought it essential that old methods of teaching history be abandoned: if history-teaching was to achieve its aims, it must be made interesting. Merely to burden students with loads of facts was to defeat the purpose of historical education; and if a child disliked history the fault rested with those who wrote the books, taught the lessons, and in the process deprived history of its human interest and its human beings, said Jay, who was familiar with the essay "Why Do Children Dislike History?" by Thomas Wentworth Higginson, the popular historical writer.[21] Jay was sure that once the "scientific method" of teaching history came to be generally adopted remarkable results would follow, for "nothing could more tend to strengthen and confirm the American character of our common schools, so absolutely essential in fitting our youth for their duties as American citizens, and the historic training to that end will no longer be confined to the select few who enjoy the higher education given in our colleges and universities, but will be shared by the masses, 'the plain people,' who

20 *Rome in America: An Address before the Bible Society at Mount Kisco, New York, September 21, 1868* (New York, 1869), p. 3; *Rome, the Bible and the Republic: Mr. Jay's Reply to the Strictures of the Rev. M. W. Newman on Mr. Jay's Address before the Bible Society of Westchester County, New York* (Mount Kisco, 1879), pp. 41, 46.

21 "Why Do Children Dislike History?", in G. Stanley Hall, ed., *Methods of Teaching History* (Boston, 1884), pp. 227-29.

constitute the great majority, whose character and life are to raise or to lower the standard of our civilization, and whose votes are to elect the rulers and determine the destiny of the republic."

Nor did Jay think that Americans could delay in introducing the needed changes. He was speaking in the period of the "new immigration" from southern and eastern Europe—at a time when students of population statistics were predicting that in a few generations several dozen Romanian or Italian peasants would produce a horde of descendants, while the number of off-spring of several dozen Harvard and Yale men would be negligible in the same period of time.[22] Small wonder that Jay found it unsafe to postpone the revision of conventional standards in the teaching of history. True, some of the new immigrants welcomed the common school which would "fit them for American citizenship, and raise them politically and socially to a higher plane of civilization"; but there were always the others, constituting, in Jay's words, "a vast multitude who in their ignorance are ready to subvert our institutions, to supersede our national principles and rights, which they do not understand, and even in some cases to force into our public schools not only un-American ideas, but a foreign tongue." Though Jay had been American minister to the Habsburg monarchy, he had obviously not taken a liking to the sounds of the Slavic, Italian, and Romanian languages.

To Jay the study of United States history was not merely an academic matter. It was a solution to the problems of the melting pot; it was a weapon to be used in the struggle against "civilizations inferior, alien, and hostile to our own." American children must learn "to understand, appreciate, and defend" their country's institutions; and this they could do only if they were taught the kind of history that would properly shape their character and thought. Therefore, the American Historical Association should strive to achieve a more enlightened public opinion. It should assume leadership in making the American people aware

22 Carl Wittke, *We Who Built America: The Saga of the Immigrant* (New York, 1939), p. 406.

of the importance of their history. If, indeed, the Association played its part vigorously, it could "supply a great national want." It could help to make history become philosophy teaching by example. It could help to carry out a program of educational reform on which the future of the United States might very well depend. It could work to further the long American tradition of national aid to state education. It could fight to transform the Bureau of Education, under the Secretary of Agriculture, into a real Ministry of Public Education. Finally, it could agitate for a national university, as advocated by George Washington,[23] a university that would combat the spread of "un-American" ideas and practices; for, Jay, who had long been expressing his fears of Catholicism, was alarmed by the recent establishment in Washington of what he described as "a foreign university with a chair devoted to the canon law, a system in antagonism with the Constitution and the common law on which the entire fabric of the Republic rests." Jay found that the difficulties facing the nation in 1890 were so considerable that if the American Historical Association only stood and waited it would not serve. Unless it took advantage of the immediate usefulness of history, it would not achieve any national or practical importance.

Just as Jay made it clear in 1890 that he prized history for what it could do to foster patriotism, so, three years later, James Burrill Angell made it clear that he prized history for what it could do to foster internationalism. Angell himself had written little of the kind of history that would achieve the objective he sought; he had written little of any kind of history apart from a contribution to Justin Winsor's *Narrative and Critical History.*[24]

23 See Worthington C. Ford, ed., *Wills of George Washington and His Immediate Ancestors* (Brooklyn, 1891), pp. 89-92. Jay's successor, William Wirt Henry, also took time out in his presidential message to back Washington's proposal of a national university. Plainly, however, it was Herbert Baxter Adams who stood behind the agitation for the establishment of this national university.

24 "'The Diplomacy of the United States, 1789-1850," in Justin Winsor, *Narrative and Critical History of America* (8 vols., Boston, 1884-89), VII, 461-513.

Longtime president of the University of Michigan and a diplomat who had served in China and on the Anglo-American Northeastern Fisheries Commission, he had left himself little time for research and writing. Faced, however, with the necessity of addressing the Association, he chose to discuss "The Inadequate Recognition of Diplomatists by Historians," a subject which he had doubtless treated in his classes on international law and the history of treaties at the University of Michigan.[25]

Thinking probably of the Samoan Treaty of 1889, the first Pan-American conference, and the Anglo-American Treaty of 1892 concerning the Bering Sea seal fisheries, Angell pointed out that the historian of 1893 was living in an age of arbitration, a fact that made all the more serious his failure to place sufficient emphasis on the role of the diplomat in history; for, as long as he continued generally to ignore this role, he would continue to lose an opportunity to make history educate. To Angell's way of thinking, the gildsman should learn to take proper advantage of a study like history which could make men "catholic and cosmopolitan" in their outlook and lift them above "the narrow prejudices and conceits of provincialism." If the historian paid more attention to the activities of the treaty-maker, he could demonstrate that peaceful discussion was the desirable way to settle international disputes; and he could play an important part in perpetuating the fraternal relations of the nations of the world.

It was, however, the patriotic value of historical study that mattered above all to George F. Hoar, the Republican Senator from Massachusetts, whose political activities had not dampened his enthusiasm for the intellectual life. President of the gild in 1895, Hoar was obviously being rewarded for his services in connection with the passage of the bill by which Congress incorporated the Association.[26] He had doubtless favored this act of incorporation, approved in 1889, because of his faith that his-

25 *The Reminiscences of James Burrill Angell* (New York, 1911), p. 242.
26 A.H.A., *Papers* (New York, 1889), III, 245-46.

tory would inspire loyalty to American institutions. The fact, however, was that when he addressed the Association he was disturbed by what he called "Popular Discontent with Representative Government"; and this discontent he ascribed to the influence of newspapermen, literary men, and historians, people who were so critical of the American past and present that Hoar, "a Puritan of Puritans," wondered that any young American could feel any love for his country.

Unfortunately, Hoar did not clarify his illusions, and, by failing to name names, he weakened the substance of his argument. He may have had in mind journalists like E. L. Godkin, whose declining faith in American ideals was evident in the *Nation,* the New York *Evening Post,* and in his recently published *Reflections and Comments, 1865-1895* (1895); George W. Curtis, of *Harper's Weekly* fame, whose posthumously published *Orations and Addresses* (1894) presented a picture of the American political scene that was filled with spoilsmen, among them James G. Blaine, for whom Hoar had served as an apologist; Joseph Pulitzer, whose New York *World* specialized in the exposure of the corruption of American political leaders; Carl Schurz, whose recent articles and editorials in *Harper's Weekly* often centered on the theme of "the people vs. the politicians"; Henry D. Lloyd, whose recently published *Wealth vs. Commonwealth* (1894) suggested that American political morality left much to be desired. As for the literary men, Hoar may have had in mind writers like Henry Adams, whose *Democracy* (1880) was a vigorous indictment of American politics; Marion Crawford, whose *An American Politician* (1884) presented an unflattering picture of American democracy in action; and William Dean Howells, whose *Traveller from Altruria* (1894) contrasted democratic professions with democratic practices.

Hoar complained that the fault-finding and cynical temper of some newspapermen and some literary men was being aped by some American historians. Again he remained vague. Just as he had failed to name the iconoclasts in the ranks of American jour-

nalists and literary men, so he failed to name the iconoclasts in
the ranks of American historians. He may have been thinking of
the disparaging strain that ran through Henry Adams' *History*
(1889-1891) and of what Charles Francis Adams called the
"generally radical and somewhat iconoclastic" notions set forth
in his *Massachusetts: Its Historians and Its History, An Object Lesson* (1893). Hoar, the author of an unpublished transla-
of Thucydides,[27] feared that history, instead of becoming the
noblest of all studies, would degenerate into nothing more than
a series of vicious scandals—a story of "horse-jockies and swin-
dlers."

Hoar would have none of this approach. Himself "one of the
most high-minded and incorruptible of public servants,"[28] he insisted that public servants as a rule were motivated by considerations of the highest order. Thinking perhaps of the blasts that
Populist leaders had been directing at both Republicans and Democrats, he insisted that the conduct of public affairs was "growing
better, purer, and wiser from generation to generation." He was
even willing to compare American representative government
at its worst with any really monarchical government at its best,
and risk all that he valued on the results of the comparison. Yet
there were in the United States critics who scorned representative government, exaggerated the abuses of the party system and
the inefficiencies of legislatures, and impugned the character and
motives of American public servants. Long suspicious of appeals
to " vulgar passions," Hoar may had in mind his own experience
in 1890 with the Pittsburgh *Post,* the Democratic newspaper
which had accused him of being "an inveterate office-seeker,"
who "lived on terrapin and champagne" and "had never done
a stroke of useful work."[29] At any rate, he issued the warning

27 Edward Everett Hale, "George F. Hoar," American Antiquarian Society, *Proceedings,* New Series, XVII (1905), 151.

28 Claude Moore Fuess, *Carl Schurz: Reformer (1829-1906)* (New York,
1932), p. 204.

29 *Autobiography of Seventy Years* (2 vols., New York, 1903), II, 271-73.

that the critical approach to the American present and past was having "infinitely mischievous and pestilent" effects. How could the young American love his country if he was exposed to unflattering treatments of its history and moral character? Mustering what rhetorical skill he could command, Hoar asked: "Is the being we love with the supremest passion of our souls altogether unlovely? Is the being we would gladly die for unfit to live with? Is the being we have imagined to ourselves a thing of beauty and of joy, simply an aggregate of all falseness, and greed, and meanness?" It was not enough that Hoar knew the answers. The historian should also know them. More than that, he should see to it that the American people knew them. He should use his knowledge of the past to expose the exaggerations and falsehoods that detractors of American representative government were spreading. He should prove that American patriotism had "its roots and its foundations in a solid respect and honor."

The faith in the immediate usefulness of history that Hoar asserted in 1895 James Schouler reasserted two years later. Schouler, however, was better qualified to do so. One of the leading historians of his time, he had already published, among other things, five volumes of his *History of the United States of America, under the Constitution*; and in this work as well as in his *Constitutional Studies, State and Federal* (1897) he had ventured to draw lessons from the past for the present. Moreover, in his recently published *Historical Briefs* (1896), a book dedicated to the Association, he had gloried in the fact that the study of history disclosed "the grand lessons of human life," lessons which the gildsman should seek to "deduce" and to "inculcate."[30]

It was understandable that in his presidential message of 1897 Schouler should urge the American historian to remember that he lived in a democratic society, and that in such a society education was designed to prepare citizens for "a just exercise of the franchise of freedom." It was understandable, too, that

30 *Historical Briefs* (New York, 1896), pp. 33, 47.

Schouler should urge the gildsman to bring his knowledge of the past to bear on current problems, so that he might help to give "right ideas and the right impulse to popular institutions." Instead of drawing off as a member of an "exclusive aristocracy," he should make every effort to guide "the devious course of republican empire, beset by snares and pitfalls, and leaven the immense and increasing mass" of American political society.

Schouler, who lectured at Johns Hopkins,[31] emphasized that there was much that "our young men" should be taught. They should be taught that there was need for the careful selection and supervision of officeholders, that there was need for civic-mindedness.

> Our young men [Schouler continued] should be taught that the organizing skill which masses for corporate effect in the mammon of unrightness may well be employed against bad politics and politicians; that political parties in this land of freedom are not immortal, but new measures, new policies of administration, invite new bands of believers; that, however it may be with the creed of a religion, there are no fixed fundamentals in politics except those on which men of all parties may in a great emergency stand together; that true representative government is a government of laws, not of men, and far less of machinery; and that where conventions and primaries, which are, properly speaking, the mere convenient agencies of the voters, become too masterful in the hands of evil managers, it is time to revoke those agencies and direct that nominations be made more immediately by the people themselves. Finally the true 'Monroe doctrine' for the New World, as originally formulated by capable statesmen, was not for conquest but for self-conquest; that we should set before the poor and suffering communities of this New World, less favored than ourselves, the shield and spectacle of a noble national example.

Specialist that he was in American political and constitutional history, Schouler did not hesitate to issue a call for "A

31 See "Biography," *ibid.,* p. 294.

New Federal Convention," which would revise the Constitution to suit the needs of modern society. Speaking one year after the Bryan Campaign of 1896, he suggested that this convention should adopt some of the improvements embodied in the constitutions of individual American states and in the Constitution of the Confederate States of America. No conservative in matters of political reform,[32] Schouler favored, among other things, new ways to amend the Constitution; the popular election of senators; the direct election of the President by a plurality of popular votes; the enlargement of the authority of the President to permit the veto of individual items in appropriation bills; and the extension of the time-period during which the President could approve or disapprove a bill. Schouler, who had devoted many years to the study of American constitutional history, took the stand that the Constitution should be changed in keeping with the needs of the present. Drawing on his knowledge of the past, he sought to give "right ideas and the right impulse to popular institutions." Indeed, it was fitting that Schouler later reprinted his presidential message in *Ideals of the Republic* (1908), a book in which he described the basic social and political ideas that had made for American greatness and applied them to present conditions.

Schouler's immediate successors were much less preoccupied with the needs of the present in their presidential messages. Consider, for example, George Park Fisher, the church historian and textbook writer. Fisher was tempted in 1898 to investigate the impact of the Spanish-American War on American national policies, but at the same time he welcomed an opportunity to seek relief from present controversies. Perhaps he had in mind the controversies from which he had not sought relief in studies like *Thoughts Pertinent to the Present Crisis* (1861), *Faith and Rationalism* (1879), and *Outlines of Universal History* (1885), the college textbook which he had consciously and conscien-

32 Cf. Lewis E. Ellis, "James Schouler," in William T. Hutchinson, ed., *The Marcus W. Jernegan Essays in American Historiography* (Chicago, 1937), p. 94.

tiously brought up to "the present time." At any rate, Fisher made it a point to choose as the subject of his presidential address one that had nothing to do with the problems of the day, "The Function of the Historian as a Judge of Historic Persons."

James Ford Rhodes, Fisher's successor, also made it a point to avoid "mooted questions" and "disputed matters" in his presidential message. Perhaps the reason was that Rhodes had had enough of controversy in the writing of his monumental *History of the United States from the Compromise of 1850*, the fourth volume of which had just appeared. Whatever the motive for his decision to avoid controversy, Rhodes did take time out to express his agreement with the recently published *Report* of the Association's Committee of Seven, the *Report* which Henry Johnson considered "the ablest document relating to history for schools that had ever been produced in America."[33] Rhodes proclaimed his faith in the usefulness of history for the training of the citizen and the building of his character. Rhodes believed that part of the usefulness of history grew out of the sympathy for the present which knowledge of the past made possible; and, as might be expected from one who had devoted his scholarly life to what was essentially contemporary history, he did not scorn the writing of such history. He even argued that it was simpler to write about the present than about the past, and that it was possible to present the present both accurately and impartially. He deemed it one of the distinguishing characteristics of the ancient historians that they wrote what amounted to contemporary history. Surely the writings of Herodotus, Thucydides, and Tacitus presented the best refutation of the notion that contemporary history, the most useful kind of history, defied truthful presentation.

Rhodes' successor was much less kind to the ancients, and this for the reason that they failed, so far as he was concerned, to serve the needs of the present. Edward Eggleston, the Hoosier

33 Henry Johnson, *Teaching of History in Elementary and Secondary Schools with Applications to Allied Studies* (New York, 1940), p. 59.

novelist and writer of American cultural history, was convinced that except in matters of style the ancients had nothing to teach the gildsman about the writing of history in the "modern sense," about what he—long before the appearance of James Harvey Robinson's volume with the same title—called "The New History." Eggleston's point was that Thucydides, for example, suffered from an excess of war and politics; but war and politics, according to Eggleston, were the very subjects of which the scholar should try to rid history in keeping with the "great world benevolence" that would characterize ages to come. A former Methodist circuit rider and minister,[34] Eggleston considered it a function of history to cultivate the brute out of man; and he looked forward to a time when the pages of history books would no longer be covered with gore, when, instead, they would be covered with "the wisdom of diplomacy, the wisdom of avoidance—in short, the fine wisdom of arbitration, that last fruit of human experience." A long-standing hater of politics, moreover, one who, having spent a Sunday with some politicians, had feared for the loss of some of his "former spirituality,"[35] Eggleston considered it a function of history to make "good men and women, cultivated and broad men and women," not merely citizens and voters; and, in 1900, the year of the anti-imperialist campaign, he looked forward to a time when Americans, studying the right kind of history, cultural history, would be cured of politics and patriotism, that "virtue of the half-developed."

Eggleston's successor, Charles Francis Adams, agreed that the study of history could have great practical value, but he found this value not only in cultural history but in military and political history as well, the types of history, indeed, which he himself had written. A man who would doubtless have held high office in the public life of his generation if he had agreed with either

34 Eggleston's religious ideas and activities are described in detail in William Peirce Randel, *Edward Eggleston: Author of The Hoosier School-Master* (New York, 1946).

35 *Ibid.*, p. 27.

of the major political parties,[36] Adams insisted, as he had done
back in the seventies in his articles on the Tweed Ring, that it
was not from politics but from low-level politics that Americans
needed to be saved. He therefore urged the scholar not to shun
politics and political history but to talk and write them all the
more—with a view to raising the level on which current questions of public policy were being discussed. Since he himself
had not hesitated to state his opinions in "all contests over public questions of any importance,"[37] it was understandable that
he deemed ill-advised any unwritten law which would bar from
the meetings of the Association the discussion of present controversies. For the gildsman to avoid the treatment of these controversies, he argued, was for him to confess a lack of faith in his
ability to deal with live issues on a scholarly, scientific, and historical level. Especially in a democratic society, the historian could
not refuse to perform so useful a public service, so major an educational function. As a citizen in a democracy, he was under a
special obligation to do what he could to foster a better understanding of current problems—the more so because recent political debates failed to do credit to the intelligence of the American
people. Conducted on a notoriously low level, they were characterized as a rule by extreme partisanship, personal abuse, scur-
rility of language, and an intention to deceive, said Adams, who
more than most Americans knew what it was to be "brought up
in an atmosphere of politics."[38]

In order to give specific illustrations of what he had in mind,
Adams proceeded to review briefly the twelve presidential campaigns in which he had taken part, starting with 1856 and ending
with 1900. In retrospect he found these campaigns painfully disappointing and the debates to which they gave rise no less disappointing. What he saw was a series of great opportunities, but
opportunities that were lost because the trained historian had

36 Hoar, *Autobiography of Seventy Years*, I, 155.

37 Henry Cabot Lodge, "Memorial Address," in *Charles Francis Adams,
1835-1915: An Autobiography* (Boston, 1916), p. lii.

38 *Ibid.*, p. 31.

neglected to participate actively in the debates. Yet to some, if not all of these debates, the historian could have made valuable contributions, applying the teachings of history "with results manifestly beneficial."

Even in the great slavery debate, which Adams regarded as the best conducted and most educational in American history, the historian made hardly any contribution at all. In the more poorly conducted debates over reconstruction and monetary questions, debates which could have benefited from the judiciousness and calm of the scholarly approach, he again failed in his duties to the public, with the result that the lessons of the past were again largely ignored. Adams did not overlook the services of men like Carl Schurz and Andrew D. White, both of whom, during the campaign of 1896, had cited from history the dangers of tampering with the currency. Unfortunately, these were only isolated examples, and when 1900 came the gildsman again neglected to bring to bear the lessons of history on such major issues as imperialism, trusts, and silver.

Having completed his review of the presidential elections that he remembered, Adams suggested that the members of the Association do some reviewing of their own. He was convinced that no gildsman would be able "to recall a single utterance [in a post-Civil War campaign] which has stood the test of time, as marking a distinct addition to mankind's intellectual belongings,—the classics of the race." Here, no doubt, Adams was setting up unreasonable standards, but at any rate he did not seek, like Fisher, "a respite of an hour from present controversies," nor, like Rhodes, the avoidance of "mooted questions." Showing the same distrust of the *au-dessus de la mêlée* spirit that he had indicated in pamphlets like *Imperialism and the Tracks of Our Forefathers* (1899) and *Historians and Historical Societies* (1899), he pressed for a shift in gild policy. The American Historical Association, he insisted, was equipped to handle controversial issues. The fact of differences of opinion among gild members would guarantee the full and vigorous presentation of all sides of any question, so that the Association, with its scholarly and scientific approach, could exert a beneficial and elevating influence, especially during a political contest. It could turn a campaign from a "babel of the commonplace" into a healthy, educational experience. The gildsman himself would appear in "his proper character and place,—the scholar having his say in politics; but always as a scholar, not as an officeholder, nor an aspirant for office. His appeal would be to intelligence and judgment, not to passion or self-interest, or even to patriotism." At last the American voter would be able to hear the views of the historian along with those of the journalist and the politician.

Emphasizing that citizenship and historical scholarship went together, Adams asserted: "As citizens, we most assuredly should, in so far as we may properly so do, contribute to results, whether immediate, or more or less remote. As scholars and students, the conclusions we have to present should be deserving of thoughtful consideration. The historical point of view, moreover, is, politically, an important point of view; for only when approached historically—by one looking before, as well as after —can any issue be understood in its manifold relations with a complex civilization." Accordingly, Adams proposed that the Association schedule a meeting for the July preceding every presidential election, a meeting at which the various campaign issues would be analyzed from the historical standpoint. Complete freedom of discussion would be required; and those historians whose research best qualified them to tackle the problems at hand would have the opportunity to speak their piece. These authorities, Adams felt sure, would raise the level of the political debate, "bringing the calm lessons of history to bear on the angry wrangles and distorted presentations of those whose chief, if not only, aim is a mere party supremacy." Certainly different historians would draw different lessons from the past; but Adams, as a good social Darwinist, was convinced that the soundest lessons would survive as "the most fit."

Adams' successor, Alfred T. Mahan, was no less intent on drawing practical lessons from history; he had gone out of his way to draw such lessons in almost all of his writings—writings which not only described the course of history but shaped it as well.[39] In his first major work, *The Influence of Sea Power upon History, 1660-1783* (1890), Mahan had tried to drive home to the layman the "permanence of the teachings of history." In *The Influence of Sea Power upon the French Revolution and Empire, 1793-1812* (1892), he had sought to "impart to the subject of Naval History an aspect which, in this very utilitarian age, should not be opened to the ready reproach of having merely archaeological interest, and possessing no practical value for men called upon to use the changed materials of modern naval war."[40] He had also sung the glories of naval preparedness in studies like *The Interest of America in Sea Power, Present and Future* (1897) and *Lessons of the War with Spain and Other Articles* (1899). He was determined that the layman should be made conscious of the importance of an adequate fleet.

What Mahan stressed in his message of 1902 was that historical lessons of any sort had to be drawn for the layman; but frequently the layman could not understand what the historian had to say. Mahan, therefore, preached the need for artistry in historical writing. The gildsman should see to it that he emphasized his central idea in such a way that it would stamp itself plainly on the mind of the reader. He should also see to it that he subordinated his details so skillfully that the reader would not receive a wrong impression as to the relative importance of individual facts. Mahan was convinced that facts had to be massed no less than troops, if they were "to prevail against the passive resistance of indolent mentality," if they were "to penetrate and

39 *From Sail to Steam: Recollections of Naval Life* (New York, 1907), pp. 325-26; William D. Puleston, *Mahan: The Life and Work of Captain Alfred Thayer Mahan, U.S.N.* (New Haven, 1939), p. 327.

40 *The Influence of Sea Power upon the French Revolution and Empire, 1793-1812* (2 vols., Boston, 1892), I, iii.

shatter the forces of ignorance or prejudgment, which conservative impression has arrayed against them."

When the historian lacked artistry, when he lacked the ability to subordinate details and to emphasize a central theme, he lessened his usefulness as a teacher; and his writings, Mahan remarked, were essentially wasted because they were not likely to be understood by the layman. Influential public servant that he was, Mahan believed that such remarks were very much called for in 1902. For the gildsman was not only worshipping accuracy for the sake of accuracy, but he was shying away from the generalizations that the public sought. As a consequence, the layman was failing to develop a proper appreciation of the usefulness of history.

Henry C. Lea, the next president of the Association, agreed that history generally had a lesson to teach; but, unlike Mahan, he preferred that the lesson "educe itself from the facts." In a sense this was a strange preference for Lea to express, for in his many writings on Roman Catholic ecclesiastical institutions he had not hesitated to state the lessons of history, as he understood them; so much so, that one offended professor of dogmatic theology charged that he wrote "to prove a thesis, to gain a cause, to misrepresent an adversary."[41] At the very time that Lea headed the Association, his writings were playing no mean role in the French religious struggle that was soon to culminate in the Separation Law of 1905. A translation of his *History of the Inquisition of the Middle Ages* was being circulated in an inexpensive edition to serve as an anti-clerical campaign document.[42]

Yet Lea made it plain in his presidential message that he was opposed to making history into "a Sunday-school tale for chil-

41 P. H. Casey, *Notes on A History of Auricular Confession: H. C. Lea's Account of the Power of the Keys in the Early Church* (Philadelphia, 1899), p. 79.

42 *A.H.R.*, VI (1901), 834; Edward Sculley Bradley, *Henry Charles Lea: A Biography* (Philadelphia, 1931), pp. 269-70.

dren of larger growth." It was for the reader, he insisted, to determine just what the teachings of history were. Possibly because he himself had turned to the study of church history in the period of the great debate between science and religion, Lea was sensitive to one particular danger that often accompanied efforts to exploit the immediate usefulness of history: the danger of injecting present conceptions into a past that frequently lacked those conceptions. Though Lea had participated actively in the public life of his times, he emerged as the first president who used his message to point out the menace of present-mindedness in historical study.

Issuing his call for past-mindedness, he stressed the need for humility. When the gildsman approached the past, he should remember that although Christian ideals had been theoretically accepted for some two thousand years, they had not seriously been practiced until quite recently; even the efforts of the last two centuries to apply those ideals had failed more then they had succeeded. Lea, who was no mean figure in reformist circles in Philadelphia, [43] insisted that the gildsman could "well afford to cast the mantle of charity over those who in fact have been only one or two steps behind us in the application of the Sermon on the Mount." The Dreyfus affair and other current evidences of "duplicity and . . . contempt for human rights" hardly entitled moderns to throw stones at past ages.

Lea's plea for the writing of history without recourse to moralization failed to win the support of Goldwin Smith, his successor. Nor was there anything strange about this; Smith, the Anglo-Canadian octogenarian, was a publicist of many decades' standing, and in 1904 he was as much in favor of profiting from the teachings of history as in the years when he served on the staff of the *Saturday Review* and on the faculty of Oxford. A stern moralist and long-time propagandist for the doctrines

43 Arthur C. Howland, ed., *Minor Historical Essays and Other Essays by Henry Charles Lea* (Philadelphia, 1942), p. ix; Charles Homer Haskins, *Studies in Mediaeval Culture* (Oxford, 1929), p. 256.

of the Manchester School, he had often insisted that historical study was designed for the instruction and elevation of mankind;[44] and this he did again in his presidential message.

Smith had often insisted, moreover, that the morals of history needed to be clearly drawn; and this he did once more in his message. Reflecting no doubt his journalistic background, he pointed out that the morals of history must be understood by ordinary people. Hence the historian ought to pay more attention to narrative art, resisting, even in an age of science and sociology, the temptation to look down on style. For an unlively presentation placed a barrier between the scholar and the layman, a barrier that hindered the popularization of the teachings of history. In this way Smith repeated in 1904 the warning that Mahan had sounded two years before.

It was obvious that in at least one important respect Smith did not succeed in convincing Albert Bushnell Hart, who served as president of the Association in 1909. For Hart had his doubts about the extent to which history should serve as a moral influence. The expression of such doubts, coming from the author of patriotic textbooks in American history and from one of the most effective teachers in Harvard Yard,[45] was perhaps surprising. Surprising or not, Hart's conception of scientific history would never have gained the approval of Smith, who would have viewed it as destructive of the immediate usefulness of historical knowledge. For Hart insisted that it was no part of the function of the scientific historian to distinguish between right and wrong, between virtue and vice; it was no part of his function to draw moral lessons from history. Taking a stand that his friend Theodore Roosevelt would have deplored, Hart observed that the scientific historian regarded all themes simply as subjects for examination. Whether he studied the massacre of St. Bartholomew or the Great Awakening did not make any difference. He

44 *Lectures on the Study of History, Delivered in Oxford, 1859-61* (New York, 1866), p. 13.

45 Samuel E. Morison, "Alfred Bushnell Hart, 1889-1939," Massachusetts Historical Society, *Proceedings, 1936-1941* (Boston, 1942), LXVI, 435.

approached all subjects in the same spirit, never opening his mouth unless he had a handy footnote reference to a reliable primary source. Hart thought that the gildsman would do well to reassert the glories of the moderate and the dispassionate presentation and "to warn the world" of the dangers of unsound historical study and writing. Despite his own considerable interest in the problems of the present, an interest that was soon to be reflected in his attendance at the Bull Moose Convention of 1912, Hart urged the scholar to avoid using history for propagandistic purposes.

When Hart's immediate successors dealt with the practical value of historical study, they also dealt with it only briefly. Take, for example, Frederick Jackson Turner, Hart's new colleague at Harvard and the most influential American historian of his generation. Son of a Wisconsin newspaper editor, Turner had practically inherited an interest in current events.[46] Already as an undergraduate orator, he had declared that faith in democracy[47] which was to figure so prominently in his writings; and, as a young teacher, he had declared another faith that was to influence his approach to the past, his faith in the immediate usefulness of history. Some twenty years before his presidential message of 1910, Turner, in "The Significance of History," had made it clear that he prized historical study for what it could do to foster good citizenship and intelligent public service. Characterizing as mere antiquarianism the study of the past for its own sake, he had suggested that the historian differed from the antiquarian in that he approached the past always with an eye on "the living present." This was much the same point that Turner made briefly in his presidential message on "Social Forces in American History." Speaking in the period of Republican in-

46 Carl Lotus Becker, "Frederick Jackson Turner," in *Everyman His Own Historian: Essays on History and Politics* (New York, 1935), p. 218; Max Farrand, "Frederick Jackson Turner: "A Memoir," Massachusetts Historical Society, *Proceedings, 1932-1936* (Boston, 1940), LXV, 434-35.

47 Fulmer Mood, "Turner's Formative Period," in *The Early Writings of Frederick Jackson Turner* (Madison, 1938), pp. 7-8.

surgency, he suggested that history should "hold the lamp for conservative reform;" it should not merely preserve "curios for the . . . museum." Ignoring the dangers associated with the re-writing of history in keeping with current viewpoints, Turner urged that contemporary problems be viewed in their historical relationships and that past events be viewed from "the vantage-ground of present developments."

Turner's successor, William M. Sloane, advanced the thesis that "history must have no thesis nor be used to maintain one." Nevertheless, Sloane argued in 1911 that the purpose of his-torical study was to account for the present; hence he thought that the gildsman should discard all data that had no bearing on the current scene. Since the historian was concerned with explaining the present, he was justified in ignoring those aspects of the past that failed to throw light on the here and now. In a sense, this present-minded stand was a peculiar one for a scholar like Sloane, who had started his academic career as a teacher of Latin; but once Sloane had turned to historical writing he chose themes that reflected his conviction that knowledge of the past should serve the needs of the present. Shortly after the col-lapse of Boulangism he published his most important work, his four-volume *Life of Napoleon Bonaparte* (1896); and in the period when the Dreyfusards were agitating for anti-clerical legislation, he wrote *The French Revolution and Religious Re-form* (1901). Sloane's present-mindedness was rooted in his past.

Theodore Roosevelt, probably to the surprise of many a gilds-man, took a much broader view of the usefulness of history. Ad-dressing the Association several weeks after his defeat in the election of 1912, he observed that the wisdom of one generation was sometimes repudiated by the next; hence it was difficult to know what was most worth knowing. Roosevelt granted that a utilitarian concept should underlie all education, but he insisted that the goal of education should not be merely utilitarian.

History obviously had its practical side. It was this practical side that Roosevelt himself had emphasized in his first historical study, *The Naval War of 1812* (1882), a work which, according to Admiral William S. Sims, had a profound effect on the attitude of the American people towards their navy.[48] In other writings, too, Roosevelt had drawn lessons from the past; so much so, that in a study like *Oliver Cromwell* (1900) the world of Cromwell bulked less large than that of Roosevelt. It was not strange, then, that in his presidential message Roosevelt emphasized that history could teach lessons which would help the present-day American better to cope with many social and industrial problems.

Yet Roosevelt insisted that the practical aspect of historical study was only one of its aspects. He maintained that "history which is not professedly utilitarian, history which is didactic only as great poetry is unconsciously didactic, may yet possess that highest form of usefulness, the power to thrill the souls of men with stories of strength and craft and daring, and to lift them out of their common selves to the heights of high endeavor." Apart from its immediate usefulness, Roosevelt valued history for its power to inspire "broad human sympathy" and "lofty and generous emotion."

Roosevelt's successor, William A. Dunning, also protested briefly against overemphasis on the immediate usefulness of history. Though Dunning was an authority on the period of the Civil War and Reconstruction—what in his own lifetime was still recent American history—he was also an authority on the development of European political thought; and it was doubtless his familiarity with the way in which the political ideas of one generation often called forth the scorn of subsequent generations that prompted him to warn of the dangers of present-mindedness in historical study. Probably there were other influences, too: Dunning had studied under present-minded Treitschke at Berlin and no less present-minded Burgess at Columbia; he was

48 H. J. Thornton, "Theodore Roosevelt," in William T. Hutchinson, ed., *op. cit.*, p. 229.

for many years the colleague of Burgess, to say nothing of Sloane and James Harvey Robinson; and he had an aversion to what Charles E. Merriam has called "contact with political affairs."[49]

Dunning pointed out that it was one thing to study the past in order to find examples and conditions which would instruct and enlighten the present; it was quite another thing to distort the past in order to glorify the present. Often, to be sure, it was hard for the gildsman to respect the ideas of earlier generations; but Dunning cautioned that the view of the present as the high-water mark of all historical evolution was fatal to the study of the past. For when the gildsman took excessive pride in the achievements of his own age, he was likely to take a warped view of previous ages. Ignoring the complexities of the past, he was likely to regard with interest only those ideas that anticipated current ideas, only those that threw light on the present and were immediately useful. Dunning was convinced that the past could never be understood as long as it was viewed as a staging-area for the present, as long as it was examined chiefly for fore-shadowings of the words and deeds of "the wonderful twentieth century." For the reading of the past in present terms was destructive of sound historical study.

If the gildsman needed anything, Dunning declared in 1913, he needed humility. He could not understand the past, if he spent his time admiring recent demonstrations of the simple-mindedness of former ages, if he spent his time scorning what was done and said before the modern era. Dunning insisted that the historian should stop parading his contempt for those accomplishments of the past which did not anticipate the present and serve its immediate needs. In one of the most stimulating addresses ever delivered before the Association, he defended historical study even when it failed to explain developments on the contemporary scene; and in so doing he joined the ranks of the few presidents who had not sought to justify history mainly on the basis of its immediate social utility.

49 Charles Edward Merriam, "William Archibald Dunning," in Howard W. Odum, ed., *American Masters of Social Science* (New York, 1927), p. 136.

CHAPTER II

THE IMMEDIATE USEFULNESS OF
HISTORY: WAR AND POSTWAR YEARS

IT was one thing to be alive to the dangers connected with the attempt to profit from the immediate usefulness of history. It was quite another thing, especially in the years after 1914, to avoid those dangers. For, with the coming of the War, the gildsman could hardly overlook his social responsibilities. He was a citizen as well as a historian, a citizen who would be tempted to combine business and service, a citizen who would be tempted to put his historical knowledge to work in the world, a citizen who would be tempted to subordinate history to current events.

Consider the case of Andrew C. McLaughlin, for instance. That McLaughlin, as president of the Association in 1914, would choose to discuss "American History and American Democracy" could perhaps have been anticipated. This was a subject with which he had dealt as chairman of the Committee of Seven and of the Committee of Five, the Committees of the Association whose purpose it had been to recommend changes in the history courses taught in American secondary schools. "American History and American Democracy" was, moreover, a subject with which McLaughlin had dealt recently in *The Courts, the Constitution, and Parties* (1912), in the new edition of his high-school textbook, *A History of the American Nation* (1913), and in the *Cyclopedia of American Government* (1914), of which he was co-editor. Especially in his textbook McLaughlin had revealed his concern over the future of popular government; and though he asserted that the historian should not permit his views of the present and his hopes for the future to color his account,[1] he made it clear at the same time that the

1 *A History of the American Nation* (New ed., New York, 1913), p. v.

past should serve the needs of the present. Nevertheless, when McLaughlin addressed the Association in 1914, he confessed that he felt guilty about his choice of topic; he suspected that as a historian who had faith in objectivity he should not be issuing any kind of special plea. Reassured, however, by the preoccupation of many Americans with the problems of popular government, he would face the risks involved; and even if, as he apologized, he could not be original in his presentation, he counted at least on not being distant from the thought of other gildsmen.

McLaughlin observed that Americans were viewing the whole democratic framework with more hope and also with more fear than perhaps at any other time in recent decades. On the one hand, they were heartened by the belief that a country which recognized that men should be free to work out their own future would in the long run meet the needs of the masses and not the demands of privileged elements. On the other hand, Americans were disheartened by the fear that democracy, with all its wastefulness, could manage neither to survive nor to spread in an atmosphere of economic and social distress. Living in a world filled with international rivalries, Americans feared that a national state could not maintain itself and meet the economic and spiritual needs of its people unless it was led by technical experts and statesmen whose authority was assured. In these circumstances, McLaughlin considered it no academic matter to re-examine the achievements and failures of American popular government. If, as at no previous time, he felt impelled to undertake such a re-examination, the reason was that American institutions, far from being glorified, were being widely assailed.

McLaughlin did not deny that there was much confusion about the meaning of America; it was even possible that America had a meaning of which it was unaware. But this did not alter the fact that more than other peoples Americans thought they had a mission, a mission inseparable from the ideal of human betterment; and unless the historian understood this, he was not likely to capture the spirit of the American past. McLaughlin considered it one of the duties of the historian to help his nation to achieve self-awareness; this was part of the practical value of historical study. Small wonder, then, that he could view George Bancroft with a sympathetic insight that was rare among the gildsmen of his time. What he saw in Bancroft's *History* was an expression of the self-confidence of the Jacksonian era and an effort to understand the American spirit.

McLaughlin's point was that every historian was constantly at work in a cultural setting. He was often meeting with circumstances that undermined his attempt to be objective; he was often prompted to use the past to serve the needs of the present. When slavery was a major subject of public discussion, he frequently turned to history to throw light on the present problem of slavery. Just as he had previously dealt with the colonial period from the vantage point of Yorktown, so he came to treat of ante-bellum years from that of Appomattox. Hermann Von Holst, for example, wrote with his gaze fixed steadily on secession. A lover of union and liberty, he generally viewed the events of the first decades of the nineteenth century as a preparation for Jefferson Davis and Lincoln. Nor was Von Holst alone in this. Many a historian did essentially the same thing, reading backwards by the reflected light of a later time.

McLaughlin emphasized that the historian made his selection and interpretation of materials with "something central and determinate" in mind. Often he studied the American past in order to explain some particular matter that had a timely interest and a topical importance; he studied the past to supply the needs of the present. Yet the difficulty with this approach was that material which at one time was immediately useful was often much less so at a later time. For instance, said McLaughlin in 1914, the year after the publication of Beard's *An Economic Interpretation of the Constitution of the United States,* the latest tendency in historical interpretation was to regard constitutional development as little more than a phase of economic history. This, however, McLaughlin viewed as an example of the present-mindedness that often made more for enlivenment than for enlightenment.

One can find no fault [he said] with the desire to trace the development of economic conditions, or with the wish to see how economic forces have played through political institutions or toyed with constitutions and parties. The story is there for someone to tell, convincingly if he can and truthfully if he is able to see the light. The ever present danger is the old one—the temptation to find in the past the present, not simply conditions out of which the present came, and to find just what we expect to find and not the almost infinite variety of motive and interest and of personal and social character which changed and changed again under the new environment and responded to new suggestions.

McLaughlin did not pretend that he himself was anything but a being rooted in time. He recognized that he was reflecting the temper of his age, and that he was attempting to take advantage of the immediate usefulness of history when he suggested that the events of the American past should be viewed with the American sense of mission and the American democratic ideal chiefly in mind. Voicing his concern over the condition of popular government, he pressed for the reworking of the American past in the light of democratic ideals and realities and in the light of that growth of the American spirit which too many historians had tended to ignore. From the adoption and application of his approach, McLaughlin granted that some distortion was sure to result. Such a risk he was willing to assume. "If this be distortion," he asserted, "I must make the best of it; for whether the historians of the future have the problem or not, we certainly are to-day interested in what has gone before us, primarily, I believe, with this experiment in self-government in mind, with all that it involves, or with all that we find to be wrapt up in it—social and individual justice, right as God gives us to see the right, and human conditions." This did not mean that McLaughlin wished to discard everything that bore no relationship to the development and functioning of American democracy: all that went into the making of America deserved to be considered.

Even so, McLaughlin, who as a professor at Michigan and at Chicago had long been aware of the need to weigh the "Western ingredient in our national character,"[2] considered it indisputable that "the very genius of American history" was the optimistic frontiersman, with his faith in progress, his belief in freedom, and his hatred of the tyranny of the past. This frontiersman underwent many changes as the wilderness gave way before civilizing institutions; and these changes, which McLaughlin was later to discuss in *Steps in the Development of American Democracy* (1920),[3] he urged the historian to examine. He acknowledged, to be sure, the importance of the contributions of his friend Frederick Jackson Turner. But much as he admired Turner, he noted, and perhaps not altogether accurately, that by reason of Turner's emphasis on the relationship between the frontier and individual self-reliance another relationship had been generally obscured, that of the frontier and privilege; and this relationship McLaughlin suggested that the historian should explore. Obviously, then, there remained much unfinished business for the scholar who wished to bring his knowledge of the past to bear upon the problems of the present. He ought to analyze discrepancies between American ideals and realities. He ought to study the justifications of popular government. In the face of the growth of strata and classes in society, he should reexamine the nature of democratic equality. McLaughlin held that the American historian must always remember that at bottom the history of a democracy was an account of the struggle to become and to remain a democracy. Having used the past to serve his own day and the future of his students,[4] McLaughlin, in effect, urged other historians to do likewise.

2 *Lewis Cass* (Rev. ed., Boston, 1899), p. v.

3 *Steps in the Development of American Democracy* (New York, 1920), chaps. VII and VIII.

4 *A.H.R.*, LIII (1948), 434.

Not that McLaughlin's successor, English-born H. Morse Stephens, needed any urging. The truth of the matter was that Stephens, drawing on his knowledge of French and Indian history, had often used the past as a guide to present actions. The study, for example, of the French Revolution, the subject he probably knew best, he had recommended because it provided, he thought, the most valuable lessons in the political history of the world;[5] and the study of Indian history, which he had done much to encourage as editor for a time of *India, A Journal for the Discussion of Indian Affairs,* he had also recommended because it could give answers to present riddles.

Stephens had long stressed the need to explore the origins of nationalism and the part played by the historian in stirring up nationalist sentiment; his presidential message of 1915 on "Nationality and History" was, in some respects, only a generalized version of an article that he had written almost thirty years before on "Modern Historians and Their Influence on Small Nationalities."[6] But what distinguished the article of 1887 from the address of 1915 was that in the intervening years nationalism itself had changed, taking on an increasingly menacing character. In the meantime, too, Stephens had changed: his faith in historiographical objectivity, a faith that he had expressed in many of his earlier writings,[7] had waned. So much so, that by 1915 he believed that the first obligation of the historian was to understand his limitations. He lived in the present, and the present was going to influence his thought about the past. Indeed, what made necessary the rewriting of history was not so much the accumulation of fresh material as the changing interests and needs of new generations. The historian found himself unavoidably dominated by the atmosphere of his time. He was biased not only by his education and his personal back-

5 *A History of the French Revolution* (2 vols., New York, 1886-91), I, iii.

6 *Contemporary Review,* LII (1887), 107-21.

7 See, for example, his article on "History," in Stephens *et al., Counsel upon the Reading of Books* (Boston, 1900), pp. 66-69.

ground but also by the attitudes of the age in which he happened to live. He might well make a genuine effort to find out the truth about the past; but unless he was "a self-deceived fanatic," deep down he knew that it was impossible to overcome his personal limitations, that he could come only more or less close to the truth.

Stephens did not question the honesty of the protestations of love of truth and objectivity that decorated the preface of many a historical work, but the mere fact that a historian found it necessary to make such protestations indicated at once that he doubted that he "should be implicitly believed." And the truth was that all the while the historian really saw and used the past in the light of his own present. Neither the medieval writer, nor the Reformation publicist, nor Gibbon, nor Voltaire, could free himself from his own times. Neither could the nineteenth-century historian, who lived in an atmosphere that was permeated by the idea of nationality. Influenced by that idea, he worked, whether consciously or unconsciously, to foster enmity among nations. Just as in former times the historian had helped to intensify religious and political fervor, so in the period since the French Revolution he helped to create and encourage "national fanaticism." Though in many cases he simply voiced the views of his fellow-countrymen, he still had to bear his portion of the blame for dividing the nations of the world against one another. He had to recognize himself for what he was, a Lord High Executioner of international cooperation.

Quickening the rise and growth of the national spirit, Henri Martin, Augustin Thierry, Jules Michelet, and François Guizot taught Frenchmen that they had a national character and a national indentity that dated back many centuries. Molding that fiery nationalism which culminated in the annexation of Schleswig-Holstein and Alsace-Lorraine, writers like Dahlmann, Droysen, Sybel, and Treitschke taught Germans that despite political separatism the German nation was a historical unit with solid roots in the past. Small wonder, thought Stephens, that Bismarck was reported to have declared that, apart from the Prussian army, professors of history contributed most to the making of the new Germany under Prussian leadership. Nor were nationalist historians confined to France and Germany. Spain and Italy could hold their own. So, too, could England, said Stephens, who had been born and educated there. A writer like John Richard Green, he pointed out, had tried to make it clear to Englishmen that they had a national personality and a national unity that dated from antiquity. As for American nationalist historians, Stephens thought it "ungracious in this presence" to consider them in any detail; and so he contented himself merely with the mention of two former presidents of the Association, Schouler (1897) and McMaster (1905), to both of whom he ascribed more of a nationalistic impulse than the facts warranted.

Stephens did not wish to overlook the historians of the smaller nationalities, who, keeping pace with their more powerful historian-neighbors, sought to revive noble memories of happier days. It was, for example, the growth of interest in the Portuguese past, associated with the name of Alexandra Herculano, that smashed the possibility of a successful Iberian unionist movement, said Stephens, himself the author of *The Story of Portugal* (1891) and of a biography of Albuquerque (1892). Similarly, it was the growth of interest in the Czech past, associated with the name of Franz Palacký, that guaranteed unrest in Bohemia; and it was the growth of interest in Romanian, Finnish, Polish, Croatian, Swedish, Belgian, and Danish history that enabled the scholar to draw on the past for the purposes of the present.

Thus, consciously or unconsciously, the nineteenth-century historian succumbed to the nationalist atmosphere of the period. Just as the medieval chronicler had taken for granted the truth of Christianity, so the nineteenth-century historian took for granted the righteousness of nationality. Yet the important thing was that, in reworking the past for his own age, he encouraged the inhumanity of nationality to nationality. He advanced the notion that civilization and progress worked only through the unit of the nation. He fostered the belief that it was the duty of every nation to spread its distinctive civilization—and to use force when necessary. Naturally, these beliefs found their way into the schools; and without question they encouraged the decline of the idea of a common Christianity and of the idea of the brotherhood of man.

Goldwin Smith had been encouraged back in 1904 by the "vast improvement" that he discovered in American treatments of relations with Britain.[8] Shortly after the Boer War he found that the British lion's tail was being less often twisted in American textbooks. But Stephens, an ex-Britisher himself, shared none of Smith's optimism, declaring in 1915 what was soon to be substantiated in Charles Altschul's study of *The American Revolution in Our School Text-Books* (1917): that by means of the study of United States history Americans were being indoctrinated with a hatred of the British.[9] Not that Stephens thought any better of his ex-countrymen. They, in turn, he recognized, suffered from a nationalist disease that was being made worse by the study of history. Yet the Anglo-American hatred was mild when compared with the Franco-German hatred that historical study had done so much to intensify. Ranke knew what he was saying when he told Thiers in 1871 that "the Germans were fighting against Louis XIV."

The moral of all this, said Stephens in 1915, was that something must be done about the "hymns of hate" that the nationalist historian had incorporated into his writings. By all means the gildsman must overcome his unpreparedness for the task of re-education that lay ahead. As Stephens phrased it in a frequently quoted paragraph:

8 *A.H.R.*, X (1905), 511.

9 Charles Altschul, *The American Revolution in Our School Text-Books: An Attempt to Trace the Influence of Early School Education on the Feeling towards England in the United States* (New York, 1917). See the recent remarks of George Macaulay Trevelyan in *History and the Reader* (London, 1945), pp. 21-22.

Woe unto us! Professional historians, professional historical students, professional teachers of history, if we cannot see, written in blood, in the dying civilization of Europe, the dreadful result of exaggerated nationalism as set forth in the patriotic histories of some of the most eloquent historians of the nineteenth century. May we not hope that this will be but a passing phase of historical writing, since its awful sequel is so plainly exhibited before us, and may we not expect that the historians of the twentieth century may seek rather to explain the nations of the world to each other in their various contributions to the progress of civilization and to bear ever in mind the magnificent sentiment of Goethe: 'Above the nations is humanity.'

In this way Stephens denounced the nineteenth-century attempt to exploit the immediate usefulness of history, and set forth his own suggestions for exploiting its immediate usefulness.

The first two wartime presidents tried to use history to throw light on the problems of democracy and nationalism. Nor were the problems of freedom to remain long neglected: George Lincoln Burr saw to that in 1916. Editor of *The Witch-Persecution* (1896) and of *Narratives of Witchcraft Cases, 1648-1706* (1914), Burr probably knew as much about the rise of religious liberty as any scholar of his time; and it was to the great regret of his fellow gildsmen that he failed to finish his book on this subject as well as on the others that he had "made his own."[10] In part, this failure grew out of Burr's loyalty to Andrew D. White, whom he had assisted in numerous projects, most notably in the preparation of *A History of the Warfare of Science with Theology in Christendom.* Nevertheless, the two men held quite different views of the usefulness of history. Back in the nineties, Burr, to be sure, had prepared, on White's recommendation, the report for the Venezuela Boundary Commission, which J. Franklin Jameson considered "as fine a piece of historical research and

10 Cf. J. Franklin Jameson, "Introduction," *Persecution and Liberty: Essays in Honor of George Lincoln Burr* (New York, 1931), pp. xvii-xviii.

criticism as ever was buried in a government report."[11] But Burr's approach to the past was not the present-minded one that White's was; unlike White, he did not seek to use the past mainly to throw light on the present. History he valued for its own sake and for what it could do to broaden experience. This he made clear in what was otherwise none too clear a presidential message.

Reversing his usual procedure for the purposes of this message, Burr dealt not with the history of freedom but with "The Freedom of History"; and if his address bordered at times on the nebulous, the complexity of the subject would seem largely responsible. To start with, Burr conjectured that from the earliest times history must have caused concern to those authorities who sought to restrict liberty. By its very nature, it must have invited interference from these authorities, for its propaganda value could hardly have escaped them. Obviously, then, human thought had first to achieve considerable freedom before the birth of history could take place. And Burr suggested that it was no accident that history was born at a time when Greek freedom was at its height, adding that while Greece alone was ready for the step that Herodotus took, even Greece was none too ready.

Burr believed that there could hardly be any adequate acknowledgment of the contribution of Herodotus: scarcely had a fresh approach ever been conceived with a clarity or stated with a vividness to match his. Though, by modern standards, he was overly credulous and reverential, Burr thought it well to remember that he enjoyed only a limited freedom. Even as he wrote his *History,* the Athenian populace was striking at those whose opinions seemed to subvert religion or government, so that the very credulity and reverence which prompted many a modern historian to brush Herodotus aside were probably instrumental in gaining for him an audience in his own day; and so effectively did he educate this audience in the ways of the new study that Thucydides "found history free." Assured of a hearing, he could

11 Quoted in Roland H. Bainton, *George Lincoln Burr: His Life* (Ithaca, 1943), p. 88.

think not merely of a temporary triumph but of a product of everlasting value.

If, in Roman antiquity, no further steps were taken in the direction of the freedom of history, Burr found the explanation largely in an inertia that made possible the domination of history by rhetoric, an inertia to which even a Polybius succumbed. What still passed for history became, in the Roman world, the weapon of politicians, special pleaders, and men of letters, people who sought to profit by its immediate usefulness. To be sure, the Roman writer of history was "not yet wholly free." The trouble was that the history-reading public had not reached proportions sufficiently large to assure the historian of financial independence. That the difficulty was largely economic was suggested, Burr thought, by the fact that those Romans who came closest to realizing the ideals of historical truth were fairly well-to-do. Even so, there was no overlooking the divorce between the Roman ideal and the Roman practice of history. Though Cicero recognized that history should risk no lie nor hide a truth, the fact of the matter was that the Romans failed largely to grasp its nature and its value. Seeking to take advantage of its practical side, they used it for propagandistic and literary purposes.

From the sterility of Roman rhetoric, Burr pointed out, history was partially liberated by Christianity; but what emerged from the liberation was "not truth, but *the* Truth." History came to provide the link between earth and heaven, and all that clashed with Holy Writ had to be rejected. Submerged in theology, history came to be valued for the "deeper meanings" it could disclose. Not that in medieval times history was altogether without liberty: writers like Einhard, Villehardouin, and Joinville proved that. Just the same, Burr thought that what worked above all against the freedom of history in the medieval setting was not so much intolerance as inertia. If revelation sufficed, what need was there for historical research?

Even the growing study of the ancients did not, at the outset, greatly benefit the freedom of history. The humanist who was employed to write a biography of his prince or an account of his

prince's dynasty hardly found himself in a position to deal criti
cally with the past. The same was true of the humanist who wa
commissioned to trace the history of some urban community
Nevertheless, even as a Petrarch sifted charters and a Valla ex
posed forgeries, producing the immediately useful results which
their patrons had ordered, they succeeded in developing soun
methods of research. Burr was inclined to date modern freedon
of inquiry from the time when Valla picked flaws in sacred Vul
gate and in hardly less sacred Livy. For the revival of the spiri
of Herodotus and Thucydides meant that the freedom of histor
had once again come into its own. Even the resurgence of theol
ogy during the Reformation did not long submerge interest i
the truth about the human past. This might not have been s
if either Catholicism or Lutheranism had achieved a unite
Christendom, for Burr suspected that in this event history woul
once more have come to serve as a handmaid to theology. A
things were, both religious camps had other uses to which t
put history. As a historical religion, Christianity had to be vin
dicated by both Catholic and Protestant on the basis of facts, s
that each group engaged in research in order to find evidenc
to satisfy the faithful, humiliate the faithless, and persuade th
wavering.

Naturally, said Burr, the freedom of history was really in
separable from the freedom of the historian. A divided Christian
ity made travel dangerous, hindered research, and hampere
cooperation among historical investigators. State and church
moreover, recognizing the present usefulness of history, fre
quently joined forces to stifle the historical press when it faile
to serve their needs. Although attempts to muzzle history ex
plained at times the caution and the silence of the historian, th
time did come when such attempts publicized a work and guar
anteed its success. Yet if the highest usefulness of history wa
to be realized, it was clear, Burr thought, that the freedom o
history and of the historian must be vigilantly maintained—
especially by reason of the fact that censorship, intolerance, an

theories of collectivism and of governmental omnipotence were in the ascendant in Europe.

Burr delivered his message a few months before the United States entered the first World War; when his successor, Worthington C. Ford, addressed the Association, the United States was a participant of almost nine months' standing. Ford spoke at a time when Clio had joined the Creel Press Bureau and the National Board for Historical Service—at a time when gildsman after gildsman was cutting loose and working up not altogether historical words to win the war.[12] Yet if Ford could be as fair-minded and moderate as he proved to be in his presidential message, the explanation was perhaps that, as the editor of numerous volumes of sources and as the editor of the Massachusetts Historical Society, he had seldom dealt with the present and the recent past in his scholarly work. Possibly, then, what helped to explain his composure, even in the war setting, was the fact that he had spent so much time on the journals of the Continental Congress, on the writings of George Washington and of John Quincy Adams, and on other documents remote from the contemporary scene.

Ford cautioned that the historian who dealt with current affairs could hardly hope to produce definitive works, for he lacked not only perspective but uncolored material. Ford granted that the historian seemed to have an advantage over the average journalist or public official. His knowledge of the past, his experience in analyzing historical characters, his familiarity with research techniques, all these helped him in his search for "some solid foundation in the welter of to-day." Furthermore, the long-range view in which he was trained tended to make for a most desirable moderateness of approach. Having long tested the deeds and utterances of the politician, for example, he was in a position

12 C. Hartley Grattan, "The Historians Cut Loose," in Harry Elmer Barnes, *In Quest of Truth and Justice: De-Bunking the War Guilt Myth* (Chicago, 1928), pp. 142-64; James R. Mock and Cedric Larson, *Words that Won the War: The Story of the Committee on Public Information, 1917-1919* (Princeton, 1939), pp. 158-86.

to learn and teach the lesson that from the start of American history "the country has been in a chronic state of crisis, requiring the election of this or that man to office, demanding sacrifices which constitute the stock claim of the politician to reward; that the years are strewn with such sacrifices, and that the number of pretended and willing saviors of the country would fill several Valhallas." The historian was likewise in a position to draw the lesson that families, governments, and censors were powerless against time; they could not suppress the unpleasant items that deserved to be remembered.

The important thing from Ford's point of view was that the historian, especially in time of war, should set the example for those unaccustomed to the ways of critical scholarship. He should keep an open mind; he should be cautious in his criticisms so as to avoid injustices, exercising "the same patience and restraint under wrongs and violations of good faith as have placed our country with an unsoiled record at the front of a world movement." The deluge of propaganda with which wartime America was being swamped made it all the more urgent for the historian to cultivate sober-mindedness and non-partisanship; in the absence of much pertinent information and with the sober weighing of evidence a long way off, he had a superb opportunity to make history not so much philosophy as caution teaching by example. Conceding that it was difficult to refrain from taking sides at a time when hot debates were raging, Ford deplored the presence of some scholars in extremist camps. While he would not impugn the integrity of the extremist, he did condemn his violent language. Happily, the long-range viewpoint offered the consolation that much that passed for history in 1917 would speedily be forgotten—only to be disinterred from time to time in order to illustrate what misguided enthusiasm and faulty thinking could do to the study of the past.

No doubt one of the extremists whom Ford had in mind was his friend and successor, William R. Thayer, the leading American authority on Italian history and one whose love of Italy was matched only by his hatred of Germany. No preacher of Ford's sweet reasonableness, Thayer, proud of his English ancestry, had long been expressing his Germanophobia. Militantly pro-Ally ever since the start of the War,[13] he had attempted to bring his knowledge of the past to bear on present American policies; and it was appropriate that when some of his wartime writings were later reprinted, they appeared under the title, *Volleys from a Non-Combatant* (1919), for volleys they certainly were. In *The Life and Letters of John Hay* (1915), Thayer had tried to expose the German menace; in fact, he had asked Theodore Roosevelt for evidence of German perfidy in connection with the Venezuelan dispute of 1902.[14] In *Germany vs. Civilization: Notes on the Atrocious War* (1916), he had tried to drive home what he called "manipulating Teutonic traits." In the preface to *Out of Their Own Mouths* (1917), he had tried to point up Prussian mendacity and cruelty.

All this he tried to do again in his presidential message of 1918, the first postwar message prepared for the Association. Making much the same point that he had made in *The Collapse of Superman* (1918),[15] Thayer lashed out at the German attempt to reduce history to a neat pattern and exploit its present usefulness; and he used the recent German experience as evidence of the menace of fitting history to a theory. If not for the German obsession with the theory of the survival of the fittest, Thayer contended, the recently-ended, German-made War might not have attained the tremendous scale that it did, and perhaps might never even have been waged. Yet the theory did obsess the Germans, whose conceit, pedantry, doctrinairism, and envy made it possible for their rulers to convince them that they were the nation best fit to survive. Did not their scientists, moreover, offer the guarantee that this survival was an established law of biol-

13 Charles Downer Hazen, ed., *The Letters of William Roscoe Thayer* (Boston, 1926), pp. 231-32.

14 Henry F. Pringle, *Theodore Roosevelt: A Biography* (New York, 1931), pp. 285-86.

15 *The Collapse of Superman* (Boston, 1918), chap. III.

ogy? Far be it, then, from the devoutly materialistic Germans to challenge an alleged scientific law, particularly one that was so flattering. In the circumstances it was easy for the Prussian militarists to use education and military service to make the Germans into a warlike nation; it was easy to teach them that war was man's chief duty and noblest undertaking, and that war left no place for moral or humanitarian considerations. Increasingly, the Germans put stress on physical strength and brute force in order to realize their objective of ruling the world. Out went Goethe; in came Hindenburg. All in all, said Thayer, the German experience showed what awaited those who "would make history and biology their accomplices in the most frightful crimes ever committed against laws human and divine." Although Thayer was seemingly unaware of the dangers of his own use of history, he was well aware of the dangers of the German use of it.

This was apparent not only in his first presidential message but in his second as well, for Thayer's strong views on the German question remained strong even a year after the Armistice; and in his second message, which was made possible by the postponement of the Association's meeting of 1918, he showed that he had continued to nurse his wrath to keep it warm. This time Thayer lashed out at the German study of psychology, insisting that it was designed in the last analysis to prepare for German world domination. Nor was it only German psychology that was suspect; suspect, too, were the many historical and biographical studies which had been affected by its sinister influence.

Thayer did not believe the German historian's protestations of impartiality; German historical writing offered only further evidence of the German deceit that he had sought for years to expose. It was perhaps debatable that Theodor Mommsen, when he wrote his chapters on Caesar, consciously aimed to idealize the Prussian state, but there was no question that he did so. As for Sybel, he worked unashamedly to glorify Hohenzollerns and Junkers. So, too, Treitschke used history for propaganda purposes; and, of all German historians, it was Treitschke, writing of the past with his eyes on the present, whom Thayer credited with having exercised the most "diabolical influence."

Thayer believed that the War pointed up the need to renounce the German approach to history. Apparently ignoring his own recent activities, he condemned the use of history as a bludgeon; and he asserted that the determination of the truth about the past was the simple goal of historical study. This was not to say that he wished to abandon the diligence and meticulousness with which German scholarship had come to be associated; but he protested against the notion that the Germans enjoyed a monopoly of diligence and meticulousness. He recognized, moreover, that some of the greatest historians of all times, Carlyle, Macaulay, and Grote, for example, were far from impartial. Yet what mattered, said Thayer, introducing a distinction between good and bad partisanship, was that the writings of these English historians were honest and not designed to pervert, corrupt, and deceive. Their partisanship he found to be of the sort that could often disclose the truth with a remarkable degree of accuracy; it was different from the perverting, corrupting, and deceiving partisanship of the modern German historian.

Just as the War taught the need to be wary of the German approach to history, so, too, it taught the need to be wary of the use of *a priori* arguments in the interpretation of history. But Thayer complained that such arguments continued to be used: witness the appeals of supporters and opponents of the League of Nations and of the Peace Treaties. Thayer, therefore, deemed it well to think back to the prewar period when the *a priori* reasoners had their heydey. Even the outbreak of the Balkan disturbances did not overly alarm them; they continued to sing "as sweetly as the sirens their song of peace." Divorced from the realities of their times, they reasoned that the gigantic size of armies guaranteed the peace as did the tremendous advances in technology and the economic ties of the world of nations. Things were getting better and better, they argued, and war was ruled out by the very nature of the twentieth-century atmosphere. In this way they deduced a lasting peace from a situation that soon produced war.

At this point, Thayer, the biographer of Cavour, John Hay, and Theodore Roosevelt, proclaimed his lack of faith in the statesman's power to predict. He thought it simply a question of applying an easy test: that of asking the statesman to predict whether or not war would come in a stated period of time. If the statesman was honest and wise, he would confess his ignorance; if not, not. Time was when reasonably accurate predictions were not so hard to make. During the period of monarchical absolutism, when traditional policies tended to hold, it was relatively simple to foresee some aspects of the future. A statesman did not have to be a prophet to determine how Louis XIV would act towards Austria. In more recent times, however, too many variables entered into the picture. With the growth of democracy, moreover, Thayer suggested that it would become increasingly difficult to predict the antics that the future would play in the realm of politics. Hence he suspected the claims of both supporters and opponents of the League of Nations and of the Peace Treaties. No one, he said, had reason to be so sure of anything as those special pleaders were of everything. Convinced of the unpredictability of politics in the modern world, Thayer could "assert no more about the future than that it some time will be the present." He granted, nevertheless, that there were some qualities of human nature that could be considered immutable. Righteousness, loyalty, friendliness, and self-sacrifice, for instance, were so basic to human nature that "if you have assembled these in your treaty or your league, nothing can prevent the dawning of the Utopian day; if you have not, you can no more attain peace than you can twist ropes of sand."

Though Thayer had his doubts about using knowledge of the past to predict the future, he risked the prediction that the usefulness of history promised to increase. It was discouraging that, despite the existence of records for so many centuries, the power of history to guide the statesman had been so ineffectively demonstrated in the past. Certainly history did not repeat itself. On the other hand, Thayer observed, certain elements did recur frequently; and it was this recurrence that accounted for the hope that the didactic possibilities of history—and of economics—would in time come into their own. If knowledge of history so rarely served to guide and caution mankind, the explanation, according to Thayer, was perhaps that the historian had not given sufficient emphasis to the ethical foundations of politics. Morals, after all, had the same relationship to politics that the rocky bottom had to the stream that flowed over it; and to the extent that the historian placed stress not only on surface manifestations but on foundations, to that extent would he command a wider audience. Thayer was not in favor of applying a Sunday-School approach to historical writing. On at least three grounds he found that approach harmful: it helped to create an imaginary world; it helped to make the historian a frightful hypocrite; and it helped to turn children into "precocious prigs." Therefore, if the gildsman sought to get below the surface of history, he should do so without recourse to Sunday-School techniques.

Thayer believed that the gildsman who started out in search of a moral purpose deserved to be criticized. Yet while he sided against the scholar who wedded "the false standards of a spurious ethics to the truth of facts," he sided with the scholar who defended the permanent facts of human nature as they were revealed in the past. Thayer thought that logic had an ardent champion in the historian; for he would repel all assaults, those of enthusiasts who equated Wilson and Washington as well as those of Bolsheviks who, ignoring the lessons of history, pronounced the abolition of God.

Thayer's hope that the past might guide the present led him to counsel the gildsman to go beyond externals in his effort to understand things historical. And in some respects his successor, Edward Channing, did just that; but it is doubtful that

Channing's "Hisorical Retrospect" of 1920 had quite the ring that an individualist like Thayer would have desired. Addressing the Association the year before the appearance of "The Period of Transition, 1815-1848," the fifth volume of his already classic *History of the United States,* Channing did not fail to draw on this study for the purposes of a presidential address which, because it took him away from the "Great Work," he probably considered a nuisance.[16] Nor did he fail to draw on the past for the guidance of the present; he could have boasted, after all, that he was the author of *The United States of America, 1765-1865* (1896), the small book which in translation had been read aloud in Russian revolutionary circles, and which, according to Maxim Gorki, had helped to undermine the Tsarist government in 1905.[17]

By and large the results of Channing's inquiry of 1920 into some of the main factors in the last hundred years of American development provided scarcely the kind of guide that a self-glorifying present would accept from the past; his investigation equipped him not so much to guide the present as to challenge and deflate it. Despite the highly-praised achievements of recent times in matters educational, for instance, the Harvard professor had his doubts as to just how superior the present school system was to the one that trained men of the calibre of Emerson, Poe, and Irving. Back in 1905, when Channing brought out the first volume of his *magnum opus,* he had seen in history forces that were "always struggling onward and upward toward that which is better and higher in human conception"; but in 1920 it was not so clear that things were getting better and better. Perhaps Channing was simply using one of his favorite classroom devices—and the device of his former teacher at Harvard, Henry Adams—that of attacking "tradition, myth, and

16 Cf. Samuel Eliot Morison, "Edward Channing: A Memoir," Massachusetts Historical Society, *Proceedings, 1930-32* (Boston, 1932), LXIV, 281.

17 *Ibid.,* p. 271.

historical humbug."[18] At all events, he suggested that, from the political, spiritual, mental, moral, and physical standpoints, present-day Americans were possibly not "happier and better off" than their ancestors in the days of Monroe, John Quincy Adams, Jackson, Calhoun, and Webster. Channing, who had long considered it his mission "to study and write without malice,"[19] did not use history to exalt the present at the expense of the past; he showed in 1920 the same past-mindedness that he had shown fifteen years before when he wrote: "To estimate [Americans of the past] by the conditions and ideas of the present day is to give a false picture to the reader and the student."[20]

According to Channing's successor, Jean Jusserand, there was not the slightest doubt that history taught, among many other lessons, the lesson of progress. Patriotic Frenchman though he was, Jusserand granted that the great concern of the historian was the search for truth. But that search was motivated not only by the craving for intellectual pleasure, said Jusserand, himself the author of such pleasant works as *English Wayfaring Life in the Middle Ages,* (1889), *A Literary History of the English People* (1895-1909), and *With Americans of Past and Present Days* (1916), which won for him the first Pulitzer award for a historical study. The search for historical truth, Jusserand insisted, as he would again do in *The Writing of History* (1926),[21] was also motivated by this idea: that to the extent that the past was better understood, to that extent could the future be more adequately anticipated, to that extent could the recurrence of past errors be more effectively avoided and the ar-

18 Samuel Eliot Morison, ed., *The Development of Harvard University Since the Inauguration of President Eliot, 1869-1929* (Cambridge, 1930), p. 169.

19 *The United States of America, 1765-1865* (New York, 1896), p. viii.

20 *A History of the United States* (6 vols., New York, 1905-25), I, vi.

21 "The Historian's Work," in Jusserand *et al., The Writing of History* (New York, 1926), pp. 28-31.

rival of happier times hastened. Jusserand viewed the past as "a great reflector" that should be kept bright; and its light should be "turned toward the future."

Because of his faith in the immediate usefulness of history, the French Ambassador to the United States regretted in 1921 that he had had so little to do as president of the gild. He confided that never before had he held an office which afforded "more pleasure with less trouble." Nevertheless, it was to the profession of the ambassador, one which gave more trouble and less pleasure, that Jusserand devoted his presidential address. He made sure to note, however, that there was no preparation more basic than history for one who planned to be an ambassador. For history taught the worthwhileness of truth and persuasion; it taught the reality of progress; and it taught an understanding of the problems of other nations. The study of the past figured so prominently in "The School for Ambassadors" that Jusserand, with consummate diplomatic skill, expressed the hope in 1921 that "history in the making will more and more have the same ideal and motto as history in the telling, the same as our American Historical Association, *Super omnia veritas*."

Appropriately enough, the French Ambassador to the United States and former medievalist had as his presidential successor Charles H. Haskins, the prominent American Francophile and medievalist's medievalist.[22] A most cautious scholar, Haskins had not hesitated, nevertheless, to use the past to guide the present. As the territorial specialist on Western Europe at the Paris Peace Conference, he had played an important part in determining the eastern frontier of France; and doubtless it was this recent practical service, which Haskins described in *Some Problems of the Peace Conference* (1920), that awakened him all the more to the need for a greater number of American experts on European history. But Haskins had long been urging

22 Cf. Lynn Thorndike, "Charles Homer Haskins (1870-1937)," *Isis*, XXVIII (1938), 55; *A.H.R.*, XLII (1937), 857.

the American scholar to do more research in European history. From the time of his first contributions to the *American Historical Review,* he had criticized the American gildsman who confined his researches to his own country's past.[23] And this note he struck once more in his presidential address on "European History and American Scholarship."

According to Haskins, the American gildsman who worked in European history could perform a real service. He could encourage respect for American scholarship, its fair-mindedness and its originality. No less important, he could help Europeans to understand Americans. Unfortunately, however, the drift away from scholarly provincialism in the United States was not proceeding rapidly enough. The result was that the American people continued to learn too much of their European history from European writers. As long as this state of affairs lasted, the dignity, independence, and creativity of American historical scholarship would continue to suffer; and Europeans and Americans would be less able to understand each other.

Haskins did not deny that it was natural that the historian should, as a rule, concentrate on his own country's past. In his fervor, however, for the writing of more non-United States history by the American scholar, Haskins made sure to stress that while America was the main concern of the gildsman it was far from being his only concern. If the narrowly national view of history had held sway in the past, the literature of history would have been much poorer. Without Gibbon, Grote, Ranke, Mommsen, Renan, and Champollion, European historiography would have suffered serious losses. If Prescott, Motley, Lea, Gross, and Mahan had failed to overcome their national prepossession, the literature of history would likewise have been woefully impoverished. Haskins did not deny that many difficulties awaited the American investigator whose historical interests refused to be bounded by his nation's borders. There was the obstacle of distance, and there were linguistic and

23 "The Vatican Archives," *ibid.,* II (1896), 40-58; "Opportunities for American Students of History at Paris," *ibid.,* III (1898), 418-30.

financial difficulties; but these could be overcome if the gildsman wished to "help Europe to understand the American mind."

Haskins pointed out that the American historian who sought to explain Europe to the American people needed much in the way of "steadying vision." Serving as an interpreter between nations, he should view Europe from the standpoint of the problems common to the individual European states. Furthermore, he should view the United States as a portion of the larger European unit, emphasizing that the distinction between European and American history was arbitrary and existed only for reasons of convenience. Unfortunately, said Haskins in 1922, there were still those who had persuaded themselves that the history of the United States was "providentially cut off from Europe by Columbus, or the Revolution, or the rejection of the Treaty of Versailles." This, however, merely showed how important it was for the historian "to tie Europe and America together in the popular mind."

To some extent this tying together was being accomplished for the colonial and Revolutionary eras, Haskins noted, thinking no doubt of the contributions of Osgood, Beer, and Andrews; but much remained to be done for the later periods of American history. In time of war, certainly, the fundamental ties between America and Europe were too prominent to be overlooked. In time of peace, on the other hand, it was all too easy to relapse into false notions of isolationism. There was all the more reason, therefore, for the historian to familiarize the layman and the official with the vital links connecting Europe and America. After all, said Haskins, Europe and America were "in the same boat, along with the still older Orient, all common material for history. The historian's world is one; let him interpret it as one, in relation both to scholarship and to the molding of public opinion!"

Just as Haskins wished to take advantage of the immediate usefulness of history, so, too, did his successor, Edward P. Cheyney, the leading American student of Elizabethan England. A specialist in the study of social and economic changes in history, Cheyney was a reformer and humanitarian at heart, a scholar who radiated "warm human sympathy."[24] And Cheyney was convinced in 1923 that if the gildsman was to bring his knowledge of the past to bear on the problems of the present, he must overcome his wariness of generalizations. He must seek to discover the laws of history, laws which would apply not only to the past but to the present and the future; for only when the gildsman established such laws would he be in a position to function as a valuable member of society. Several years after his presidential address of 1923 on "Law in History," Cheyney was to indicate that before the first World War he had been content as a rule to study and teach history for its own sake and for the love of learning. But since the War he longed increasingly to make historical knowledge "directly serviceable"; he wished to protect civilization against the many dangers that threatened it and to help men to advance to "the possibilities that lie before them."[25]

It was in this spirit that Cheyney, with the great capacity for generalization that he had shown in his writings on English history, ventured in his presidential message to draw up a list of six historical laws—laws which will later be described in connection with the idea of a science of history. All these laws had tremendous implications for the present, Cheyney insisted, showing courage, not to say rashness, of a sort that has rarely figured in a presidential address. The law of continuity demonstrated that it was impossible for a nation to make "any complete break in historical development," he said, speaking in the period of the New Economic Policy in Russia. The law of impermanence demonstrated that conservatism destroyed rather than preserved institutions, so that an isolationist America,

24 William E. Lingelbach, "Edward Potts Cheyney (1860-1947)," American Philosophical Society, *Year Book, 1947* (Philadelphia, 1948), p. 243.

25 *Law in History and Other Essays* (New York, 1927), p. vi.

scorning the League of Nations, might not be in a position to survive. The law of interdependence demonstrated the absurdity of nationalism and the unwisdom of French policy toward Germany. The law of democracy foredoomed the regimes of Mussolini and Lenin. The law of necessity for free consent guaranteed the failure of the Treaty of Versailles. The law of moral progress guaranteed the triumph of ethical considerations in human affairs.

Cheyney was not dogmatic in the presentation of his six laws; he viewed them merely as suggestions. The important thing was the "great value" of historical laws in general: they would serve human needs; they would provide man with a guide to action; they would make for human happiness. No longer would knowledge of the past have little practical value; laws would give man clues to the future, and they would enable him to heal the nations of the world and to handle intelligently current political, social, and economic problems. So went the reflections of what Cheyney was later to call his "ever-growing inclination . . . to make the present explain the past and to bring the past to bear on the present . . . ."[26]

Cheyney's successor was Woodrow Wilson; but some months before the meeting of 1924 took place Wilson died. Accordingly, on its fortieth anniversary, the Association was addressed by Vice-President Charles M. Andrews, the gildsman who had approached the American colonial period from the standpoint of both the colonist and the contemporary Englishman, something that "no one ever did . . . so well before."[27] Appropriately enough, Andrews devoted his message to a review of some of the major developments in historiography in "These Forty Years" since the founding of the Association. A product of the Johns Hopkins of the eighties and a leader of the gild prac-

26 *Ibid.*, p. v; Cheyney, "Introduction," in Lucy Maynard Salmon, *Why Is History Rewritten?* (New York, 1929), p. xiii.

27 J. Franklin Jameson, "Preface," *Essays in Colonial History Presented to Charles McLean Andrews by His Students* (New Haven, 1931), p. xii.

tically from the start of his academic career, he was certainly equipped to undertake this review. A scholar's scholar, a gildsman who had done much to reorient the study of American colonial history in a direction that could hardly please professional patriots, he was eminently qualified to discuss the period during which scientific history came into its own in the United States.

Andrews was distressed that the present-day layman had so little appreciation of the nature and usefulness of scientific history and that recent advances in historical study had not gained the public recognition accorded to recent advances in the study of science, philosophy, and psychology. It was bad enough that the layman showed the historian none of the respect shown to other specialists; worse still, he continued to believe that every man could serve as his own historian, and that the historian could write as he pleased. Failing to understand the changed character of historiography, the layman placed Hume, Gibbon, Prescott, and Bancroft in the same category with the carefully trained present-day historian, and viewed them as worthy of commanding as much confidence. This, Andrews thought, was most regrettable; and so he made sure to differentiate sharply between the historical works of recent decades and those of earlier times— all in an effort to demonstrate that history, like science and philosophy, had moved in the direction of "higher canons of criticism and interpretation, better balanced judgments, and more rational methods of presentation." If Andrews then proceeded to indicate a broad familiarity with the history of historical writing in general, the explanation no doubt was that he dated from an era when the young gildsman did not categorize himself from the start as an American history specialist or as a European history specialist.[28]

Andrews noted that the eighteenth-century historian had many failings: an inability to appreciate the workings of the great historical forces that shaped the past, an inability to grasp the role of continuity in history, an inability to go beyond the externals of history. The credulity of the eighteenth-century historian, his childishness, his blinding biases, his susceptibility to neat theories, his unfounded generalizations, his carelesness, his uncritical reliance on anecedotes and gossip, his fabrication of motives, his unawareness of evolutionary conceptions, his tendency to judge the standards, ideals, and viewpoints of the past in the light of his own time, all these failings of the eighteenth-century historian detracted from the value of his works.

Even the historian of the first half of the nineteenth century, Andrews continued, produced few historical works that managed to survive—despite his almost unbelievable productivity. Like the eighteenth-century historian, he was frequently actuated by the wrong motives; he frequently used history for "inferior ends—to prove, to justify, to defy, to glorify, or to abuse." A man of strong ideas, he sought to profit by the immediate usefulness of history. Pamphleteer that he was, he often used history to uphold some religious, political, philosophic or national cause. Viewing history as "an armory of weapons with which to carry on the attack," he used those sources which seemed best suited to the objectives he had in mind. Unwilling to permit the past to retire from service to some present cause, he could not avoid shaping his material to prove some point; he could not avoid omitting and falsifying portions of his material; he could not avoid being a moralist; and he could not avoid reading the present into the past.

This was not to say that Andrews thought that the contemporary historian had overcome all traces of partisanship. There would always be some unhistorical-minded writers who in their zeal to throw light on the present would throw the past out of the past and the present into it. There would always be those who would write history for racial, sectional, and nationalistic ends. Yet as far as Andrews was concerned there can be no doubt that he would have wanted said of himself what he had recently said of George Louis Beer, his co-worker in the field of American colonial history: "Loyal American though he was, he would not demean history by compelling it to serve as an object lesson for the cultivation of patriotic virtues."[29]

Andrews had no intention of overstating the archaism of historical works that antedated the mid-nineteenth century. Some of these works gave signs of a serious-minded approach to the past; some showed an awareness of the essentials of historical criticism. Already there were writers who sought to free themselves from dogmatic and theoretical prepossessions, shunning the controversies of their own times when they delved into the past. Only rarely, however, did there emerge a man like Ranke who thought it worthwhile to study history for the sake of history and not for the sake of society or a reading public. Andrews' view of Ranke was quite different from that which Charles Beard was later to present in "Written History as an Act of Faith," the view of Ranke as a conservative helping the cause of the German ruling classes who in the period after the French Revolution "did not want to be disturbed."[30]

Andrews defended what he thought was Ranke's approach to the past. He believed that historical study should be its own reward, that history should be studied for its own sake. To study the past to explain the present was often to distort the past in the interest of the present. On the other hand, to study the past to understand the past, this was to study history. And it was history studied in this way that Andrews hoped laymen, university trustees, and philanthropists would come to appreciate. But he would doubtless have done just as well to hope that more gildsmen would come to appreciate history studied in this way. He seemed not to realize that even in historical circles his approach, the historical-minded, past-minded approach, was relatively rare.

29 *George Louis Beer: A Tribute to His Life and Work in the Making of History and the Moulding of Public Opinion* (New York, 1924), p. 37.

30 *A.H.R.*, XXXIX (1934), 221.

Contrast Andrews' views with those of Dana C. Munro and James Harvey Robinson, two of his successors in the latter part of the twenties. Munro was a medievalist whose knowledge of the history of the Crusades was perhaps unrivalled.[31] Although he published disappointingly little during the course of his career, apart from texts and source books, he had done much to further the cause of medieval studies in the United States; and to the success of his activities as a sponsor many of his students at Pennsylvania, Wisconsin, and Princeton have testified.[32] During the period of the War, Munro had served actively as a researcher and publicist for the Creel Press Bureau and for the National Board for Historical Service; he was one of the authors of such widely circulated pamphlets as *German War Practices* (1917) and *German Treatment of Conquered Territory* (1918). Yet the memory of his own wartime activities did not keep him from condemning in his presidential message of 1926 the use of history for propaganda purposes. If he could do this apparently without self-consciousness, the reason perhaps was that he himself had been responsible, in the words of Cheyney, "for preserving in many government publications a tone of moderation in criticism of German actions and policy ...." [33]

Munro made it clear in his message on "War and History" that he was aware of the dangers of the partisan use of the past. The conflict over lay investiture, he noted, for example, inspired an enthusiastic, if barren, study of history. It inspired a quest for precedents to justify either imperial or papal claims to hegemony; and the sterility of the attempts of the special pleaders, said Munro, showed "how little they could know of history." Similarly, if, with the exception of the Florentines, many sixteenth-century writers failed to produce satisfactory works, the

31 A. C. Krey, "Preface," Dana C. Munro, *The Kingdom of the Crusaders* (New York, 1935), p. v.

32 Louis J. Paetow, ed., *The Crusades and Other Historical Essays Presented to Dana C. Munro by His Former Students* (New York, 1928), p. vii.

33 Edward P. Cheyney, "Dana Carleton Munro," *Dictionary of American Biography*, XIII, 331.

explanation was much the same. Interest there surely was in historical writing but chiefly for reasons of propaganda. History was merely a bludgeon to be used against an opponent. In an atmosphere dominated by religious strife, the search for precedents that would help in current controversies figured as the chief characteristic of historiography.

For all his awareness of the danger of using the past for present purposes, Munro continued to be attracted by the possibility of increasing the immediate usefulness of history. A close friend and former colleague of Cheyney and James Harvey Robinson at the University of Pennsylvania, he sought to draw on the past to guide the present, to bring historical knowledge to bear on current problems, and to overcome the lag of the social sciences behind the natural sciences. The great problem, he declared, was to learn how to go about organizing modern government and administration to meet the complexities of a civilization based on science. So it was that in 1926, three years after the formal establishment of the Social Science Research Council, Munro suggested that the historian should assume leadership among social scientists and that all should work for the answers that would "make life better worth living."

These, of course, were the very suggestions that James Harvey Robinson, president of the Association in 1929, had been making for some twenty-five years. Back in the first decade of the century, Robinson had come under the influence of Charles A. Beard, his young colleague at Columbia. Beard, who had recently returned from England, was concerned by what he had seen of the impact of industrialization on the lives of working-class elements; and this concern he communicated to some of his friends at Columbia, among them, Robinson.[34] The upshot was that the old Robinson of *An Introduction to the History of*

34 See Carlton J. H. Hayes, *British Social Politics: Materials Illustrating Contemporary State Action for the Solution of Social Problems* (Boston, 1913), p. iv; and Harry Elmer Barnes, "James Harvey Robinson," in Howard W. Odum, ed., *American Masters of Social Science* (New York, 1927), pp. 332-33.

Western Europe (1902-1903) came to differ basically from the new Robinson of Robinson and Beard, *The Development of Modern Europe: An Introduction to the Study of Current History* (1907-1908). This new Robinson came increasingly to value history for what it could do to throw light on contemporary problems and to aid the cause of human betterment and social justice.[35] He sought consciously and constantly to subordinate the past to the present. He sought "to enable the reader to catch up with his own times; to read intelligently the foreign news in the morning paper; to know what was the attitude of Leo XIII toward the social democrats even if he has forgotten that of Innocent III toward the Albigenses."[36] Nor was it only in Robinson's widely-used textbooks that this preoccupation with the present bulked large. It also bulked large in *The New History: Essays Illustrating the Modern Historical Outlook* (1912), *The Mind in the Making: The Relation of Intelligence to Social Reform* (1921), and *The Humanizing of Knowledge* (1923). And it bulked large in his presidential message of 1929 on "The Newer Ways of Historians."

In at least one respect Robinson was aware of the danger of using the past for the purposes of the present. For by the time he addressed the Association, World War revisionist historiography had scored several major triumphs; and Robinson did not let pass the opportunity to deplore the uses to which history had been put in the wartime setting. He recalled that everywhere the historian had been unable to subdue his particular brand of tribalism. He swallowed nauseating propaganda, and everywhere he was as "easily sold out" as the layman, for his study of the past had not equipped him to meet the emotionalism of a war crisis.[37]

35 Luther Virgil Hendricks, *James Harvey Robinson, Teacher of History* (New York, 1946), pp. 35-38.

36 Robinson and Beard, *The Development of Modern Europe: An Introduction to the Study of Current History* (2 vols., Boston, 1907-08), I, iii.

37 See Harry Elmer Barnes, *A History of Historical Writing* (Norman, 1937), chap. XI.

Robinson found consolation in the thought that wartime intolerance had taught the gildsman peacetime tolerance. The gildsman, he said, became increasingly aware of the provincial and anachronistic character of the strictly national approach to the past and of the inadequacies of the old divisions of history and of the need to study general and world history. And this was only right, for civilization was essentially what H. G. Wells had called it, "the common adventure of mankind." Robinson deplored the ignorance that had permitted a Fichte to console Germans with thoughts of their originality; and he deplored the ignorance that had permitted a Freeman to urge the teachers of Liverpool to impress on their students their Mercian origins. Man had done so much wandering through the ages that terms like autochthonous and aboriginal could not be applied to any people for whom records existed. In fact, said Robinson, setting forth one of the favorite notions of James H. Breasted, his textbook collaborator, every people at every stage of its history owed "most of its knowledge, skill, art and *mores* to other peoples including those of a very remote past." Robinson condemned the use of history for nationalistic purposes; he had other purposes for which to use it.

One of the most successful and influential textbook writers of his time, Robinson did not fail to introduce the subject of textbooks into his presidential message. For he believed that the growing insistence on recent coverage in history textbooks was among the most important of recent educational changes. At the beginning of the century, he noted, the past and the present seemed to be two different things, so that the textbook writer did not have to bother with the contemporary scene; he could permit his narrative to end for all practical purposes with the Franco-German War. The reader had to find out only what had taken place before his birth; he was expected to be familiar with his own times. No doubt Robinson exaggerated the lack of up-to-dateness in late nineteenth and early twentieth-century textbooks, but he certainly did not exaggerate the stress on recent coverage in textbooks since the first World War. In these volumes, he declared, the treatment of the contemporary scene had to be "posted like ledger," for a work copyrighted in 1925 was sure to be considered woefully antiquated by the time 1929 rolled around.

What this meant, said Robinson, was that from the time the historian began his textbook he had to choose his material so as to make "close connections with the morning newspaper the day that he releases his plate proof...." Nor did Robinson bemoan this state of affairs. Quite the opposite; he argued that it would serve to develop in both the writer and the reader "a thoroughgoing historical sense," encouraging them to view genetically all kinds of persistent problems. If Robinson failed to understand how destructive of "a thoroughgoing historical sense" was this view of the past in the light of the morning newspaper, the explanation doubtless was that he himself enjoyed being immersed in his own times. He believed that what concerned the world of the twenties offered the best standard for selecting materials from the past; and it was a present-minded kind of history, an immediately useful kind of history, that he considered necessary in every educational scheme that aimed at a general preparation for an intelligent life.

Discussing the recent revision of *The Development of Modern Europe,* he emphasized that any modern treatment of the eighteenth and nineteenth centuries should take into account directions and movements which have become clear only with the passage of time. Krupp and Stinnes, he pointed out, gave added significance to the Prussian acquisition of some Ruhr villages back in the days of the Congress of Vienna. Similary, the momentous results of European imperialism called for a reconsideration of the history of overseas regions—so much of a reconsideration that Robinson and Beard renamed their revised volume *The Merging of European into World History* in keeping partly with a suggestion from Egyptologist James H. Breasted, who recognized that the history of Western Europe formed only "a chapter in world history."

Nor was the Europeanization of the world the only major fact that called for a rewriting of the past; there was also the growth of science. Robinson was inclined to place science on a par with church and state in historical accounts; he suggested, in fact, that science "should mayhap be accorded a larger place than they in reviewing the changes of the last two or three centuries." And just as the growth of science and the Europeanization of the world required a readjustment of historical accounts, so, too, did the emergence of organizations like the League of Nations, the World Court, and the World Bank. For these organizations had to be regarded—even by the skeptic—as steps in the direction of "human unification." Robinson, in a word, was contemptuous of the idea of studying the past for the sake of the past, the relatively new idea that Burr and Andrews had upheld in recent years. Instead, he was sold on the very, very old idea of studying the past for the sake of the present; this, indeed, was fundamental to his "New History." Accordingly, he added his own suggestions to the many his presidential predecessors had made in their efforts to increase the practical value of historical study.

CHAPTER III

THE IMMEDIATE USEFULNESS OF HISTORY: DEPRESSION AND WAR YEARS

As in the war years and the postwar period, so in the depression years and the period of the second World War, many presidents defended the study of the past in the interests of the present; few defended its study in the interests of the past. It seemed to matter relatively little that a particular president happened to be an ancient historian, a medievalist, a modern European historian, or an American historian. With rare exceptions, all urged that historical knowledge be used to throw light on the present; all pointed up the immediate social utility of history; all searched the past for solutions to contemporary problems; all seemed anxious to avoid the charge of antiquarianism and to disprove the dictum of Fustel de Coulanges that *"l'histoire ne sert à rien."*

Evarts B. Greene, for example, the author of such important studies as *The Provincial Governor in the English Colonies of North America* (1898), *Provincial America, 1690-1740* (1905), and *The Foundations of American Nationality* (1922), chose as the subject of his presidential message of 1930 "Persistent Problems of Church and State." For Greene this choice was a natural one. Son of a New England missionary who had served long and well in Japan, Greene never lost interest in the problems of religion. As a layman, he worked for the improvement of inter-group relationships; and in his classes at Illinois and Columbia and in his writings on American colonial history he often tried to throw light on the problem of church and state.[1] Yet Greene did not justify the choice of his presidential theme on

1 Richard B. Morris, ed., *The Era of the American Revolution: Studies Inscribed to Evarts Boutell Greene* (New York, 1939), p. vi.

the basis of its own merits or on the basis of his personal interests; he justified it on the basis of the needs of the contemporary scene, so that the aspects of American religious history which he described he used merely as "a point of departure."

Emphasizing the continuing importance of church and state relations in the twentieth-century world, Greene insisted—as he was again to do in *Religion and the State: The Making and Testing of an American Tradition* (1941)—that those relations were "not so comfortably settled" as had been supposed. Thinking perhaps of James Harvey Robinson,[2] he pointed out that there were those who predicted that the advance of science would mean the decline of religion. He himself, however, did not subscribe to this view. Ideas frequently lingered much beyond the date set for their expiration by wishful thinkers; and the fact was that "issues long regarded by most Americans as completely dead, or dying, now seem very much alive." Speaking in 1930, Greene had little need to press his contention that church and state relations had not ceased to present all kinds of difficulties, for the teaching of evolution in the schools, the Al Smith episode, and the activities of the Ku Klux Klan were still live matters. Just the same, Greene made sure to point out that in Britain, France, Germany, Italy, and Soviet Russia, as well as in the United States, religious conflicts could not be submerged. In the sphere of education and of social welfare, for example, there were serious clashes. In short, the formal separation of church and state did not dispose of "issues deeply rooted in human experience and human psychology"; nor did disestablishment remove religion from the realm of politics.

Modest and meticulous scholar that he was, Greene had his doubts about the advisability of using history "to point a moral." Only recently, in *A New-Englander in Japan: Daniel Crosby Greene* (1927), his biography of his father, he had made it clear that the historian should try "to explain rather than to pass

2 See James Harvey Robinson, "Religion," in Charles A. Beard, ed., *Whither Mankind: A Panorama of Modern Civilization* (New York, 1928), pp. 264-86.

judgment"; he should try to present the past as it was, not as he wished it might have been.[3] Yet while Greene believed in studying the past for the sake of the past, he was convinced that historical studies could place current developments in "more reasonable perspective." He was also convinced that the historical point of view could help mankind to go beyond mere partisanship; for it depended on a desire to penetrate past ways of thinking, even if they happened not to be congenial to the historian. And just as the historical point of view· required a willingness to understand, so real tolerance had the same prerequisite. Therefore, if past tragedies were not to be repeated, more and more people would have to develop this willingness to understand, the key to tolerance and to the historical approach. So thought Greene, a citizen who had voted for Smith in 1928 because he hated intolerance. So thought Greene, a scholar who had worked hard to promote an understanding of Japanese culture in the United States.[4]

Carl L. Becker, Greene's successor, was much more determined to make historical knowledge serve the needs of the present. Trained by Frederick Jackson Turner, he had long subscribed to one of the chief notions of his teacher: that history should "hold the lamp for conservative reform."[5] Indeed, engrossed as Becker was in the problems of the present, distressed as he was that American democracy seemed to have failed from the economic point of view,[6] he could have little sympathy for an antiquarian approach to the past. Despite this, he produced

3 *A New-Englander in Japan: Daniel Crosby Greene* (Boston, 1927), p. vii; Theodore C. Pease, "Evarts Boutell Greene, 1870-1947," Illinois State Historical Society, *Journal*, XLI (1948), 15.

4 Carlton J. H. Hayes, "Evarts Boutell Greene (1870-1947)," American Philosophical Society, *Year Book, 1947* (Philadelphia, 1948), p. 252.

5 George H. Sabine, "Carl Lotus Becker," in Becker, *Freedom and Responsibility in the American Way of Life* (New York, 1945), p. xxvii.

6 *Ibid.*, p. xxxiii; Carl Becker, *The United States: An Experiment in Democracy* (New York, 1920), pp. 331-33.

several of the most past-minded studies of his time in books like his *Beginnings of the American People* (1915), *The Eve of the Revolution* (1918), and *The Declaration of Independence* (1922). But Becker's present-mindedness was unmistakable in "Everyman His Own Historian." Addressing the Association in 1931, he spoke at a time when it would have been difficult for anyone to defend an antiquarian approach to the past; and Becker, who had been critical of history for its own sake in time of prosperity, was all the more critical of it in time of depression.

Defining history simply as "the memory of things said and done," he suggested that even without having taken a history course at college, even without ever having read Gibbon, every normal individual knew something about history. The gildsman tried his best to hide this hateful fact; and so, in his best professorial style, he announced that some graduate student knew no history when what he really meant was that the candidate failed his Ph.D. examination. But the truth was that Mr. Everyman as well as Mr. Gildsman had some remembrances of things said and done; without such historical knowledge, his present was sure to be purposeless and his future meaningless. Mr. Everyman did not have to prepare a lecture when he awoke in the morning, so that he did not have to remember the Sanders Mission or the Pseudo-Isidorian Decretals; but he did have to remember enough of things said and done for orientation in his own world, things which, if they lacked the importance of the Pseudo-Isidorian Decretals, were still enormously useful to Mr. Everyman.

This did not mean that Mr. Everyman's memory of things said and done was confined strictly to practical and personal matters; he also held memories of things that he had not experienced personally. And what mattered was not that these memories were full or fully accurate; what mattered was that they were of use to Mr. Everyman. For he was likely to remember those things which harmonized with his conception of himself and his place in the world. After all, it was his memory of things said and done that made possible the enrichment of his life; and it was his memory of things said and done that connected in his mind the future and the past.

Becker subscribed to the idea of Benedetto Croce that all living history was contemporaneous.[7] The remembrance of the past and the anticipation of the future were inextricably linked; so much so, that the memory of things said and done could not be exactly the same for those who lived at the same time, much less for those who lived at different times. As a product of the imagination, history varied from layman to layman and from gildsman to gildsman. Fustel de Coulanges liked to think that *he* was not speaking, but that history was speaking through him. Yet it was plain enough, especially to later generations, that Fustel was conditioned by the nationalistic atmosphere of his times, an atmosphere that disposed him to challenge the Germanic origins of French institutions. "And so," said Becker, "it must always be. Played upon by all the diverse, unnoted influences of his own time, the historian will elicit history out of documents by the same principle, however more consciously and expertly applied, that Mr. Everyman employs to breed legends out of remembered episodes and oral tradition."

Nor was it only this that the historian should recognize. He should also recognize that he had either to adjust his books to meet the needs of Mr. Everyman or else see his books go unopened. Becker, in short, took his stand in opposition to a scholar like Andrews. Proclaiming his lack of sympathy for research for the sake of research, he asserted that historical knowledge which lay inactive in unread books had no influence in the world; the historical knowledge that did have influence was the living kind that contributed to the enrichment of Mr. Everyman's life. Hence Becker rejoiced that every generation had inevitably to view both past and future on the basis of its own limited experiences; he rejoiced that every generation had inevitably to "play on the dead" any tricks that made for "its own

7 Benedetto Croce, *History: Its Theory and Practice* (New York, 1921), pp. 11-12.

peace of mind." Nor did he think that this detracted from the value or dignity of history. Here was simply society's way of arriving at an understanding of its present actions in the light of both its past and future actions.

According to Becker, the business of the gildsman was "to correct and rationalize for common use Mr. Everyman's mythological adaption of what actually happened." His function was "not to repeat the past but to make use of it." And make use of it Becker surely did in the books he brought out in the years after his address of 1931. In volume after volume—*The Heavenly City of the Eighteenth-Century Philosophers* (1932), *Progress and Power* (1936), *Modern Democracy* (1941), *New Liberties for Old* (1941), *How New Will the Better World Be?* (1944), and *Freedom and Responsibility in the American Way of Life* (1945)— he tried to take advantage of the immediate usefulness of history. Now and then, to be sure, he had his doubts—as when he noted that he had never written a popular work, much less a best-seller, and that he was unfortunately not sufficiently familiar with the needs of the non-professional reader.[8] By and large, however, he held to the position that he had taken in his message of 1931; for, if his early writings were "a conscious reaction" against history for the sake of history,[9] his later writings were all the more so.

Becker's successor, Herbert E. Bolton, the historian of the Western Hemisphere, was likewise intent on using the past for the purposes of the present. And in his presidential message of 1932 Bolton said nothing about the practical value of historical study that he had not been saying for years in his large classes at the University of California and in writings like *The Colonization of North America, 1492-1783* (1920) and *History of the Americas: A Syllabus with Maps* (1928). Yet if Bolton

8 *The Declaration of Independence: A Study in the History of Political Ideas* (Reprint ed., New York, 1942), p. xvii.

9 Sabine, *op. cit.*, p. xxiv.

92 HISTORIANS AND THEIR CRAFT

simply repeated in "The Epic of Greater America" a point of
view for which he had long been pioneering, there can be no
question that the situation in the early thirties justified the repetition. For few historians had had the courage to do what
Bolton had done: to depart from the way of treating United
States history that he had learned as a student of Turner and
McMaster.[10] Few historians had learned what Bolton had discovered early in his career, that a study undertaken in United
States history would frequently defy present-day national
boundaries.[11]

As in his *Syllabus,* so in his message, Bolton stated his opposition to the scholar who concentrated on the strictly national
history of the various American powers. It was plain that European history could not be properly understood on the basis of
the separate investigation of the individual past of the individual European powers; it was just as plain that American history
could not be properly understood if approached from the point
of view of Brazil, Chile, Mexico, Canada, or the United States.
For two reasons, above all, Bolton thought the teaching and
writing of national history in the United States deserved to be
condemned. Not only did national history becloud many of the
broader aspects of the development of the United States, but it
served to rear a chauvinistic nation.

It was for two reasons also that Bolton thought the synthetic
approach to the history of the Western Hemisphere deserved to
be supported. First of all, it was justified by the dictates of sound
historiography. Secondly, said Bolton, returning in 1932 to a
theme on which he had often harped,[12] it was justified by the
need to foster better inter-American relations; for it was "not

10 "Herbert Eugene Bolton: An Appreciation," in *New Spain and the
Anglo-American West: Historical Contributions Presented to Herbert
Eugene Bolton* (2 vols., Los Angeles, 1932), I, x.

11 *Wider Horizons of American History* (New York, 1939), p. xiv.

12 Bolton and Thomas Maitland Marshall, *The Colonization of North
America 1492-1783* (New York, 1920), p. v; *History of the Americas: A
Syllabus with Maps* (Boston, 1928), p. iii.

a matter of indifference to know that European influence in
South America today far outweighs that of Saxon America,
and that Europe is bending every effort to draw the Southern
continent more and more into the European circle and away
from its northern neighbors." To counteract this tendency,
Bolton recommended that less attention be given to the writing
of national history and that more attention be given to the writing of Greater American history. He also recommended a basic
reorganization of American history courses, the same reorganization that he had suggested in his *Syllabus*. Students should
first be exposed to an overall view of the whole Western Hemisphere: then, after having studied what the American countries
had in common, they could move on to the study of the history
of any particular American nation. In these ways Bolton tried
to make use of the past in order to meet the needs of the present.

Nor was it strange that Charles A. Beard, who followed
Bolton as president, also emphasized the practical side of historical study. One of the most influential historians of his time,
Beard had written much on both European and American history; and though he had done his doctoral dissertation on a
subject that took him back to the Middle Ages, *The Office of
Justice of the Peace in England in Its Origin and Development*
(1904), he became increasingly absorbed in recent and current
history, something that his position as professor of politics at
Columbia did little to lessen. Yet while Beard valued history
for the light it could throw on the present, he continued to be
more sympathetic to history for its own sake than Becker, for
example. Partly perhaps this was because Beard associated such
history with scholars like Osgood and Dunning, whom he admired greatly, and who stood by him in the period of storm
that followed the publication of *An Economic Interpretation of
the Constitution of the United States* (1913).

Addressing the Association in 1933, one of the most critical
years of the depression, Beard suggested that the historian who

studied the length of wigs in Restoration England or cotton prices in the Alabama of the fifties "would be a strange creature if he never asked himself why he regarded these matters as worthy of his labor and love, or why society provides a living for him during his excursions and explorations." To Beard's way of thinking, there were more worthwhile activities for the historian to undertake. Above all, he should try to determine whether the world moved, and, if it did, the direction in which it moved. In other words, Beard thought that the historian should try to throw light on the present as well as the future. Was it with capitalist or proletarian dictatorships or with collectivist democracies that the future lay? Beard ventured his own guess; but this, as well as other aspects of "Written History as an Act of Faith," will be described in more appropriate places.

William E. Dodd, Beard's close friend and successor, also tried to use the past for the sake of the present and the future. Unfortunately, however, "The Emergence of the First Social Order in the United States" failed to do justice to the author of *Statesmen of the Old South* (1911), *Expansion and Conflict* (1915), and *The Cotton Kingdom* (1919). Dodd himself noted in his *Diary* that he had had to prepare his message "under pressure." As Ambassador to Nazi Germany, he was providing the German people with what President Roosevelt had called a "standing example" of American liberalism; [13] and he was too busy making history to give much time to trying to recapture it. Dodd avoided the discussion of Germany in his message of 1934; but another subject about which he felt strongly—democracy—he did not avoid. An old-time Wilsonian liberal whose democratic sympathies outstripped those of his hero, Dodd had long feared that great concentrations of wealth might wreck the Republic; but he had continued to believe that the greatest work of democracy lay in the future.[14]

13 William E. Dodd, Jr., and Martha Dodd, eds., *Ambassador Dodd's Diary, 1933-1938* (New York, 1941), p. 3.

14 Charles A. Beard, "Retrospect and Recollection," *ibid.*, pp. x-xiii.

This belief was plainly reflected in his presidential message. Drawing on the study that was later to be published as *The Old South: Struggles for Democracy* (1937), Dodd distinguished two fairly well-defined social orders in United States history: one that extended from 1660 to 1865, a second that ran roughly to 1929. By 1934, however, there seemed to be slowly emerging a third social order, in which democracy was "to be tried at last on a national scale." In short, critical times were compelling Americans to test the validity of their inherited philosophies; and Dodd thought it would be useful to reexamine the first social order now that a third was coming into being in the United States. Dodd thus justified his choice of subject on the basis of the needs of the contemporary scene, hoping perhaps, as he had once written, "to strengthen the appeal of History to a generation too little prone to think and assess."[15]

Dodd's successor was Michael I. Rostovtzeff, one of the foremost ancient historians since Mommsen's time; and he, too, tried to take advantage of the immediate usefulness of history. In his classes at Wisconsin and at Yale and in his monumental writings on the social and economic history of antiquity, Rostovtzeff had often ventured to draw on the past for the purposes of the present. He doubted that the study of history would enable the gildsman to foresee the future,[16] but he was convinced that its study would enable him to point out lessons and give warnings.[17] Rostovtzeff had had a brief experience with Soviet rule and a brief taste of "proletarian culture," all of which had prompted him, in a pamphlet he wrote under the auspices of the Russian Liberation Committee, to implore God to save Russia and to "protect the rest of the civilized world from

15 *Lincoln or Lee: Comparison and Contrast of the Two Greatest Leaders in the War between the States: The Narrow and Accidental Margins of Success* (New York, 1928), p. viii.

16 *Out of the Past of Greece and Rome* (New Haven, 1932), p. x.

17 *The Social and Economic History of the Roman Empire* (Oxford, 1926), pp. 486-87.

the same sufferings!"[18] Devoted to the cause of private capitalism and disturbed by growing evidences of state intervention,
he found it impossible to keep the present out of the past and
the past out of the present and future.

Addressing the Association in 1935, he explained that "in
these days of unsettled and chaotic economic conditions, of an
acute economic crisis which prevails over all the civilized
world, when all sorts of remedies are suggested for healing the
wounds, and among them, under the label of the last word in
economic science, some age-old and many times tried devices,
it is perhaps not inappropriate for a student of ancient economic
history to recall to mind the remote past of Greece and Rome
where similar crises were not infrequent and where many devices were tried in the hope of solving them." Turning to the
description of some aspects of the economic evolution of Hellenistic times, Rostovtzeff boldly projected modern conceptions
into the ancient world.[19] He dealt with the Egyptian "planned
economy" and "New Deal"; he dealt with Hellenistic strikes,
crises, inflationary tendencies, and movements of passive resistance.

Ancient capitalism, to be sure, never reached the modern industrial stage; and for this Rostovtzeff found the chief explanation
neither in the defectiveness of ancient science, nor in the feeble-
ness of the ancient capitalist spirit, nor in the presence of slave
labor. He found the explanation in the condition of the market.
It happened rarely, he said, that "the market for goods was
steadily expanding and its buying capacity steadily increasing";
and the reason for this Rostovtzeff found in a strictly non-eco-
nomic factor. Politics, he argued, as he had often done before,
hindered the development of additional capitalist techniques and
forms of organization. Pursuing the kind of deadly parallel that
often figured in his writings, the world's leading authority on
ancient economic history ended his message with this question:

18 *Proletarian Culture* (London, 1919), p. 18.

19 Cf. Meyer Reinhold, "Historian of the Classic World: A Critique of
Rostovtzeff," *Science and Society*, X (1946), 363, 367-68, 372, 390.

"We on our part have greatly developed what we inherited from antiquity or independently created, but are we sure that our economic progress will last forever, that it will never be terminated by events brought about not by economy but by the development of our mentality and our emotions?"

In the early thirties, then, president after president—Greene, Becker, Bolton, Beard, Dodd, and Rostovtzeff—tried to use history to supply the needs of the contemporary scene. The past, it seemed, existed above all for the purpose of throwing light on the present. Yet while the past-minded position that Andrews had taken in 1924 fared poorly in the early thirties, it did find a defender in 1936. This defender, as might perhaps have been expected, was Charles H. McIlwain. Author of *The High Court of Parliament and Its Supremacy* (1910), *The American Revolution: A Constitutional Interpretation* (1923), and *The Growth of Political Thought in the West from the Greeks to the End of the Middle Ages* (1932), McIlwain owed much to some of the most past-minded scholars of recent times, Englishmen like Maitland and Tout and Americans like Charles Gross, George Burton Adams, and Edward Channing.[20] This is not to say that McIlwain's past-mindedness was of the sort that ruled out interest in the present. In his most important scholarly study, he had suggested that if the American judicial system was to be understood and improved, it was essential to know something of the development of the legislative activities of English courts.[21] In his edition of *The Political Works of James I* (1918), he had suggested that no thoughtful observer of the contemporary world could dismiss the study of the divine right theory of monarchy as being "insignificant or antiquarian."[22] McIlwain was

20 *The High Court of Parliament and Its Supremacy: An Historical Essay on the Boundaries between Legislation and Adjudication in England* (New Haven, 1910), pp. xiii, xviii-xix.

21 *Ibid.*, pp. viii-ix.

22 *The Political Works of James I, Reprinted from the Edition of 1616* (Cambridge, 1918), p. x; cf. *Constitutionalism and the Changing World: Collected Papers* (New York, 1939), p. vii.

not averse to using history to throw light on the present, but he considered this only an incidental function of the historian. As a devoted follower of Maitland, he believed that the all-important function of the historian was to understand the past in the light of the past, not of the present. This he certainly made clear in 1936 when he discussed "The Historian's Part in a Changing World."

McIlwain doubted that there had ever been a time since the founding of the Association in 1884 when the gildsman, as a professional man, was so deeply moved as in the thirties to come to the aid of his country and the world in general. The gildsman of the thirties could surely appreciate what Thomas Fuller was driving at when, during the period of the Cromwellian Protectorate, he prefaced his *Church History of Britain* with the remark, "An ingenious Gentleman some months since in Jest-earnest advised me to make haste with my History, for fear (saith he) lest the Church of England be ended before the History thereof." Like Fuller, the gildsman was often tempted to hurry along with his history for fear that the institutions he was describing might end before he finished writing; and he was often tempted to apply the lessons of history to some current crisis. According to McIlwain, however, the contribution which the gildsman could make lay in another direction. It lay in combating the widespread view that what was needed was merely the lessons of history and not the history. McIlwain granted that as long as human beings were what they were they were likely to draw lessons from history and act on the basis of the lessons drawn, but the historian should try to determine whether the alleged lessons were in reality "the lessons *of history*."

McIlwain was critical of the notion that the gildsman should adapt his writings to the changing needs of his times. The historian's job, he emphasized, was to discover, insofar as the sources permitted, what actually took place. If the gildsman denied this, if he harped on the unattainability of objective truth, he was really wasting his time in the field of history. As far as

McIlwain was concerned, the logical result of the notion that the past should be revised in keeping with the purposes of the present was the kind of propagandistic history that was in full bloom in Germany, Italy, and Soviet Russia. McIlwain did not deny that in some respects the rewriting of history was justified from the scholarly point of view. The modern preoccupation with economic matters, for example, made possible a more adequate understanding of the role of economics at other times. Always, however, the historian must guard against distorting the past; he dared not assume that at some former time economic considerations were necessarily just as important as in his own time. McIlwain favored the rewriting of the past in keeping with present interests provided that the interests of the past were closely protected.

Nevertheless, it was his main thesis that the chief flaws in many historical works grew out of the "untimely intrusion of modern ideas." If studies of institutional history, for example, were long inadequate, it was because modern ways of thinking about past institutions had not been suppressed. Obviously, the hazards of injecting the present into the past were greater for some types and periods of history than for others; but doubtless the most flagrant instances of "retrogressive modernism" occurred in the study of medieval institutional development. Because many present-day institutions stemmed from medieval foundations, the historian was often tempted to overlook basic differences between what institutions once were and what, many centuries later, they had come to be. Yet if he was to succeed in gaining any real insight into some aspect of institutional history, he had to bury himself in the records of his period; and having done this, he was likely to discover to his surprise that the thoughts, motives, and institutions that he found revealed in the sources failed to harmonize with what he had been led to anticipate on the basis of the standard modern studies. McIlwain himself recalled how upset he was to find that when Elizabethans talked of parliament they had in mind a body that differed con-

siderably from what he had had in mind. It was a blow to learn
that those who actually made history or recorded it contempo-
raneously often said, did, and thought things altogether different
from what the historian had reason to expect, and, worse still,
altogether different from what the historian had been telling
others was history.

Small wonder that McIlwain regarded as historically disre-
putable the view that "because they were political liberals, St.
Thomas Aquinas must now be made over into a modern Whig
and Cardinal Bellarmine into a democrat; because they believed
in a restricted royal prerogative, men like Sir John Eliot and Sir
Matthew Hale have to be turned into preposterous parliamentary
Austinians." Using the past this way made possible certain lessons, but they were hardly what could correctly be termed the
lessons of history. For, if the scholar started out by putting the
present into the past, he was going to find it there quickly and
surely, if not properly.

McIlwain's argument was that the gildsman, as a scholar,
was concerned with history rather than with the applications of
history. Especially in times of distress, however, he was always
tempted to use the experiences of the past to help out his own generation. McIlwain did not object to the search for lessons from the
past; but he emphasized that the world crisis of the thirties,
with all its "unpredicted, if not unpredictable," features, provided the scholar with a much needed "lesson in humility." More
than that, he emphasized that the gildsman should recognize
that often he spoke not as a historian but as a citizen. When he
set forth his lessons, therefore, it was well for him to bear in
mind the statement of an English pamphleteer of the Civil War
period: "When a Patient lies sicke under the destroying parox-
ismes of a Fever, every stander-by will be telling his Medicine,
though he be no Physitian: O then let no Sonne of this State
account it presumption in me, for putting in my judgment, and
speaking that which I conceive might, if not remove, yet miti-
gate this fatall distemperature of our common Mother: at an-

other time perhaps it might be censurable, but in this exigence laudable."

McIlwain's successor, Guy Stanton Ford, agreed that the historian should not carry "the present as baggage on excursions into the past"; he should not "etch the features of the present on the tables of the past." But Ford valued history mainly for what it could do to throw light on contemporary developments; during the course of his career he had often made this plain. A former student of Frederick Jackson Turner at Wisconsin, he had shifted to European history by reason of his interest in the social welfare measures of Bismarckian Germany.[23] But in 1913, before he managed to publish much, apart from his doctoral dissertation on *Hanover and Prussia, 1795-1803: A Study in Neutrality* (1903), he was appointed to the deanship of the graduate school at the University of Minnesota.[24] Then, when war came, he was chosen by George Creel to play a major part in "America's Fight for Public Opinion." He served as Chief of the Division of Civic and Educational Publications of the Committee on Public Information and as one of the leaders of the National Board for Historical Service. Thus, Ford, whom Creel considered "admirably fitted by temperament and training" for the task,[25] helped to mobilize American historians for the greater damnation of Germany; though, it should be added, Ford had cautioned that wartime pamphlets be prepared in such a way that historians would not wish to disown them "twenty years after the war."[26] The result of all this administrative activity was that Ford did little historical writing. Even when

23 *A.H.R.*, XLIII (1938), 265.

24 George E. Vincent, "Guy Stanton Ford: An Appreciation," in Ford, *On and Off the Campus* (Minneapolis, 1938), p. 17.

25 George Creel, *How We Advertised America: The First Telling of the Amazing Story of the Committee on Public Information that Carried the Gospel of Americanism to Every Corner of the Globe* (New York, 1920), p. 101.

26 "America's Fight for Public Opinion," in Ford, *op. cit.*, p. 97.

he left Washington to return to his academic duties, he found that administration left little time for research, so that, except for *Stein and the Era of Reform in Prussia, 1807-1815* (1922), he wrote little of a scholarly nature. He did, however, keep up with what others were writing; and so, when he addressed the Association in 1937, he ventured "Some Suggestions to American Historians."

Disagreeing with the gildsman who regarded current problems as no part of his business, he announced that his chief aim was to trace the features of contemporary America and "catch the direction of its gaze and the expression of its countenance." Obviously, however, without history, no society could understand its present actions. Ford, therefore, sought to determine some of the ways in which historical knowledge could help the thoughtful American to understand the factors that were likely to influence the survival of the American experiment. For the United States was losing its youth and some of its youthful self-confidence. In fact, Ford suspected that what the American historian had been writing about Europe he would soon have to be writing about his own country. Convinced, however, that Americans would solve their problems with greater confidence and intelligence if they made more use of history, Ford urged the American gildsman to work for "that detachment, that necessary aloofness, that elevation" which would enable him to distinguish between the transient and the abiding features of American life; for the supreme lesson of history, if there was such a thing as a lesson of history, was that changes were taking place endlessly within society itself and in man's relation to his physical surroundings.

Ford had some concrete proposals to offer. Above all, he advocated the study of fields wider than United States history alone, counselling the gildsman to investigate the European past, especially in the period since 1787. Yes, thought Ford, to study history was to travel; and if the gildsman looked abroad, he was likely to look homeward with greater penetration. For instance, the European powers in the last century and a half had seen much the same scientific, industrial, and economic changes as the United States. The American scholar could therefore develop his perspective as he studied the history of countries which adapted themselves to these changes more rapidly than the United States. He had several decades of European experience on the basis of which to view factors and tendencies that had become apparent only recently in the United States.

Ford did not expect the aftermath of industrialization in European countries to be precisely duplicated in the United States. Full well he appreciated the differences, as well as the parallels, in European and American development. The United States continued to cling much more than Western Europe to the individualistic social thought and outlook of the Age of Reason. Ford even suggested that from the start ideas of individualism and *laissez-faire* seemed superficial and out of place in the European setting; but these ideas found a happy home with "a frontier people" like the Americans, said Ford, himself, as has been noted, a former student of Turner. Still, the important thing, he pointed out in 1937, as he had done before in his addresses, "Are Revolutions Necessary?" and "Science and Civilization,"[27] was that rugged individualists were

unconscious of a changing mood in the nation, apparent since 1870 and increased sharply since the turn of the century. Now, since the World War, their fear and their lack of a social philosophy defensible in the forum of public opinion leave them little but a vituperative vocabulary and a blind and dangerous insistence that any change or social adjustment is revolution. They would imperil all loyalty to government and the Constitution by using them as defenses for their individual or group acquisitiveness. They give little evidence of realizing that, at the close of a century and a half under the same Constitution and under the dynamics of an industrial civilization ruled by science and machinery, we are passing, as President

27 *Ibid.,* pp. 61-72, 101-26.

Hoover pointed out, 'from a period of extremely individual-istic action into a period of associational activities.'

This phrase, indeed, summarized the major theme that Ford thought the American gildsman should develop with a view to supplying the needs of the present: the decline of individualism and the rise of the idea that individualism "must yield in large areas to common action for the general welfare." Nor did Ford, who had recently edited *Dictatorship in the Modern World* (1935), find it irrelevant to add that democracy was "dependent on enlightenment by scholarship," and that "historical scholarship without freedom to speak the truth about our national history would become here, as it has in many lands, a mute testimonial of the decay of all scholarship and all liberty."

Ford's successor, Frederick L. Paxson, also used his address to throw light on the contemporary scene; and for Paxson, too, this was very much the thing to do. For, though he had written on the Civil War and on the West—he won the Pulitzer Prize in 1925 for *A History of the American Frontier*—he had increasingly immersed himself in the study of contemporary developments.[28] He wrote a *Recent History of the United States* (1921) which looked "toward the future rather than the past" and included those facts that were "useful for a full understanding of the United States of today"; and he gathered materials for a multi-volume account of *American Democracy and the World War*. In fact, in his presidential message on "The Great Demobilization," Paxson dealt with a theme that he was later to treat at length in *Postwar Years: Normalcy, 1918-1923* (1948), the long-delayed third volume of *American Democracy and the World War*.

Paxson recalled in 1938 that the Association had failed to meet twenty years before; and President Thayer, though armed with a message, had lost a chance to speak, if not to be read. Nor

28 See the bibliography in *The Great Demobilization and Other Essays* (Madison, 1941), pp. 159-81.

did Paxson regret in retrospect that this meeting of 1918 had failed to take place. His point was that the wartime gildsman—himself included,[29] though he did not mention this—had been so geared to the explanation of war issues that he was hardly capable of impartial historical analysis. Certainly no Hearst could find reason to crusade against him for neglecting the patriotic possibilities of history. Quite the contrary, said Paxson; the gildsman needed to be urged not to write under war conditions pieces that he was later likely to deplore.

When Paxson turned to his main theme, "The Great Demobilization," he made sure to pronounce as tentative his efforts to recapture the spirit and flavor of postwar readjustments: it would take many decades of careful research before reliable estimates of the "calamity" of demobilization would be possible. Even so, Paxson was speaking shortly after the Munich Agreements of 1938 had been arranged, so that he ventured to predict that in case of another war the Allies might well achieve victory; and he ventured to add that his study of "The Great Demobilization" led him to doubt that "American society, or any society, could win another 'peace'."

By the time Paxson's successor addressed the Assocation in 1939, the second World War had been on for several months. But William S. Ferguson paid no attention to it in his message. Instead, he dealt with the ancient world, continuing to maintain the highly scholarly standards that had been associated with his name ever since the appearance of his first study, *The Athenian Secretaries* (1898).[30] A gildsman who had done much to further an understanding of Greek chronology, *Hellenistic Athens* (1911), and *Greek Imperialism* (1913), and to stimulate interest in ancient history at Harvard, Ferguson did not apologize for remaining with antiquity in his presidential ad-

29 Creel, *op. cit.,* p. 108.

30 For a list of Ferguson's writings, see *Harvard Studies in Classical Philosophy* (Cambridge, 1940), LI, 1-9.

dress. Nor did he attempt to justify his choice of subject on the basis of the needs of the contemporary scene. Ferguson, indeed, long before his presidential message, had cautioned that historical-mindedness was "not a boy's birthright."[31] In addition, he had cautioned that there were many pasts and that the historian should not treat them as being "one in spirit with the present."[32] Small wonder that his address on *"Polis* and *Idia* in Periclean Athens: The Relation between Public Service and Private Activities" proved to be one of the most past-minded pronouncements in the history of the Association.

While Ferguson did not attempt to meet the needs of the present in his message, his successor, Max Farrand, definitely did. Editor of one of the monuments of twentieth-century American scholarship, *The Records of the Federal Convention of 1787* (1911-1937), and author of *The Framing of the Constitution of the United States* (1913) and *The Fathers of the Constitution* (1921), Farrand had demonstrated that he was no narrow-minded patriot. Long intent on using history to foster better Anglo-American relations, he had written, in the period of the first World War, *The Development of the United States from Colonies to a World Power,* a book which he dedicated to the Allies. In the post war period, even though as director of research at the Huntington Library he took on numerous administrative responsibilities, Farrand continued to work actively for a better American understanding of English civilization. The Library itself he considered "not a mere museum or mausoleum, but an active force."[33] In view of his intense Anglophilism, to say nothing of his detestation of Nazi Germany, it was no surprise that in his message on "The Quality of Distinction" he tried to make use of the past for present purposes.

31 "The Office of the Ancient Historian," *Classical Journal,* V (1910), 265.

32 *Greek Imperialism* (Boston, 1913), p. 109.

33 *A.H.R.,* LI (1946), 412.

Contrasting the position of the gildsman in 1917 with his position in 1940, Farrand suggested that the period of the first World War was a time of distress for the historian who longed to use his subject-matter and training in the struggle for victory. What the historian could do as a historian seemed slight when compared to "the more immediately effective service" of scholars in other fields. In 1940, on the other hand, Farrand thought, the historian was much more favorably placed to meet his obligations and responsibilities. Concerned as he was with the study of ideas, the search for truth, and the investigation of values, he must inveigh against the menace of totalitarianism. Indeed, the sad truth was that, with much of the world at war, only the American scholar found himself in a position to encourage the ideals of scholarship and the values that formed so basic a part of the New World inheritance from Europe; and it was Farrand's hope that the historian would assume leadership among all brands of scholars in the fight to preserve the things without which scholarship itself was doomed.

American democracy, according to Farrand, was faced with several major problems: first, the discovery of able leadership, second, the achievement of the submission that effective leadership demanded, and, third, the raising of standards. When it was a question of meeting the first two of these problems, the historian as historian had only to record what had taken place in the past; but when it was a question of upholding and raising standards, the historian as historian had an active part to play in a democracy. Though Farrand deplored the widespread confidence of Americans in "the efficacy of merely going to school and college," he recognized that the historian could work to raise standards only through educational channels. He insisted, however, that these channels should be broadly interpreted in a world where the transmission of ideas was closely linked with technological changes. Thus, for the first time in the history of the Association, a president used his message to advocate the popularization of historical knowledge by means of the radio and the

motion picture. Farrand granted that so far the historian had
made no impressive showing along these lines. Yet when one
appeared who could write and speak with a popular appeal, Farrand urged that he be welcomed, not banished. And he added
that "The Story behind the Headlines," the radio program
sponsored by the Association, was a step in the right direction.[34]

As the director of one of the world's leading research foundations, Farrand made it clear that what mattered was the
laborious research that lay behind the popularization of knowledge. Nevertheless, the real need, as he saw it, was not for more
historical output but for output of greater distinction. Like the
poet, the artist, and the composer, the historian travelled in a
"world of values"; and, for him, as for them, "salvation" lay
in the improvement of qualitative production—the more so because the American of 1940 was growing increasingly aware of
"the seriousness of the present crisis." The gildsman, then,
should face the magnitude of his responsibilities, realizing that
"there never was a greater need than at present for the accurate
recording of historical events and for adequate and truthful
interpretations of history"; and the younger scholar in particular
should try to meet present needs by cultivating that "quality of
distinction" which would give to his works a long life.

Arthur M. Schlesinger, president of the Association in 1942,
likewise attempted to make use of the past for the sake of the
present; appropriately enough, his message was later reprinted
in *Paths to the Present* (1949), a volume of essays that was advertised as being concerned with the "usable past." Author of
what has often been considered one of the best doctoral dissertations ever produced in the United States, *The Colonial
Merchants and the American Revolution, 1763-1776* (1918),
Schlesinger had ventured in his post-doctoral days to abandon
the concreteness of economic history for the insecurities of

34 See Evelyn Plummer Read, "Broadcasting History: The Story of the
Story behind the Headlines," American Association for State and Local
History, *Bulletins,* I (1943), 161-88.

social history; and in his presidential message the co-editor of the *History of American Life* series turned to a favorite theme of the social historian, that of national character. For, with the United States at war, he thought it especially urgent to search for further answers to Crèvecoeur's question of American Revolutionary times, "What then is the American, this new man?" Schlesinger, obviously, had courage; otherwise, he would not have broached a subject that Tocqueville and Bryce had made peculiarly their own. But he was sure that European observers had not exhausted the possibilities of investigating the American character. There was need for further observations and diagnoses —the more so because of the growing role of the United States in world affairs.

In his analysis, one that showed little of the "painstaking, fundamental research" that he had thought would be necessary if social history was to have "substance and validity,"[35] Schlesinger ascribed an all-determining importance to the rural setting of American life. He emphasized that self-sufficient farming in a land of abundant physical resources and of labor shortages went a long way to explain the American's traits: his glorification of work and his disparagement of idleness; his view of members of leisured classes as tramps; his inability to relax; his view of spare time as an occasion for useful activities; his apathy along aesthetic lines; his worship of mechanical skill; his respect for versatility and his disdain for specialization; his rapid shifting from one job to another; his wastefulness except in times of crisis; his acceptance of corruption; his veneration of women; his powerlessness to stay put, which turned the pursuit of happiness into "the happiness of pursuit"; his belief in social mobility; his faith in equality of opportunity; his individualism; his conception of government as an umpire; his evasion of the law; his worship of wealth which made the class struggle a "struggle of Americans to climb out of one class into a higher one"; his worship of financial success; his idealism and humani-

---

35 "History," in Wilson Gee, ed., *Research in the Social Sciences: Its Fundamental Methods and Objectives* (New York, 1929), p. 234.

tarianism; his optimism and faith in progress; his habit of bragging.

Naturally, said Schlesinger, the decline of the rural setting and the growth of the urban community worked to modify the traits of the American. Though many of his old-time characteristics survived undisturbed, others, despite the brief duration of urban supremacy, were already undergoing transformation. It was, then, to the impact of urbanization and industrialization that the latter-day American owed some of his more recently acquired traits: his reverence for things cultural; his respect for the specialist and the expert; his enthusiasm for group activities; his distrust of individualism as a panacea; his view of government as the guarantor of equality of opportunity; his belief not merely in the habit of work but in the right to work. Here, then, was the new American, as Schlesinger pictured him in 1942, an American whose traits, though best adapted to peaceful pursuits, promised to serve well in time of war.

Even Nellie Neilson, Schlesinger's successor and the first woman to head the Association, yielded to the temptation to exploit the immediate usefulness of history. This was novel for Miss Neilson, who had taken her doctorate at Bryn Mawr under Andrews and who had often applauded her teacher's study of history for the sake of history.[36] As a former student of Maitland, moreover, she had become all the more alive to the dangers of using the past to throw light on the present. It was, in fact, her ability to keep the present out of the past that accounted in large measure for the high caliber of her publications on the economic and legal history of medieval England.

Yet when Miss Neilson addressed the Association in 1943, the year of the invasion of Sicily and the fall of Mussolini, she was obviously not content to be "hopelessly mediaeval," as she had once referred to herself;[37] and she went out of her way to

36 *Essays in Colonial History Presented to Charles McLean Andrews by His Students* (New Haven, 1931), p. 3.

37 *Ibid.*, p. 1.

explain why she chose "The Early Pattern of the Common Law" as the subject of her message. Noting that preceding presidents of the Association had frequently preferred to generalize about the nature of history rather than discuss some specialized historical theme, Miss Neilson announced that she would cling to the Middle Ages—especially since they offered "material pertinent to our own time." There were, to be sure, those who held that medieval English law, for example, was so far removed from the present-day world that the subject could readily be ignored until the war's end once more permitted "the pleasant pursuit of the nonessential." Miss Neilson, however, countered with the view that the subject be studied "not only for its own sake but also for the growth of political and social ideas whose birth lies hidden in the remote past but whose influence has had an important share in forming present opinions and actions resulting therefrom." With so many difficult problems to solve, no American in the year 1943 could ignore the truism that the roots of the present were to be found in the past.

Pointing out that much of England's history was America's history, Miss Neilson thought it urgent to re-examine the things that differentiated the English past from that of other countries. It was important to study the development of self-government and the growth of civil liberties, all of which formed so fundamental a part of the American inheritance from England. English law, legal procedure, and legal thinking, to say nothing of English lawbooks and legal dictionaries—all had so profound an influence on United States history that it was necessary to understand something of the models from which all these borrowings were made.

With a view to spreading the kind of knowledge that was "especially essential to us Americans in war and in peace," Miss Neilson focused her attention on the early pattern of the common law. Concentrating on the two centuries following the Norman Conquest, she explained that this period had intrinsic interest. Secondly, it was frequently viewed unhistorically and endowed with characteristics that belonged to subsequent times. Above all, Miss Neilson selected the period for the illustrations it had to offer of "the English method of gentle change." The interplay of the king's courts and old customs could still be studied profitably for an understanding of how the free governments of "the English-speaking peoples have come into being." After all, said Miss Neilson in 1943, Englishmen had found in the common law protection against tyranny; and "nurtured in the common law we Americans too have pledged against what seems to us to be tyranny 'our lives, our fortune, and our sacred honour.' "

While Miss Neilson justified her choice of subject chiefly on the basis of current needs, her successor, William L. Westermann, offered no such justification. Like Ferguson, a scholar who had helped to shape his outlook, Westermann viewed his message as a vehicle for the presentation of some of his recent findings. True, during the course of his career, he had used and abused the past for the purposes of the present. In the period of the first World War, for example, he had contributed an impassioned article to the University of Wisconsin War Pamphlets[38]—something for which he was later to be reprimanded, he thought rightly, by C. Hartley Grattan in "The Historians Cut Loose."[39] At the Paris Peace Conference, moreover, Westermann had served as an expert on Turkish and Near Eastern problems; and even in the years after the Conference he was frequently called upon to stop work on his papyri so as to advise, write, and talk on the Near East. Westermann, however, much preferred to stick to ancient history, which he studied not in the interests of the present but in the interests of the past. The very nature of his scholarly work testified to this, for his numerous articles on ancient economic history dealt, as a rule, with subjects that only a small

38 University of Wisconsin, *War Book: Papers on the Causes and Issues of the War* (Madison, 1918), pp. 253-66.

39 "The Historians Cut Loose," in Harry Elmer Barnes, *In Quest of Truth and Justice: De-Bunking the War Guilt Myth* (Chicago, 1928), p. 158.

number of specialists could understand. And it was to one of these subjects, ancient slavery, on which he had written most notably in a *Supplementband* of Pauly-Wissowa, that Westermann turned in his message of 1944.

Calling it "Between Slavery and Freedom," he concentrated on the status of those ancient Greeks and Romans who were part slave and part free. Briefly, however, he discussed slavery and freedom as phenomena that continued through the centuries, commenting, for instance, on recent restrictions on the occupational and spatial mobility of the British and American peoples. Even so, it was not the current importance of freedom of movement that concerned Westermann; it was its importance in the ancient world. Westermann used his address to throw light on the past. If in the process he threw any light on the present, that, from his standpoint, was only incidental, for he viewed historical study as its own reward.

By the time Westermann's successor delivered his message in December, 1945, the military phase of the second World War had ended; and it was the coming of peace that encouraged Carlton J. H. Hayes to reconsider the problem of American isolationism in its relation to the frontier. Recently returned from his wartime mission to Madrid, he was anxious to bring the past to bear on present problems. For Hayes this was nothing new. Deeply influenced in the early part of his career at Columbia by Robinson and Beard, he had come to value history for what it could do to throw light on the difficulties of the contemporary world.[40] Abandoning the Germanic invasions, on which he had done his doctoral dissertation, he edited a source book on *British Social Politics* (1913); he wrote widely used textbooks that were closely geared to the explanation of recent developments; he undertook studies of the origins of modern nationalism; and by reason of his effective classroom teaching he stimulated scores of graduate students to undertake similar studies. As a leading

40 "The Propriety and Value of the Study of Recent History," *History Teacher's Magazine*, IV (1913), 243-48.

Roman Catholic layman, moreover, and an active member of the National Conference of Christians and Jews, he often tried to draw on what he called "the contribution of history to group relations."[41] Hayes was being consistent, then, when, in his presidential address on "The American Frontier—Frontier of What?," he tried once more to take advantage of the present usefulness of historical knowledge.

It was high time, he thought, for the American gildsman to widen his view of the frontier and to ask the question, of what was the American frontier a frontier? Scholars like Dixon Ryan Fox, William R. Shepherd, and Herbert E. Bolton had already asked and answered the question; but the answer, though obvious, had captured the enthusiasm of very few specialists in United States history. In a small minority were those who regarded frontiers in North America—and in South America, Australasia, and South Africa—as frontiers of Europe; in the overwhelming majority were those who viewed the frontier as the area west of the eastern United States.

According to Hayes, this narrow conception of the frontier was both a result and a cause of "growing intellectual isolationism" in the United States. Naturally, isolationism had many sides and explanations; and inseparable from it was American nationalism, the growth of which had fostered an isolationist outlook. But Hayes wished to emphasize that this outlook American historians had done much to encourage. In fact, he referred to the years since 1875 as the period of the "Babylonian Captivity" of American historiography, a period which saw a trend away from European subjects and a trend toward purely American themes. In the last two decades, for example, Hayes said, monographs and doctoral dissertations in United States history outnumbered those in European history by at least a twelve-to-one ratio. In former years, even the specialist in American history was given "some basic training" in European his-

41 See Newton Diehl Baker, Carlton J. H. Hayes, and Roger Williams Straus, eds., *The American Way: A Study of Human Relations among Protestants, Catholics and Jews* (Chicago, 1936), ch. VIII.

tory; recently, however, Hayes complained, dissertations were being prepared "in a state of comparative innocence" about what had taken place outside the United States. In the circumstances, it was not surprising that the wider implications of the American frontier were being neglected.

There were those who believed that the isolationist and nationalist tendencies in American historical study were not proceeding with all possible speed and effectiveness. And so, seizing on the New York *Times* survey of what students did not know about the American past, politicians were enacting laws and educators were revising curriculums. Yet the irony of it all, Hayes thought, was that the rising American generation that would have to meet so many recently assumed international obligations was the same generation that would be exposed to more schooling in United States history and to less schooling in any other kind. Hayes was convinced that "the backbone" of the formal education of young Americans should be "solid, vertebrate history," not some substitute product. He was equally convinced that no appreciable improvement would result from running the high-school course in United States history for two or three years instead of one, especially since this was sure to mean the reduction of the remainder of man's history to the status of a one-year or even a semester-long course. Hayes made it clear that he had no use for the over-simplifications and generalizations that went by the name of world history. Nor did he have any use for the college and university courses that were grouped as "American civilization"—unless those courses could equip students and scholars for "enlightened participation in the transcendent responsibilities of the United States as a world power," and this presupposed courses which would bring American civilization into close relation with the original civilization of which it formed only a part.

If something was not done to combat intellectual isolationism, Hayes anticipated a further popularization of the myth of the American way as "something entirely indigenous, something

wholly new, and something vastly superior to any other nation's."
He also feared an intensification in the United States of a "missionary and messianic impulse, which will have far greater scope
and far greater opportunity for expressing itself in the current
aftermath of the second World War, and which, if unattended by
realistic knowledge of other peoples and their historic cultures,
may lead to the most dangerous consequences for the United
States itself." Hayes found it shocking that, despite the developments of the last years, Americans had learned so few lessons
and that intellectual isolationism should have become intensified
at a time when the United States was moving away from political and economic isolationism. But the truth was that most
Americans, even most intellectuals, still thought in isolationist
terms.

Time was when Americans knew that in addition to being
Americans they were Europeans who inhabited a frontier of Europe. The members of the Philadelphia Convention knew this. In
fact, Hayes suggested that, unlike most present-day senators or
Ph. D.'s in United States history, the American Founding Fathers could have handled themselves admirably in stiff doctoral
examinations in European history and comparative government;
and American political and economic achievements in the whole
period from 1775 to 1825 Hayes ascribed "less to American
aloofness from Europe than to the informed statecraft of Americans who were then in familar touch with Europe and equipped to
treat with it intelligently and realistically." Nor was it only the
statesmen in the period from 1775 to 1825 who had an awareness
of the interrelationships of Europe and America. Teachers, students, writers, merchants, and cotton planters had that awareness, too. No doubt the frontiersman of the time considered himself first of all an American, but even he could never escape from
his indebtedness to Europe; for he inhabited an "evanescent phe-
nomenon," and the influence of tradition and continuity directed
the transit of culture "not so much *from* as *to* the frontier." Besides, the frontier had exercised an important historical influence

in countries other than the United States. Virtually every European nation had had a frontier past conditioning its historical evolution.

Hayes did not deny that Americans of the United States differed from European peoples, but he contended that the differences were "not greater in kind, and hardly greater in degree" than those that divided Englishmen and Spaniards or Germans and Italians. The development of nationalism, to be sure, had involved a heavy emphasis on the idea of unique and peculiar cultures; and it had operated to becloud the European culture in which all the national cultures shared. This, however, made it only more urgent for the historian to reassert the glories of European culture, that "unifying fact and force" which made Englishmen, Frenchmen, Germans, Spaniards, and Americans fundamentally Europeans. "More than ever before," then, Hayes suggested, the historian should make a comparative study of frontiers, melting pots, and nationalisms in Europe and America; "more than ever before" he should emphasize that the differences among the nations of European tradition were fewer in number and significance than their similarities.

As used by Hayes, the word *European* referred to the "cultural community" that arose originally in the Mediterranean area and then came to embrace the Atlantic, giving rise to what Walter Lippmann termed the "Atlantic Community. "In the past Americans had inherited as well as developed the civilization that formed the basis of this Atlantic Community, but it was probable that in the future they would lead it. And the success or failure of this leadership, Hayes was convinced, would depend on the extent to which the ties of the Atlantic Community were strengthened or weakened. Indeed, the end of the second World War meant that the Atlantic Community would assume "a crucial and very practical importance," for it could serve as "the balance between Eurasian Russia and the Far East, on one hand, and ourselves, on the other." Agreeing with Walter Lippmann, Hayes voiced his conviction that a solidly united Atlantic

Community offered the best guarantee of a peaceful world and a secure United States. After the first World War, American myopia weakened the Atlantic Community. And even after the second World War, Hayes was distressed to note, the belief continued in the United States that European disputes were the affairs of Europe; the belief continued that European disputes could be avoided to a large extent if a United States of Europe were formed. Such a federal union, some Americans assumed, would make possible the attainment of "the happy goal of America for the Americans and Europe for the Europeans."

Hayes found it lamentable that such "fantastic" beliefs could manage to survive in the United States. Peace and security, he could not emphasize strongly enough, were to be achieved not through a United States of Europe but through the Atlantic Community. As for the widespread American faith in Pan-Americanism, Hayes argued that it lacked real foundations outside the framework of a "larger Atlantic Community." Especially in the atomic age, American security demanded the defense of the entire Atlantic basin. Hayes' point was that the Pan-American Union could not possibly function successfully without British, French, Dutch, Spanish, and Portuguese participation, for history and geography had decreed inexorably that these Europeans were members of the Pan-American Union. He suggested therefore that the alliance projected at Chapultepec be expanded to include the powers of the Atlantic Community. Not that he thought that such a step would work against the United Nations. On the contrary, he was convinced that, once Americans recognized and assumed their place in the Atlantic Community, they could work all the better with all of the United Nations.

According to Hayes, there was much for the historian to do. He should fight against intellectual isolationism in the United States. He should help Americans to understand their "historic setting and current responsibilities." He should help them to understand conditions in foreign countries and to overcome he provincialism that jeopardized the United Nations. With a view to lessening prejudices of all kinds—racial, political, religious, and nationalist—he should concentrate more on the use of the comparative method in historical study. The specialist in United States history should investigate the history of some foreign country which he could then compare and contrast with that of the United States; and the student of a subject like nationalism, slavery, democracy, or the frontier should also learn to benefit from the comparative method. Thus, like so many of his predecessors, Hayes tried to use the past to supply the needs of the present. Continuing in the tradition that Andrew D. White had established some sixty years before, he took his stand in favor of an alive and active history, one that would do work in the contemporary world.

CHAPTER IV
HISTORY AS LITERATURE

SINCE so many presidents placed so much emphasis on the practical side of history, it would seem logical to suppose that many of them would also have placed much emphasis on its literary side; for, if the past had immediate social utility, if it had messages for the present, those messages, it would seem, should be written in a way to command the attention of the layman. Yet relatively few leaders of the Association dealt with history as literature in their messages. By and large they took the subject for granted or considered it only incidentally. And though some presidents dealt with it in relation to the practical value of history, others dealt with it simply for esthetic reasons. Still others took the stand that the historian should not worry about style because he had too many more important things to do.

James Ford Rhodes, fourteenth president of the Association, was the first to devote his message to any serious consideration of the literary side of history. The subject had been left almost totally undiscussed in the messages of his predecessors: even George Bancroft and Henry Adams had ignored it. Rhodes, therefore, had a wide open field at his disposal. Yet even the fondest admirer of the Cleveland iron manufacturer who had turned historian would not dwell long on his stylistic virtues. His friend, J. Franklin Jameson, for many years editor of the *American Historical Review,* found in his books "no great charm of literary style, beyond the attractive power of a manly simplicity";[1] and his sympathetic biographer, M. A. DeWolfe Howe, found in them "comparatively little of grace, ease, and beauty."[2] Yet while Rhodes did not write particularly well, he had certain-

1 *A.H.R.,* XXXII (1927), 677.

2 M. A. DeWolfe Howe, *James Ford Rhodes, American Historian* (New York, 1929), p. 99.

ly tried to train himself as a writer; and doubtless it was his awareness of the artistic shortcomings of his *History of the United States from the Compromise of 1850* that prompted him to discuss history as literature in his presidential message of 1899.[3]

Rhodes did not pretend to be issuing any earth-shaking revelations. He confessed that the long history of historiography made him suspicious of attempts at originality. History was such an old subject and one that had attracted so many fertile minds through the centuries that a historian would have to be pretty vain to think that he could say something new about the way to write it. Rhodes hoped only to arrange "the commonplaces in some different combination." Nor did he wish to exaggerate the intellectual demands that history made on its students, stating at the outset that it was not "the highest form of intellectual endeavor." He thought, for instance, that it would be better to lose every history book that had ever been written rather than lose Homer and Shakespeare. Nevertheless, Rhodes, whose practice it was to fill his scrapbooks with passages from gifted writers,[4] hastened to classify Homer and Shakespeare as "great historians of human nature," from whom the gildsman had much to learn about the art of narration and of character description. Nor was it only literature that Rhodes rated more highly than history; he rated the mathematical and physical sciences more highly, too. But if, when compared with literature and science, history was only a "modest enterprise," it was still a secure one, for it preserved the memory of man's deeds.

Yet how well was the modern historian carrying on this enterprise? By "modern" Rhodes meant the historian who lived in the period after the publication of *The Origin of the Species*, the historian who had the advantage of exposure to Darwin's theory of evolution. Was this modern historian giving a better performance than the pre-Darwinian historian? Though Rhodes

3 *Ibid.*, pp. 95-96.
4 *Ibid.*, pp. 98-99.

seemed to be renewing the quarrel over the relative merits of
the ancients and the moderns, he really found little about which
to quarrel. For he was confident that if English, German, and
American historians voted to determine the two all-time favor-
ites of their craft, a fairly large majority would cast their vote
for Thucydides and Tacitus. Third place, Rhodes added, would
doubtless fall to Herodotus or Gibbon. In other words, all the
successful candidates would date from the pre-Darwinian era—
an indication that, despite the advantages the moderns enjoyed
the excellence of the ancients remained unexcelled. Himself a
scholar's scholar, Rhodes granted that the moderns outstripped
the ancients along certain lines: "in the connection of materials
in criticism and detailed analysis, in the study of cause and effect
in applying the principle of growth, of evolution." Even so, the
superior position of the ancients remained unchallenged.

How to explain this? Certainly Herodotus could be recommended neither for the accuracy of his details nor his critical
sifting of facts, nor, least of all, for his skepticism; but he could
be recommended, Rhodes thought, for diligence, honesty, narrative power, and literary talent, a combination of qualities that
kept him alive while Polybius went unread or was read "as a
penance." Thucydides and Tacitus, moreover, thought Rhodes—
and not quite correctly—could be recommended for their accuracy, their love of truth, their impartiality, and their diligence
These, however, were qualities in which they were surely
equalled by some modern historians. For example, said Rhodes
selecting a historian about whom he had written recently in "A
New Estimate of Cromwell,"[5] Samuel R. Gardiner was on a
level with Thucydides in impartiality and love of truth. Why
then, should Thucydides continue to be placed in the top position? Rhodes found the explanation in the skill with which
Thucydides—as well as Tacitus—could say so many meaningful
things in so few words. Thinking no doubt of his own *History*
the first four volumes of which covered only the period from

5 *Historical Essays* (New York, 1909), pp. 317-23.

850 to 1865, Rhodes remarked that the compressed narratives of the ancients made modern works look "really curious"; or the modern ones that dealt with long stretches of time were short and those which dealt with a few years were long. Macaulay, Rhodes pointed out, covered seventeen years in five wordy volumes that offered a constant invitation to exercises in paraphrasing. Thucydides, on the other hand, covered twenty-four years in a narrative that was so concise as to defy paraphrasing. The account of the plague in Athens has been studied and imitated," said Rhodes, whose own classical training was negligible, "and every imitation falls short of the original not only in vividness but in brevity. It is the triumph of art that in this and in other splendid portions we wish more had been told." Having devoted a life of long reflection to the composition of a single volume, Thucydides could assimilate his materials and write a pithy and vigorous narrative, an account unparalleled in all the literature of history. Tacitus also placed no importance on production for the sake of production; like Thucydides, he was able to mull over his materials and make conciseness an instrument of historiographical policy. Indeed, if all of his works had survived, Rhodes estimated that they would have filled only four volumes of moderate size. The ancients, in short, took time out to think about what they were writing. Scornful of the quantitative approach to historiography, they were able to produce thoughtful and well-written works.

Unfortunately, "the periods of fruitful meditation" that the ancients knew did not seem to be "a natural incident of our time," Rhodes complained in 1899. Actually, he had less reason to complain than most historians of his period, who lacked the financial independence that permitted him to devote so much time to research. At all events, Rhodes regretted that the modern guildsman was plagued by an atmosphere that encouraged him to rush into print. He worried about deadlines; he worried about the pressures of publishers. Small wonder, then, that Tacitus and Thucydides more than continued to hold their own. Yet if the

historian was interested in outstripping the ancients, he wou
be well advised to know their works thoroughly; he shou
understand that their preeminence grew out of their concis
ness and that their conciseness grew out of their thorough ma
tery of materials.

The ancients received no such tribute from Rhodes' successo
Edward Eggleston, who dealt only briefly with history as liter
ture in his address on "The New History." This address, pr
pared during the illness that was shortly to bring on his deat
gave few hints of the literary talent that Eggleston had shown
his novels, his books for children, and his historical writings; b
despite the unevenness of its style and the faultiness of its o
ganization,[6] it showed traces of the vigor that had characteriz
the prose of the former Methodist clergyman.

Eggleston did not deny the artistry of the classical historian
he granted that Herodotus, Thucydides, and Tacitus were ma
ters of language. But they were not much more than that from h
point of view. In fact, he was determined to break their dom
nation once and for all. Obviously, he said, there were moder
writers who, like the ancients, had admirable stylistic gifts. Mo
than that, these modern writers had meaningful subject-matte
something which the ancients, with their emphasis on war an
politics, lacked. Interested as Eggleston was in the history
the customs and manners of the people, he found his models
writers like Raleigh, Macaulay, and Green, writers who lavishe
their artistry on the right kind of material.

Eggleston was a latecomer in the field of history; but his pr
vious experience as a novelist doubtless encouraged him to tal
stylistic grace pretty much for granted. This was not true, how
ever, of Alfred T. Mahan: though, like Eggleston, Mahan can
late to history, unlike Eggleston, he had had little previou
training as a writer, and so the matter of form that the auth

6 Cf. William Peirce Randel, *Edward Eggleston: Author of The Hoosi
School-Master* (New York, 1946), p. 225.

f *The Hoosier School-Master* could take essentially for granted
ae naval officer could not. Mahan's own style, to be sure, has
alled forth widely varying reactions, ranging from the state-
ient that "it was deplorable in any language to Theodore Roo-
evelt's generous praise."[7] Just the same, Mahan was convinced
hat lack of literary merit in a historical work was a sure ob-
tacle to the popularization of knowledge. Therefore, he found
: "especially necessary" in 1902 to remind the gildsman that
historical work should not only be truthful but artistic as well.
pokesman that he was for the cause of naval preparedness,
Iahan pointed out that if the gildsman was to make himself
seful as a teacher, he should devote much time and thought to
is "preliminary work as an artist." He should strive for unity,
mphasis, and subordination in his writings; for, if he lacked
rtistry, if he failed to bring order to an unshapely mass of dis-
onnected facts, he would fail to communicate his message to
is reader.

Nor did Mahan think that artistic historical writing was
imply a matter of composing a vivid narrative. The important
hing, he believed, was to avoid the vague and general impres-
ions that resulted from an inability to select and group material.
According to Mahan, the gildsman should scorn the Froissarts
1 history—the Froissarts whose works had "neither beginning,
iiddle, nor end, only surface ebullition." Doubtless Mahan was
nduly harsh on Froissart; doubtless, too, he was overly gen-
rous in his evaluation of Bishop Stubbs' literary talent. How-
ver that may be, he conceded that there were probably as few
orn historians as there were born artists; but he added that the
istorian did not have to be a genius to achieve unity, emphasis,
nd proper subordination in his presentation. An "artistic
rouping of subordinate details around a central idea" he re-
arded as within the reach of many whom he hesitated to call

7 W. D. Puleston, *Mahan: The Life and Work of Captain Alfred Thayer
Iahan, U.S.N.* (New Haven, 1939), p. 331; Albert B. Hart and H. R.
erleger, eds., *Theodore Roosevelt Cyclopedia* (New York, 1941), pp.
26-27.

artists, but who were capable of rising above the level of chro
iclers or narrators. Wisely, Mahan conceded that, in contra
to other fields, his own, that of military history, was characte
ized perhaps by "more pronounced definiteness of human pla
more clearly marked finality of conclusion, and withal a certa
vividness of action," all of which made possible the unity a
emphasis that he sought in historical writing. He insiste
nevertheless, that political, economic, and social history cou
also be artistically presented.

The artistry that Mahan preached in 1902 found anoth
advocate two years later in the person of Goldwin Smith, t
Anglo-Canadian publicist and one-time journalist for the *Satu
day Review*. Having studied history with a view to instructi
and elevating mankind, Smith had long emphasized the ne
for attractive historical prose. In the inaugural lecture that he d
livered in 1859 as regius professor of modern history at Oxfo
he had argued that "to command beautiful and forcible langua
is to have a key, with which no man who is to rule through opi
ion can dispense, to the heart and mind of man."[8] Yet for a writ
who was so style-conscious Smith produced disappointingly fe
literary gems: his writings on English and American histor
exhibited all too frequent signs of hasty composition; and h
presidential message disclosed, in addition, symptoms of a
vancing age, which was not surprising, for when he addresse
the Association on "The Treatment of History," he was ov
eighty.

As a good nineteenth-century Manchester liberal and inte
nationalist, Smith reacted unfavorably to the rhetoric a
Fourth of July spirit of a George Bancroft. In general, howeve
what he found wrong with American history books was not
much their patriotic bias as their dryness of style. It was Thom
Carlyle's lack of dryness, among other things, that prompt

8 *Lectures on the Study of History, Delivered in Oxford, 1859-61* (Ne
York, 1866), p. 28.

Smith, who disliked Carlyle personally,[9] to commend his account of the French Revolution as a model and to recommend its study for the training of the gildsman's "historical sense." He acknowledged that from the standpoint of accuracy of detail the work was open to just criticism, but this he forgave in view of Carlyle's insight and breadth and his ability to write picturesquely and vividly.

Smith, who had written for different audiences in England, Canada, and the United States, recognized that style should "vary with the subject, with the genius of the writer, with the intelligence of the reader." But even in an age of science and sociology, he insisted, it was clear that a historical study, in order to be widely read, must be of interest to "ordinary minds." Smith deplored the tendency to look down on narrative art. He did not deny that Stubbs, his successor at Oxford, was a master of research; but he insisted that *The Constitutional History of England* could be read only by a serious student—something, he might have added, that Stubbs himself had recognized. David Hume's *History of England,* on the other hand, for all its inaccuracies, said Smith, continued to have much in its favor. For the fact was that, unlike Stubbs, Hume had popularized history. His attractive style and narrative skill had gained for him and for history "countless readers." The same was true of William Robertson. His study of Charles V was doubtless incorrect in some of its details, but in its time it had served to popularize history; and this Smith found most commendable.

George Burton Adams, however, was opposed to the suggestion of both Smith and Mahan that the gildsman court popularity among lay readers. This opposition doubtless grew out of the fact that Adams worked in a field that had only recently, in the hands of Stubbs and Maitland, started to come into its own.[10]

9 *Reminiscences* (New York, 1910), pp. 141-42, 167-68.

10 See Nellie Neilson's comments in *Essays in Colonial History Presented to Charles McLean Andrews by His Students* (New Haven, 1931), pp. 1-2.

Since much remained to be done, Adams was convinced that re-search, more research, and still more research were in order. A scholar's scholar, he had been disturbed by the movement to con-vert the *American Historical Review* into a popular journal. This, he feared, would have endangered its scholarly character.[11] Not that Adams failed to appreciate good prose. He himself was an admirably clear writer, who had not hesitated to take to task the historian whose style was "needlessly uninteresting."[12] As a rule, however, his great preoccupation was a simple one: to in-crease knowledge of the past. Of this he left no doubt in his presidential message of 1908.

Adams would not yield to those "estimable gentlemen" who at the end of a hard day wanted to do some historical reading that was at once relaxing, entertaining, and enlightening. He thought that such gentlemen were in no small measure respon-sible for the frequently voiced demand that history be written as an art and not as a science. This dichotomy Adams resented: it hinged on the absurd notion that history as art and history as science were antithetical. Obviously, however, any gildsman who had a feeling for the beauties of language could write literary history.

Adams was anxious for history to continue, as in the past, to maintain its position as "one of the highest branches of litera-ture." He was convinced that a time would come when man's past would be "unfolded in a great work of art, immortal in it-self like all great works of art." He was also convinced that this time could come only when the facts of history were definitively ascertained. Without such established facts, a historical work could lay claim neither to truth nor to "permanence as art." Adams' point was that in the long run the work of the gildsman who wrote history as literature would be more short-lived than the work of the obscure gildsman who dug up and established

11 W. Stull Holt, ed., *Historical Scholarship in the United States, 1876-1901: As Revealed in the Correspondence of Herbert B. Adams* (Baltimore, 1938), p. 245.

12 *The Growth of the French Nation* (New York, 1896), p. iv.

facts. While Adams did not wish to disparage overly the emphasis on the literary side of history, he did wish to stress the continuing need for additions to the sum of historical knowledge, additions that some of those who sought to produce the "finest art" were not making.

Adams' views gained little support from his successor, Albert Bushnell Hart. Nor was this really surprising in view of the vast temperamental differences between the two men. Hart was probably the most colorful historian of his time. At Harvard, where he gave the general course in American history, he put on a show that delighted students and drove assistants frantic—especially when the time came for them to gather his notes and place them in the appropriate colored folder.[13] As a teacher, Hart was sensational. As an editor, he was tremendous, for he knew how to get the best out of those whose works he was editing. But as a researcher Hart was not in a class with a scholar like Adams. Perhaps it was that he lacked patience; perhaps it was that in general he did not find research sufficiently dramatic. Whatever the explanation, he certainly wanted the results of research to be presented dramatically or at least in good literary form. He had pointed out in his pioneering multi-volume source book, *American History Told by Contemporaries* (1897-1929), that he chose his documents on the basis not only of accuracy but of stylistic merit. Similarly, in his introduction to *The American Nation: A History from Original Sources by Associated Scholars,* he made it a point to note that the series was designed not only to instruct the layman but to entertain him as well, for it would be both accurate and readable.

Returning to the subject of style in his presidential message of 1909 on "Imagination in History," Hart complained that scientific history often resembled the teacher who could teach but could not win the affection of students. The upshot was that

13 Samuel E. Morison, "Albert Bushnell Hart, 1889-1939," in Massachusetts Historical Society, *Proceedings, 1936-1941* (Boston, 1942), LXVI, 435-36.

the layman found history books, history books everywhere, but hardly an attractive tome to read. Logically, Hart saw no reason for the dullness of scientific history, but even so sound and discriminating a pioneer as Stubbs could hardly be termed "enlivening." The English constitutional historian knew how to write accurate and truthful prose, but not the kind of prose, said Hart, that would move poets to odes or peoples to revolutions. Though Stubbs had a sound grasp of facts, he lacked imagination, a gift that Hart considered indispensable in historical writing.

If Hart deplored the lack of imagination that frequently made the scientific historian dull, he likewise deplored the excess of imagination that made the picturesque historian grossly inaccurate. In an attempt to draw word pictures that would enable the reader to visualize what was being described, a Froude was not averse to supplementing the sources with details that he himself invented, details which made for a more striking picture and for an "impression of constant excitement." Though Indians were not always engaged in scalping operations, and though Cossacks were not always setting fire to villages, the picturesque historian often concentrated on heroic and startling events, omitting commonplace matters like the social and economic aspects of history which did not lend themselves readily to imaginative literary description.

To Hart's way of thinking, the scientific historian and the picturesque historian were plainly inferior to the dramatic historian. For the scientific historian contented himself with presenting facts; and the picturesque historian contented himself with presenting striking facts; but the dramatic historian contented himself with nothing less than transmuting "the lifeless lead of the annals into the shining gold of the historian" He aimed for vital historical writing, the kind that gave new life to the people of former ages. Hart singled out for special praise five writers of dramatic history: Motley, Tacitus, Macaulay, Parkman, and Gibbon. Motley, for example, knew how to select, arrange, and state his facts, but he also knew how to apply imagination to a narrative. He was indisputably a master of the art of dramatic history. So, too, was Tacitus, Rhodes' ideal of a historian. While Rhodes had emphasized his conciseness, Hart emphasized his dramatic energy and his "power to seize men and things and group those that belong together, to describe men in their habits, to separate them from other men . . . ." Of Macaulay, the most prominent writer of imaginative history, Hart had this to say: "The arousing style, the prodigality of knowledge, the real interest in, acquaintance with, and love for, historical characters (though he may have misjudged them as we misjudge our acquaintances) combine to put Macaulay in the front rank of the world's historians. He is great because of his dramatic power; his people are all taking a part in a mighty movement; one after another speaks his lines, telling us himself why he is on the stage, or by indirection making us aware of his assignment."

Yet even more than the dramatic sense that linked Macaulay with Shakespeare, Hart stressed another gift that few historians possessed: insight. The genius of a Parkman, he suggested, depended on his insight into the dramatic character of man's life; he understood the elements that made for genuinely imaginative history. Such was Hart's enthusiasm for Parkman that he maintained that "few writers have ever established such sympathy and understanding between themselves and the personality of men whom they never saw." Just the same, it was Gibbon, according to Hart, who combined most of the traits of the first-rate historian; and Gibbon's writings offered incontestable proof that great history presupposed large imagination. "Gibbon was a grand man, the prince of historical writers, who, whatever he is writing, is always describing a triumph; for his sentences rank themselves right-forward and fours-right; his paragraphs succeed each other in platoons and squadrons; his chapters are army corps moving forward to the sound of trumpets and cymbals, banners flying, armor gleaming, commanders on caracoling horses, all moving forward steadily, resistlessly, and magnificently."

It was with Hart rather than with George Burton Adams that William M. Sloane sided in 1911. This was to be expected, for Sloane was the author of a highly publicized four-volume biography of Napoleon, a study that he had intended as a popular work. When it was reviewed by Charles M. Andrews in the *American Historical Review,* it was criticized for its lack of color and romance and for its superabundance of facts. Andrews granted that Sloane's writing was often "polished and forcible," but he found it wanting in "charm and simplicity," so much so, that he ventured to state that "such a style as this can never become popular."[14] Obviously, however, Andrews' criticisms—as well as those of other hostile reviewers—could not have made much of an impression on Sloane. For when, in his presidential address, he commented briefly on literary form, he made it clear that he considered himself qualified to speak for the general reader.

The layman, he said, demanded history that was not only truthful but entertaining; and if a historical work lacked these qualities, it was likely to be flouted and quickly forgotten. The gildsman therefore did well to make the necessary concessions to popular taste. Nor did Sloane see any harm in the layman's demand for truthful and entertaining historical writing; he viewed it as deriving from both a righteous and an artistic impulse. He saw no point in bothering with historical writing that lacked immediacy, concreteness, poignancy, directness, proportion, and stylistic attraction.

Theodore Roosevelt, who succeeded Sloane, took a more moderate stand. Delivering his presidential message in 1912, the recently defeated Progressive candidate showed no traces of campaign scars. From the letter he wrote to Henry Cabot Lodge the day before he addressed the Association, it would appear that even political activities had not prevented him from devoting "much care" to the preparation of what he called a "beastly

14 *A.H.R.,* III (1898), 359.

lecture."[15] His great concern seemed to be that his address was not to be published anywhere, but this was a totally unfounded fear. If Roosevelt in the midst of a busy political life had been able to keep up with scholarly publications, he would have known that already for almost a decade the *Review* had been carrying the text of every presidential address.

That Roosevelt, for the purposes of his message, should have decided to discuss "History as Literature" was understandable enough. It was a subject about which he had long felt strongly. His own books he would have preferred to regard as contributions not only to history but to literature as well. And if he admired George Otto Trevelyan, it was, among other things, because he viewed the author of *The American Revolution* as "one of the few blessed exceptions to the rule that the readable historian is not truthful."[16] If he admired Trevelyan's son, George Macaulay, moreover, it was because the young author of the article on "The Latest View of History," later printed in *Clio, A Muse, and Other Essays* (1913),[17] shared his own conviction that history should be "literature of a very high type." Indeed, after Roosevelt read the original article, he wrote in 1904 a lively letter to Trevelyan *père*, whom he had taken to be its author;[18] and in this letter he presented a summary of the essential ideas that he was to restate in his message of 1912.

Like George Burton Adams, Roosevelt took the stand that there was no real conflict between history as science and history as art. True, discussions of the subject often generated more heat than light, but this was often the result of confused terminology. Roosevelt could certainly recognize arguments that were

15 *Selections from the Correspondence of Theodore Roosevelt and Henry Cabot Lodge, 1884-1918* (2 vols., New York, 1925), II, 427.

16 Joseph Bucklin Bishop, *Theodore Roosevelt and His Time Shown in His Own Letters* (2 vols., New York, 1920), II, 139.

17 "The Latest View of History," *Independent Review*, I (1903-04), 395-414; *Clio, A Muse and Other Essays, Literary and Pedestrian* (London, 1913), pp. 1-55.

18 Bishop, *op. cit.*, II, 139-41.

"neither mutually incompatible nor mutually relevant." He thought, nevertheless, that the gildsman who lauded the scientific side of history and ignored its literary side tended to forget that time was when history could not be distinguished from poetry or science, that time was when poetry provided a splendid vehicle for both science and philosophy. Though philosophy had not been severed in any thoroughgoing way from literature, the breach between science and poetry and between history and poetry was virtually complete. Did modern science or modern history enlist the talents of a Goethe or a Browning? Obviously not; yet the fact was, said Roosevelt, that Goethe and Browning had done much to advance the cause of philosophy. Just as Macaulay brought history to many a reader who would never have gone to a formal historical work, so Browning brought philosophy to many a reader who would never have gone to a formal philosophical treatise. Falling prey, however, to the very looseness of terminology that he had just deplored, Roosevelt announced that both philosophy and history were sciences; and he affirmed his belief that both should be presented in attractive literary form.

Roosevelt did not mean that history should be presented emotionally rather than truthfully. He insisted that deep and diligent research had necessarily to precede historical writing; for "no amount of self-communion and of pondering on the soul of mankind, no gorgeousness of literary imagery" could serve as a substitute for research. A writer like Thomas Carlyle thought otherwise, said Roosevelt, and the result was his *French Revolution,* "a splendid bit of serious romance writing." In all fairness to Carlyle, it should be added that Roosevelt could never forgive him for his attitude toward the American Civil War.[19] In all fairness, too, it should further be added that Roosevelt himself, on occasion, had gone in for the same "romance writing" of which he accused Carlyle. His biographies of Thomas Benton (1886) and Gouverneur Morris (1888) were prepared without

19 Hart and Ferleger, eds., *op. cit.,* p. 67.

much research[20]—something that his critics were quick to bring to his attention. And his biography of Oliver Cromwell (1900) called forth from Guernsey Jones the comment that "life is short and Gardiner is long, but...anyone who has not time to read and re-read Mr. Gardiner's delightful though voluminous pages has not time to write a life of Cromwell."[21] Roosevelt, at any rate, blamed a work like Carlyle's *French Revolution* for the disrepute into which literary history had fallen. For the gildsman, well aware of the inadequacies of Carlyle's brand of historiography, often came to suspect not only all romantic historical writing but all vivid historical writing. While he was correct in believing that truth should never be made to yield before the demands of a colorful presentation, he was incorrect, Roosevelt thought, in believing that a colorful account and a truthful account were incompatible.

If Roosevelt did not consider the dryness of facts and the greyness of details worthwhile in themselves, he made sure to pay his respects to the gildsman who held this view. A collector of facts and details, this gildsman had no need of literary talent. He performed an "invaluable service" to history by stressing the worth of scientific methods. Nevertheless, he performed a disservice to history when he sought to divorce it from literature, all in an attempt to ape the scientist who truculently disclaimed any links with the world of letters. Recalling Macaulay, Roosevelt urged the gildsman to overcome his distrust of the historical work that was readable; an interesting book was not necessarily superficial. Recalling Lucretius, moreover, Roosevelt urged the scientist who knew how to write to stop feeling "apologetic about it": no small measure of the success of Darwin and Huxley was due to their powers of expression.

Roosevelt recognized that there were many works on which literary and imaginative powers would be almost wholly wasted.

20 Harrison John Thornton, "Theodore Roosevelt," in William T. Hutchinson, ed., *The Marcus W. Jernegan Essays in American Historiography* (Chicago, 1937), pp. 231-33.

21 *A.H.R.*, VI (1901), 564.

Such were specialized studies which by their very nature could be of interest only to the scholar. Such, too, were history text-books, whose purpose it was to teach the privileges and responsibilities of citizenship in a democracy. What mattered in these books was content, not form. Obviously, however, there were other kinds of historical works; and in writing these Roosevelt thought that the gildsman ought to strive for the qualities that went to make for great literature. He should strive for "vision and imagination, the power to grasp what is essential and to reject the infinitely more numerous non-essentials, the power to embody ghosts, to put flesh and blood on dry bones, to make dead men living before our eyes." The task of the literary historian was "to take the science of history and turn it into literature." Through the use of his imaginative and artistic talents, he should give life not only to the heroic aspects of the past but to its hum-drum aspects as well. Unless he could arouse interest in "the gray tints of the general landscape no less than in the flame hues of the jutting peaks," he was really wasting his time studying the commonplace. For, like his good friend, Alfred T. Mahan, Roosevelt argued that if writings were not read, they were useless, and they would not be read unless they were readable. The need for artistry in historical writing impressed Roosevelt all the more because of the likelihood that the gildsman would increasingly be called upon to indicate those teachings of history that would help Americans to grapple with present-day problems. Unless the lessons drawn from the past were effectively presented, they might go unheeded.

Again and again Roosevelt insisted that the historian should combine literary talent and a thorough knowledge of the facts; attractive language was not designed to conceal ignorance and misinterpretation. Again and again he insisted that knowledge and wisdom were not enough; only the power of words could make it plain that the past once had life much like the present. Certainly the worst thing that the historian could do was to write a vivid and inaccurate account. On the other hand, if he did not

vrite vividly, Roosevelt was convinced that he could not write
ruthfully; for only the historian with imaginative gifts could
>resent the past accurately. The example of Thucydides, Roose-
velt remarked, could well serve as a constant source of inspi-
ation to the gildsman, for the Peloponnesian War continued to
.eem important because it once seemed important to a great his-
orian. Similarly, said Roosevelt:

> No poet can ever supersede what Napier wrote of the storm-
> ing of Badajoz, of the British infantry at Albuera, and of the
> light artillery at Fuentes d'Oñoro. After Parkman had written
> of Montcalm and Wolfe there was left for other writers only
> what Fitzgerald left for other translators of Omar Khayyam.
> Much new light has been thrown on the history of the
> Byzantine Empire by the many men who have studied it of
> recent years; we read each new writer with pleasure and
> profit; and after reading each we take down a volume of Gib-
> bon, with renewed thankfulness that a great writer was moved
> to a great task.

Roosevelt did not win H. Morse Stephens to his point of view.
For Stephens expressed some of the same wariness of "fine writ-
ng" that he had expressed years before, when, in an essay on
'History," he wrote: "It is almost an insult to a historian of the
modern school to say that his work can be recognized by its lit-
rary style. It is not his business to have a style."[22] Roosevelt
would have found this all the more astounding because Stephens
was an authority on the French Revolution, a subject that lent
tself readily to dramatic and literary presentation. Stephens,
however, as James Ford Rhodes has said, was the kind of
scholar who, when he wrote a sentence that struck him as being
especially good, would cross it out and rewrite it.[23] But this
was not what he asked others to do in his presidential message;

22 "History," in H. Morse Stephens *et al.*, *Counsel upon the Reading of
Books* (Boston, 1900), p. 68.

23 Howe, *op. cit.*, p. 107.

for what he had to say in 1915 about history as literature came
not as an appeal but as a description.

No unqualified admirer of the ancients, Stephens remarked
that Tacitus, for example, was a pamphleteer who used literary
history as a weapon with which to attack Roman rulers; and
Thucydides was a writer who colored his material in the interest
of a dramatic account. Stephens thought it well to offer the re-
minder that until the eighteenth century Clio was regarded as
the muse of a "branch of imaginative literature, demanding artistic presentation." The historian, to be sure, seldom neglected
to declare his impartiality and to state that his task was to find
out and present the truth about the past, but from antiquity to
the eighteenth century a piece of historical writing was judged
not by its accuracy and its disinterestedness but by its literary
qualities. In the third century, for example, Lucian of Samosata
insisted in *The Way to Write History* that the historian's business was to describe an event as it took place. Yet what did
Lucian do? He proceeded to devote the greater part of his essay
to a discussion of the literary manner in which history should
be presented—an approach of which Stephens did not approve.

It was in an incidental way, too, that George Lincoln Burr,
Stephens' successor, expressed his distrust of style. In Burr's
case this distrust may have been partly influenced by what, in
a letter to Andrew D. White, he had once referred to as his
lack of "facility in expression." Anyone who has read Burr's
letters, reprinted in Roland H. Bainton's biography, would be
quick to deny this; but Burr had told White that if he had been
more gifted with the pen, he would have gone into journalism.[24]
In a sense, then, what he considered a personal failing proved to
be a blessing for the cause of medieval studies in America.

Commenting, in his address of 1916, on the ancient view of
history as art, Burr noted that the Athenian grant of ten talents

24 Roland H. Bainton, *George Lincoln Burr: His Life* (Ithaca, 1943),
pp. 24-25.

to Herodotus was less a tribute to his historianship than to his patriotism and his artistry. When in Roman times, moreover, Herodotus and Thucydides served as models, the reason was, above all, a literary one. Burr thought that the tragedy of Roman historical writing was that the search for style took precedence over the search for truth. Even a Polybius yielded to the demands of rhetoric—to such an extent had Roman historiography been conquered by fine writing. And this tyranny of the rhetorical style reappeared in Renaissance historiography, which served primarily to display the glories of the Latin language. In short, as far as Burr was concerned, "The Freedom of History" was won only when the past was liberated from subservience to style.

It could not have come as a shock that the cause of well-written history was vigorously defended by William R. Thayer, former literary critic for the Philadelphia *Evening Bulletin,* author of several volumes of poetry, and biographer of Cavour. Thayer had long been striving for what he had once called "mastery of expression"; and when he turned to the writing of Italian history, he was determined that it should be of the literary kind.[25] It is significant that he wrote to James Ford Rhodes in 1900, congratulating him on his presidential address and on the stand he had taken in favor of well-written history.[26] And after Thayer learned that Roosevelt had said some kind things about his *Cavour,* he wrote to tell him how glad he was that they saw eye to eye on the need for vivid historical writing.[27]

When Thayer addressed the Association in 1919, he made sure to praise the gildsman's emphasis on accuracy and objectivity; but he regretted that this emphasis frequently worked to becloud the importance of style. Insisting that the way the his-

25 Charles Downer Hazen, ed., *The Letters of William Roscoe Thayer* (Boston, 1926), pp. 24, 135-36, 189.

26 Howe, *op. cit.,* pp. 106-7.

27 Hazen, ed., *op. cit.,* pp. 190-92.

torian wrote, the way he presented his material, mattered might-
ily, Thayer maintained that it was not enough to prepare the kind
of historical work that would serve as a storehouse of information, from which the reader would have to sort the materials.
Like Roosevelt, of whom he had recently published a biography,
Thayer berated those who held that an interesting historical
work could not be accurate. He thought that sloppy writing
convicted itself above all in the sense that it detracted from the
subtlety of a volume—and therefore from those subtleties of the
past which the historian ought to capture for his reader.

Thayer's ardor for well-written history was not shared by
Charles H. Haskins. President of the Association in 1922, the
Harvard medievalist had not yet brought out in book form the
studies in cultural history that Lynn Thorndike believed
"should stand for years to come."[28] Most of his writings up to
1922 had appeared in scholarly journals.[29] Haskins, in a word,
was a medievalist's medievalist—a fact that doubtless shaped the
attitude toward history as literature that he set forth in his
message on "European History and American Scholarship."

Haskins made it clear that he was disturbed by the preoccupation of many an erudite gildsman with the literary needs of the
general reader. He granted that the gildsman should always remember that "his theme is life, rich and deep and full-blooded,
and not running pale beneath his pen"; but he complained that,
as a result of the gildsman's preoccupation with the needs of the
general reader, too many historical works succeeded in satisfying
neither scholar nor layman. Haskins, indeed, ventured to suggest
his own solution to the difficulty. Rather than write the cross-
eyed history that resulted from fixing one eye on the layman and

28 Lynn Thorndike, "Charles Homer Haskins (1870-1937)," *Isis*, XXVIII
(1938), 56.

29 See the bibliography compiled by George W. Robinson in *Anniversary
Essays in Mediaeval History by Students of Charles Homer Haskins Presented on His Completion of Forty Years of Teaching* (Boston, 1929), pp.
389-98.

the other on the scholar, the gildsman would do better on the whole to plan any given work for a single constituency, either lay or erudite. In this way he would confine his truckling either to the multitude or to the clan.

If in recent times the unhurried historian was a rarity, and if, then, it was hard to find, among recent historical writings, the kind of work that the French called an *ouvrage de longue haleine,* Haskins, Dean of Harvard's Graduate School of Arts and Sciences, found the reasons not far to seek. Academic burdens and pressures, requests from publishers for popular works, heavy demands from newspapers and magazines, the textbook craze, all these went a long way to explain why the historian who took his time about his writing was a rarity. Nevertheless, like Rhodes, back in 1899, Haskins urged, cautioned, and advised that "the temptation to write much and frequently on topics of current interest—'hot stuff on live subjects'—must be withstood if the historian hopes to accomplish a considerable and finely matured work. Thucydides would have found it hard to syndicate his account of the Sicilian expedition from day to day and still produce that 'everlasting possession' which Ranke reread every year, and we may well ponder the example of one who set himself to write a book 'for all time' rather than an essay 'for the passing hour'."

Charles M. Andrews, who headed the Association two years after Haskins, was much more disturbed by the view that history should be literature. One of the most meticulous and productive scholars of his time, Andrews, whether he wrote on medieval England, modern Europe, or the American colonies, was not one to use literary devices in order to attract the attention of the layman. Even when he prepared a volume for the Home University Library, he did not hesitate to adopt the kind of approach that would eliminate some of the drama from the American colonial past.[30] In other writings, too, he showed his small sym-

30 *The Colonial Period* (New York, 1912), p. vi.

pathy for the general reader. In his essay on George Louis Beer, he referred scornfully to those who read history for "its literary and dramatic qualities."[31] Similarly, in *The Colonial Background of the American Revolution* (1924), he criticized those who read history for "mental relaxation rather than mental effort."[32] Andrews had much the same reaction to history as literature as George Burton Adams, his former colleague at Yale; but he was much less gifted a writer.

In his address on "These Forty Years" Andrews pointed out that the assault on objectivity came generally from two sources: from those who could not appreciate the "anemic" and "bloodless" kind of history that did not lend itself to use as a bludgeon; and from those who could not appreciate history that was not literature, history that avoided "the midsummer madness of romantic adventure," history that was dull, colorless, and impersonal. The literary-minded assailants of objectivity wished to exploit the dramatic possibilities of the past; they wanted the historian to use "a palette of bright colored words, epigrams, and vivacious expressions." Andrews was ready to grant that thoroughgoing objectivity in historical writing could not be achieved; it was not even to be desired. Ordinarily, however, an objective account was merely a moderate and dispassionate account; and though at times it burdened the memory more than it illuminated the soul, it was to be preferred to the subjective account that was great literature but not great history. Little wonder that Andrews rejoiced that Macaulay, Carlyle, and Treitschke had had their day, that picturesque Prescott and romantic Lamartine had had theirs.

Andrews recognized that there were still those who argued that the historian had to learn not only how to read but how to write; that the historian who did not write a vivid account could

---

31 *George Louis Beer: A Tribute to His Life and Work in the Making of History and the Moulding of Public Opinion* (New York, 1924), p. 41.

32 *The Colonial Background of the American Revolution: Four Essays in American Colonial History* (New Haven, 1924), p. 175.

not write a truthful account; and that there was no point in writing a historical work that would not be read. Like George Burton Adams, however, Andrews was left unconvinced by such arguments—above all, because they betrayed a sad confusion concerning the purpose of historical study. Only incidentally was history designed to entertain, interest, benefit, and elevate mankind. Primarily, it was designed to be studied for its own sake.

Andrews denied the competence of the layman or the book reviewer to judge the manner in which history should be written. The layman, he said, was generally in no more position to judge history than he was to judge drama, music, and painting. He lacked the standards by which to evaluate any work that was not expressly prepared for his enjoyment; for even if a historical study was readable, it was not therefore artistically or intrinsically worthwhile. Like George Burton Adams, Andrews was convinced that the historian did wrong to cater to the reading public and to emphasize style. Rather than strive for literary grace and polish, Andrews thought that the gildsman should strive for historical-mindedness. He should develop the ability to view history in its own light, not in the light of its literary, political, poetic, or dramatic character. Indeed, the historical-minded scholar ignored pressures from the general reader. He did not think of history in narrative terms; he thought of it as a mass of unsolved problems. Scornful of the literary reviewer's scorn for dull and objective writing, the historical-minded scholar wrote for other scholars. Lacking the ambition to be a story-teller, he placed a low rating on the ability to clothe historical facts in brilliant prose. As if to deliver the final blow to the advocate of literary history, Andrews declared that it was the historical-minded scholar who had made "the only real progress" in the recent study of history in the United States.

Andrews' opposition to the view of history as literature was reflected in the criteria which he suggested for the evaluation of a historical work. First of all, he said, the content of the work should be truthful and significant. Secondly, the interpretations

presented in the work should grow out of the documents themselves. Finally the style of the work should suit its content as
well as the audience for which the work was prepared. Great
history was written only when content, interpretation, and form
were in harmony. Applying his criteria to some historians of
the past, Andrews emerged with results, some of which a Hart
or a Roosevelt would have found disconcerting. He rated Stubbs
and Maitland above Macaulay and Froude, Parkman above
Bancroft, and Lea above Prescott and Motley; and he pointed
out that on the basis of these criteria even a doctoral dissertation
might rank high "as a work of artistic proportions." Andrews
was pleased with the recent scorn for ornateness of presentation
in historical writing. Plainly, the contemporary gildsman was
aware that he could not content himself with producing a dramatic account that would entertain the layman with its rich and
glowing colors.

By the time Dana C. Munro addressed the Association in
1926, the report of the Committee on the Writing of History
had been published, the report whose purpose it was to make
students and their professors conscious of the "part good expression must play in enabling history to maintain a place in the world
of letters."[33] If Munro, therefore, concerned himself with history as literature in his message on "War and History," the inspiration had doubtless come from this Committee's report. For
Munro was surely not an accomplished writer. Perfectionist
that he was, he wrote little. And what he did write was notable
for its content, not for its form; his constant emphasis on "rigorous critical scholarship"[34] made his studies of medieval history
enlightening rather than enlivening.

Munro pointed out in his presidential message that wars had
often aroused the layman's interest in the past. This was true of
the wars of the Crusades, of the wars in the Italies after 1494,
and of the French Revolutionary and Napoleonic Wars. It was

33 J. J. Jusserand, W. C. Abbott, C. W. Colby, and J. S. Bassett, *The
Writing of History* (New York, 1926), p. vi.

34 *The Kingdom of the Crusaders* (New York, 1935), p. 208.

also true of the World War. In fact, Munro suggested that it was the war that prepared the way for the popular reception extended to the historical writings of Hendrik Willem Van Loon and H. G. Wells.[35] It was the war, moreover, that helped to increase the number of histories on the book lists of publishing houses. The important thing, then, Munro thought in 1926, was not only to maintain the existing interest in history but to stimulate it further. Endorsing the point of view embodied in the report on *The Writing of History,* he insisted that, if interest in the past was to be increased, history books should be attractively written. Like Wells and Van Loon, the gildsman should consider the layman; he should remember that even scholarly research was compatible with the kind of style that would capture the layman's interest and enthusiasm. Had not Henry C. Lea's work on the Inquisition sold in a popular French translation during the struggle over the Separation Act of 1905? And had not Edward P. Cheyney's study of late Elizabethan England made an unintentionally humorous reviewer express surprise that a historical work could be so well written— in spite of the fact that it was based on a critical examination of primary sources?[36]

For more than a dozen years, Munro's successors showed in their messages virtually no interest in history as literature. James Harvey Robinson went so far as to assert in 1929 that the present-day gildsman spent as little time wondering whether history was an art or a science as he spent wondering whether glorified spirits were found in "the empyrean rather than the aqueous heaven—once a matter of debate in the University of Paris." True, Carl L. Becker proclaimed the historian the heir of the bard, the story-teller, and the minstrel, and he proclaimed history itself a story that employed all the techniques of litera-

35 See his review of *The Outline of History* in *National Municipal Review,* X (1921), 192-93.

36 *A History of England from the Defeat of the Armada to the Death of Elizabeth with an Account of English Institutions during the Later Sixteenth and Early Seventeenth Centuries* (2 vols., New York, 1914-26).

ture; Becker ended his comments right there. And Charles A. Beard was even briefer. He merely voiced his opposition to labelling history an art or a branch of literature. Gifted writers like Becker and Beard could have said much of value about style. Apparently, however, the world crisis after 1929 prompted them, as well as other presidents of the Association, to concentrate on subjects of greater topical importance. So it was that the discussion of the literary side of history was not resumed in a presidential address until 1940.

Nor was the president who revived the discussion particularly distinguished as a writer. Max Farrand was above all an administrator and an editor; and with him, as with Munro, it was the meticulousness of his scholarship, his frequent use of qualifying and modifying remarks, for example, that impeded the flow of language in his articles and books on American history. Nevertheless, Farrand did not hesitate to discuss "The Quality of Distinction" in his message of 1940. The gildsman, he said, had as one of his major objectives the elevation of standards, and therefore he should try to win popular favor and stimulate popular interest in history. Farrand did not mean to champion the cause of publishing agents who encouraged many a historian to meet a production schedule for which he lacked adequate preparation. Just the same, Farrand knew that publishers were likely to be in the best position to judge popular tastes; and what they presented to the public offered a way of judging the interests of the layman. The gildsman might well pronounce as worthless the historical novels and biographies that ranked high on best-seller lists; but they did at least excite interest in the past.

Farrand argued that especially in a democracy it was urgent that the gildsman provide an accurate historical basis for the ideas of the populace; he should make it clear that many volumes which pretended to be historical were anything but that. But if Farrand held publishers responsible for the appearance of inferior historical works, he also blamed university officials, contending that as long as advancement in the university depended on quan-

titative, rather than qualitative, production, the young instructor
was going to be tempted to rush into print—probably with a sad
performance from both the literary and scholarly angles. Yet for
all the guilt of university authorities and publishers, Farrand
declared that the historian himself was chiefly to blame for the
appearance of inferior works. Though he was the judge of the
worth of historical volumes, he had not made his stand sufficiently clear. In the future, then, he should make sure that he was
heard—and heard preaching "the quality of distinction."

Thus, in the first sixty years of the life of the Association,
relatively few presidents dealt with history as literature in their
addresses. Many doubtless took it for granted that history should
be well written. A few were suspicious of style, viewing it as
dangerous and as essentially irrelevant. Others gloried in history as literature apparently above all for esthetic reasons. Still
others were convinced that unless the gildsman had style he
would not have readers and his knowledge of the past would
for all practical purposes be wasted.

CHAPTER V
FACTS IN HISTORY

ONE major obstacle to well-written history that presidents like Rhodes, Mahan, Roosevelt, and Thayer singled out was the gildsman's emphasis on facts. Accordingly, they suggested that the gildsman who wished his history to rank as literature should learn to tone down this emphasis and discard some of his facts for the sake of clarity and conciseness. Yet it was not simply as a hindrance to good writing that facts figured in the presidential messages; they figured also as a hindrance to good history. For some presidents subscribed in effect to Macaulay's view of facts as the dross of history, insisting that facts alone were meaningless, that what really mattered was their significance. These same presidents often believed that facts should be accumulated and selected to meet the needs of the present. Few presidents defended their accumulation for their own sake or for the sake of the past.

Andrew D. White, the first president of the Association, was also the first to consider the nature of historical facts in a presidential message. Nor was it odd that his attitude was far from reverential; it had been that for a long time. When White started his teaching career at the University of Michigan, he looked for textbooks that would not confuse students with "masses of pedantic detail";[1] and when he lectured, he avoided what George Lincoln Burr, his most distinguished student at Cornell, called "the barren recital of more barren facts."[2] Outside the classroom, too, White made it plain that the facts he presented were strictly incidental to the particular historical lesson that he wished to drive home: witness his booklets on

1 *Autobiography* (2 vols., New York, 1905), I, 259-60.

2 Roland H. Bainton, *George Lincoln Burr: His Life* (Ithaca, 1943), p. 18; Walter P. Rogers, *Andrew D. White and the Modern University* (Ithaca, 1942), pp. 137-38.

The Warfare of Science (1876) and *Paper-Money Inflation in France* (1876). White, in truth, lacked the time and the patience for detailed research. In his later years, indeed—when, after resigning from the presidency of Cornell (1885), he was to serve on a number of major diplomatic missions—he came to depend increasingly on the spade work of an assistant. It was Burr who did much of the digging for his *History of the Warfare of Science with Theology in Christendom* (1896); it was Burr, too, who had the job of correcting the factual errors that crept into the work.[3]

Nor were these later developments out of keeping with the stand that White had taken in his message of 1884. He complained that much too often the gildsman used the word "investigation" to mean the study of petty facts rather than the study of factual relationships. He also deplored the widespread use of the expression "the advancement of knowledge." As if knowledge was advanced only by means of the investigation of minute facts, and not by the study of factual relationships! White was convinced that the writer of general history—what he considered himself to be—advanced knowledge quite as much as the annalist who explored little, unremembered acts of diplomacy or strategy; Guizot increased knowledge no less than a scholar who solved the mystery of the retirement of Charles V or a scholar who revealed the influence of Manasseh Cutler on the Northwest Ordinance. Understandably, White had little interest in many of the facts of local history: it made no difference to him that the fire-engine house in a particular country town was originally located near the town school rather than the town pump; it did not matter to him that a particular local official had at one stage of his life leaned closer to the Presbyterians than to the Methodists.

White was scornful of surface facts and interested in factual relationships, but he did not agree with some of the views that Herbert Spencer had presented in *Education: Intellectual, Moral,*

3 Bainton, *op. cit.,* pp. 48, 53-56.

and Physical (1860). He thought that Spencer had too much faith in the value of "material statistics." Besides, he thought that Spencer's attack on "worthless facts" missed the point.[4] Unlike Spencer, White would not discard as worthless those facts that dealt with battles, treaties, and court intrigues. His contention was that military, diplomatic, and political facts—as well as all other facts—were important insofar as they contributed to an understanding of "the great lines of historical evolution." A seemingly trivial fact could be of great value if it was a "pregnant" fact; a seemingly important fact could be of little value if it was a "barren" fact. Thoroughly present-minded in his outlook, White believed that what made a fact barren or pregnant was its relationship to "the great lines of historical evolution." Condé's reception at Versailles was a tremendous fact in the age of Louis XIV, but in the light of general history it was hardly worth noting. The oratory of Rufus Choate was a major fact in its time, but the test of general history relegated it to the background. In contrast, the newspaper of William Lloyd Garrison hardly figured in its own setting, but on the basis of the standards of general history it loomed as a major fact in American history.

Reflecting further the present-mindedness that obsessed him, White emphasized the frequent relevance to a contemporary situation of a largely forgotten historical event. When Northern troops fared badly in the early part of the Civil War, it was worth recalling the fact that at the outset French Revolutionary troops had broken and fled. When wild inflationary schemes were proposed in the United States of post-bellum days, it was well to remember the *assignats,* said White, himself a vigorous advocate of sound money. Always, however, the historian should make sure not to degenerate into a petty academician bent on the mere accumulation of minute facts. He should combine specialization and synthesis in order to overcome two of the

4 Herbert Spencer, *Education: Intellectual, Moral, and Physical* (New York, 1860), pp. 65-71.

basic menaces to sound historical study: the triviality of the
annalist and the vagueness of the Hegelian brand of philosopher.

It was surely to be expected that Justin Winsor, the Harvard
librarian, would view historical facts differently from White.
For Winsor was preeminently a researcher, a digger, one who
revelled in historical, bibliographical, and cartographical details.
Beyond a doubt, his knowledge of the sources of American history was unrivalled in his time; and he believed, as Edward
Channing has said, that "the truest form of historical expression was the bare statement of fact in bald language."[5] President of the Association in 1887, Winsor was still editing that
multivolume mass of material that went by the name of the
Narrative and Critical History of America (1884-1889). Indeed, his presidential address was largely a summary of portions
of what was soon to appear as the appendix of the eighth and
last volume of the *History.*

This is hardly the place to describe Winsor's comments on
the "Manuscript Sources of American History—The Conspicuous Collections Extant." Suffice it to say that Winsor thought
that the "historic spirit" was being seriously threatened in the
United States. More than that, he thought that it would continue to be threatened until steps were taken systematically to
preserve the manuscript sources of American history. Therefore, while there was still time, he believed that the Association
should try to persuade Congress to authorize an American equiv-
alent of the Historical Manuscripts Commission which the
English had organized in 1869.[6] Speaking several years before
the Association established its own Commission, Winsor suggested that if the members of the gild descended on Washington
and pressed for action from Congress, they might be able to
avert some future tragedies along lines manuscriptal.

5 Edward Channing, "Justin Winsor," *A.H.R.,* III (1898), 201.

6 See F. J. Weaver, *The Material of English History* (London, 1938),
pp. 121-23.

Praising the efforts of Jared Sparks, Peter Force, and George Bancroft to arouse interest in the preservation of American national documents, Winsor pointed out that now it was a question of working up a similar interest. It should be recognized that public papers belonged to the government, not to the officeholder; that only the government could afford to put records beyond the risk of accident by having them printed; that only the government could afford to pay the almost prohibitive prices that were often demanded for papers in private possession. Intent on preserving the sources that enabled the gildsman to determine historical facts, Winsor presented his scheme for spending a portion of the surplus revenue that the Cleveland administration had on its hands.

William F. Poole, the Newberry librarian who succeeded Winsor as president of the Association, was quick to present a similar scheme. Poole had done much less than his predecessor to throw light on the facts of the American past,[7] but his *Index to Periodical Literature* had endeared him to many a student of history. Much more disposed than Winsor to make his appeal on a patriotic basis, Poole insisted that the United States should extend its control over public documents. Like other major countries, it should establish a separately and permanently organized department of archives that would be "worthy of this Nation." Nor was the State Department in a position to manage the proposed archives; Poole believed that real control should be vested in trained experts who would not be dropped from office each time the administration changed. Furthermore, he believed that Congress should do something about the manuscripts dealing with American history that were lodged in European archives. Unhappily, the much-needed copies, calendars, and descriptive catalogues had not yet been prepared; so

7 His writings are listed in *Memorial Sketch of Dr. William Frederick Poole* (Chicago 1895), pp. 29-34.

that the student of American history was compelled to provide
himself with the necessary materials at his own expense.[8]

Despite governmental backwardness along these lines—the
National Archives Act did not become law until 1934—Poole
noted that Americans were showing a growing interest in history. This he considered partly the result of the activities of the
well-trained professor who appreciated the importance of going
to the sources for the facts. Poole found it amazing that so much
of what had been copied by one writer after another and had
passed for history proved to be false once the original sources
were studied. Indeed, he thought that what distinguished the
contemporary historian was his determination to ascertain the
facts and then to present them with clarity and conciseness and
without fear. Unfortunately, the findings of recent monographic
scholarship were slow in being incorporated into general histories. Therefore, said Poole in 1888, the great need was for a
general history of the United States, which, drawing on specialized studies, would embody the facts and the principles revealed by scientific research.

Eleven years later, however, James Ford Rhodes complained
that modern historical works were packed with too many facts.
In his address Rhodes did not refer directly to his own *History,*
but a letter that he wrote shortly before he addressed the Association makes it clear that he had it in mind; for Rhodes regretted that his own powers of expression and compression
were not adequate to meet the challenge of recent American history.[9] Doubtless he was overly self-conscious. In any event, when
he tried in his message to account for the superiority of the ancient historians, he harped repeatedly on their ability to dis-
criminate in their selection of materials. Thucydides and Tacitus

8 See J. Franklin Jameson, "The Expenditures by Foreign Governments
in Behalf of History," A.H.A., *Annual Report, 1891* (Washington, 1892),
pp. 33-61.

9 M. A. DeWolfe Howe, *James Ford Rhodes, American Historian* (New
York, 1929), pp. 95-96.

knew what to discard "as not being necessary or important to the posterity for which they were writing." Sticking closely to their subjects, they avoided the tempting by-paths of narration, and they rejected much of the factual material they might have used. No one could accuse them of what John Morley accused Macaulay: that he described numerous events about which no reasonable person could "in the least care either how they happened, or whether, indeed, they happened at all or not."

Rhodes suggested that if the modern historian was ever to rival the ancients, he must learn not only to digest his facts but to throw many of them away, and he must learn to strive for the rigorous conciseness that was the chief glory of the ancients. That it was difficult to be selective in an age of newspapers and magazines, in an age when so many trivialities were recorded, Rhodes could appreciate full well, for his own *History* was based in large part on newspapers and magazines;[10] but he thought that the masterpieces of Thucydides and Tacitus spoke plainly to the scholar who sought to master the secrets of effective historical writing. To refuse to scrap facts that could be scrapped was to run the risk of repelling readers.

Rhodes' warning of 1899 was repeated three years later by Alfred T. Mahan in his address on "Subordination in Historical Treatment." First, however, Mahan was impelled to offer some apologies of the sort that he was again to offer in *From Sail to Steam: Recollections of Naval Life* (1907). Acknowledging that he had studied history only incidentally and only at a late stage in his career, he did not pretend that his writings had either breadth or depth. He admitted his lack of the training and equipment which, according to Lord Acton, went into the making of a first-rate modern historian. He confessed that his writings on naval history failed to satisfy the requirements set forth in 1895 in Acton's inaugural lecture as regius professor

10 "Newspapers as Historical Sources," in Rhodes, *Historical Essays* (New York, 1909), 83-87; Raymond C. Miller, "James Ford Rhodes," William T. Hutchinson, ed., *The Marcus W. Jernegan Essays in American Historiography* (Chicago, 1937), p. 175.

of modern history at Cambridge.[11] He had not displayed the diligence that Acton applauded; he had not delved feverishly into previously inaccessible materials; he had not accumulated vast stores of facts. Mahan suggested, indeed, that if he had made a real effort to meet Acton's qualifications, he would have died before ever lifting a pen—essentially what happened to Acton himself. He also suggested that it was perhaps the impressive list of citations that Acton lavished on his inaugural lecture that explained why so learned a scholar wrote so little in a life that ran into sixty-eight years.

Acton published much more than Mahan imagined.[12] Still, Mahan's point was that it did not suffice for the historian to achieve an exhaustive knowledge of his facts. These were, to be sure, his raw materials, his bricks and mortar; but in the raw state they were only the "unutilized possession of the one, or at most of the few." Even when they were out of the raw state they might still fail to become useful possessions of the many. Much depended on how the historian selected, grouped, and digested them; much depended on how effectively he achieved unity of treatment—despite the disconnected, conflicting, and unwieldy facts with which he had to work.

Emphasizing that a faithful presentation did not call for the inclusion of all facts and the omission of none, Mahan pointed to the need for emphasis. This emphasis could be achieved through the clear grouping of some facts in the foreground and others in the background. Minor and accessory facts should be clearly subordinated to a central theme. Without such subordination, it was unlikely that a historical study would make much of a positive impression on a layman. And this was condemnation indeed from Mahan's standpoint, for his faith in the immediate usefulness of history made him most sensitive to the

11 *A Lecture on the Study of History Delivered at Cambridge, June 11, 1895* (London, 1895).

12 Lord Acton's writings are listed in F. E. Lally, *As Lord Acton Says* (Newport, Rhode Island, 1942), pp. 272-300.

response of the general reader to historical literature. The function of the gildsman, he insisted, was "not merely to accumulate facts, at once in entirety and in accuracy, but to present them in such wise that the wayfaring man, whom we now call the man in the street, shall not err therein. Failing here, by less or more, the historian, however exhaustive his knowledge, by so far shares the fault of him who dies with his treasures of knowledge locked in his own brain. He has not perfectly communicated his gifts and acquirements to his brethren." Yet if the historian was to make himself clear to his reader, he had first to be clear to himself. If he was going to teach men, he had to know what to teach them. He had to know which facts to accumulate and which to present, making sure not to present all that he had accumulated. Mahan could think of no worse condemnation than that a historical work was obscured by the masses of its details.

Accuracy, no doubt, was the historian's "right arm of service," but one that was suffering from an excess of activity. After all, said Mahan, some facts could probably never be ascertained, and even if they could be ascertained, they were not important enough to justify the difficulties that would be involved. It was "troublesome enough to handle a multitude of details so as to produce clearness of impression; but to add to that difficulty a too fastidious scrupulosity as to exhausting every possible source of error, by the accumulation of every imaginable detail," this was pointless, Mahan thought. Obviously, generalizations and conclusions presupposed the careful study of large numbers of facts, but there should be a limit to the passion for exactitude. If the historian was to go on recording facts without thinking that the time had come for drawing conclusions, history would be largely useless to mankind. Mahan believed that the gildsman should not content himself with writing books that would occasionally be consulted; he should write books that would be read. But this meant that he must show discrimination in his handling of facts. Otherwise, his history would have little appeal as a guide to action and his facts would be wasted.

While Mahan, like White and Rhodes before him, criticized the gildsman's preoccupation with facts, George Burton Adams hurried to the defense of that preoccupation. Unlike his predecessors, Adams was a medievalist—and an active medievalist, who did research of his own and kept up with the researches of others. He was familiar with the numerous historical revisions that had taken place since Stubbs and Maitland had started to publish; he himself had helped to convert many an alleged fact of English medieval history into a myth. Perhaps it was as a result of all this that Adams, seeing scores of unsolved historical problems, placed so much emphasis on the discovery of new facts and the reinvestigation of old ones. Certainly he believed that factual relationships should be studied and that details should not obscure general movements;[13] but he insisted in his message of 1908 that history, far from having suffered from the scrupulous verification of its facts, had much to gain from a continued emphasis on such meticulousness. All genuine science, he declared, rested on the foundation provided by "the proved and correlated fact"; and to generalize prematurely on the basis of semi-digested data was to engage in an undertaking that was 'useless and often worse than useless."

Adams did not deny that scientific advances had sometimes been made in consequence of hasty and inaccurate generalizations; but those advances occurred only when the generalizations grew out of "the best knowledge of the fact" that contemporary scholarship could provide. The fundamental key to the conquest of the unknown was still the fact, "established and classified to the fullest extent possible at the moment." As for going beyond the fact, Adams doubted that this was scientifically possible in 1908. There were still too many sources whose reticence had to be overcome. The time when an adequate factual knowledge of the past would permit the fruitful generalizations for which the historian yearned remained far in the future.

13 *Civilization during the Middle Ages Especially in Relation to Modern Civilization* (New York, 1894), p. v.

Robert Browning, said Adams, may well have been correct when he described, in *Sordello,* the two sights that God had granted to man:

> One of man's whole work, time's completed plan,
> The other of the minute's work, man's first
> Step to the plan's completeness.

Unhappily, however, those sights granted to Browning's man lay beyond the range of the imperfect vision of the historian, who, if he was interested in making a genuine contribution to scholarship, should content himself with a most "modest ambition." For many years to come he should regard generalizations as luxuries that he could not afford because of the inadequacies of his knowledge. For many years to come he should concentrate on one chief activity: the discovery, exploration, and establishment of facts. Adams did not share the point of view of White, Rhodes, and Mahan; but, then, they had not been compelled to contend with the meager sources that had bedeviled him in his study of medieval constitutional history.

The same was true of Albert Bushnell Hart, the next president. Author and editor of numerous books on American history and government, he, too, had not been compelled to contend with meager sources in his studies; and this doubtless helps to explain why he shared only in part Adams' enthusiasm for collecting facts. Whatever the explanation, Hart gathered from the complaints of educators and employers that factual inaccuracy was a major menace to the American Republic. Newspapermen, public speakers, members of Congress, students, and even historians, all seemed to be unfaithful to the facts. As aimed at the historian, however, Hart noted that this type of complaint was only a variation on a theme that Horace Walpole had voiced in the eighteenth century: that such was the incompetence of the historian that if the dead were to come back to life they could scarcely understand what he was saying about their times—to such an extent had truth failed to enter into his toriography. Not that Walpole was alone in bewailing the misrepresentation that figured in historical writing. Actually, said Hart, it was only a question of recalling one of the milder comments of Freeman on Froude: "If history means truth, if it means fairness, if it means faithfully reporting what contemporary sources record, and drawing reasonable inferences from their statements, then Mr. Froude is no historian."[14]

Hart was more than willing to sympathize with the historian who had trouble in distinguishing between facts and falsehoods. Unfortunately, perhaps, there was no law to punish the writer who handled history with plenty of imagination but with little reference to the facts revealed in the sources. A Paul Leicester Ford wrote fiction that sounded like history and history that was unhistorical. Indeed, many an author who wrote with an eye to the public suffered from an overactive imagination—one which was not to be restrained by the facts of history; and this made it all the more important for the gildsman to move into action. To combat the crimes committed in the name of history, he should dwell on the need for careful research and warn of the dangers of unsound historiography. He should emphasize that scientific methods needed to be used if facts were to be established and generalizations formulated. He should point up the vice of credulity and the virtue of incredulity, exposing the myths that surrounded the past. In recent years, said Hart, thinking perhaps of Edward Channing, his colleague at Harvard, this blasting of myths had proceeded at such a pace that the gildsman sometimes seemed like a cannibal, who thrived on the destruction of the facts and interpretations of his fellow scholars.

Just the same, Hart thought that the gildsman should seek an escape from the "obsession of facts." This escape White had found in the principle of "the great lines of historical evolution." Mahan had found it in the principle of subordination. Hart, the editor of a series known as *Essentials in History*, found it in the principle of cogency. The facts that the gildsman

14 See Herbert Paul, *The Life of Froude* (London, 1905), pp. 147-98.

should discard, he thought, were those that lacked cogency, those that lacked historical interest. The facts that he should retain were the cogent facts, those that demonstrated whether a particular man, a particular people, a particular age, or a particular standard "carried forward civilization, opened wide the gates for thought, liberated souls." Optimistic believer in progress that he was, Hart would reject or retain facts on the basis of much the same principle as White; still, he recognized that different historians would differ in their judgments as to cogency, that a fact that was cogent to George Bancroft would often be far from cogent to James Ford Rhodes, the friend to whom he had recently dedicated his *Slavery and Abolition, 1831-1841* (1906).

In this way Hart made the point that gildsmen like Carl Becker and Charles Beard were to make increasingly in subsequent years:

> It was all very well [he said] for Ranke to begin his lectures: 'I will simply tell you how it was.' Did not his students really get 'how it was' as seen through the mind of Ranke? The dictum that history must be objective, that it consists in a proper marshalling of facts, leaves out of account the varieties of humanity in historical characters and in historical writers. What a man does is conditioned by the make-up of his mind; by what he thinks about what he does; and in addition the reader's judgment is affected by the mental peculiarities of the historian who describes that mental process.

Besides, Hart continued, even when facts were judiciously chosen and tested,they no more made history than rookies made an army. Hart, in a word, would not justify the dominion of facts in historical writing. He granted that they should be carefully selected and verified, but he insisted that they were impotent when "taken by themselves." Always, what mattered was the synthesis of facts, he said, thinking perhaps of what he himself had tried to do in his *National Ideals Historically Traced, 1607-1907* (1907).

Just as Hart found fault with Ranke's view of facts, so, too, did Frederick Jackson Turner, his presidential successor and new colleague at Harvard. Turner, to be sure, as Carl Becker has written, had an "inordinate thirst for facts" as well as an "uncanny instinct for finding them in the most unlikely places." What appealed to him, however, was not the business of arranging a succession of facts in some kind of narrative account. What appealed to him was the task of getting "behind the facts" —something, of course, that rarely makes possible mass production, something, indeed, that helps to explain why his collected writings leave "much of a five-foot shelf open to the collection of dust."[15]

Although Turner dealt only briefly with the nature of historical facts in his presidential message of 1910, he did at least make clear the present-mindedness of his approach. The gildsman, he said, could obviously content himself with presenting facts, considering it his function merely to describe the past as it really was; but the difficulty remained that the historical fact was "not planted on the solid ground of fixed conditions." It was in the middle of the currents and influences of its age; it was a part of those currents and influences; and it derived its significance from its connections with those currents and influences. These, however, were so gradual in character that frequently it was only the passage of time that made possible the disclosure of the truth about the fact and the right of the fact to be included in a historical work. Thus, Turner, who was "always occupied primarily with the present, and with the past as illuminating the present,"[16] believed that current interests played—and deserved to play—the major role in determining the particular historical facts that should be remembered.

15 Carl Lotus Becker, *Everyman His Own Historian: Essays on History and Politics* (New York, 1935), pp. 201, 226-27.

16 *Ibid.*, p. 224.

This was much the same position that William M. Sloane, the next president, took in 1911. True, Sloane's own writings on modern French history were often filled with facts that threw little light on the present—facts, indeed, that threw little light on the past; but he made it plain in his message that he believed that the task of the historian was to account for the contemporary world. He granted that the nearer the facts of the past were to the present, the less clear were the insights they afforded, the less plain their proportions and relations, the less easy their interpretation. He insisted, nevertheless, that the gildsman was concerned not with all the facts of the past but only with those that went to explain the present.

Alhough Ranke proclaimed it the function of the historian to determine "how it was," Sloane pointed out that neither he nor his disciples defined the *it*. As a rule, it was common sense and instinct that indicated the *it* that deserved to be investigated and the *it* to be overlooked. If the historian exhumed parish registers to find out the birthday of Oliver Cromwell and ignored equally accurate data concerning the birthday of some obscure village forefather, the explanation was that some facts were "pregnant of historical results" while others were not. The pregnant ones were those that enabled the historian to trace causal relationships and to establish laws. For the historian to claim "absolute impartiality" was, in any case, absurd, for no gildsman went into "the wilderness of events 'um nichts zu suchen.'" Rather, he went "with a mind furnished, ill or well furnished, but furnished, either with positive purposes or negative prejudices"; and he went to find out the truth about the facts and the meaning of the facts.

Unlike the triumvirate of Hart, Turner, and Sloane, Theodore Roosevelt, the next president, did not concern himself with the way in which the gildsman should select his facts. He was not concerned, as Hart was, with cogent facts, nor, as Turner and Sloane were, with the present as the guide to the facts that the gildsman should accumulate. Instead, Roosevelt dealt with facts as an obstacle to literary history, returning to a theme that his close friend Mahan had discussed a decade before and a theme about which he himself had long had strong feelings.[17] Of course, Roosevelt had every reason to be cautious in taking to task the gildsman who was a fact-worshipper. For some of his own writings, especially his biographies of Benton, Morris, and Cromwell, were notoriously weak on the factual side; they were hastily composed and based on a minimum of research.[18]

Perhaps, then, it was as a precautionary measure that Roosevelt emphasized in his message of 1912 that if the gildsman was to achieve a truthful account of the past, he must first acquire a thorough knowledge of the facts and their interrelationships; and this he could acquire only as a result of diligent and meticulous research. The historical work that was "worth writing at all," Roosevelt said—apparently without self-consciousness—required that many years be spent accumulating materials. Still, Roosevelt thought that the gildsman ought not to push his devotion to facts too far. Aiming his remarks at the gildsman who viewed the dryness and grayness of facts as worthwhile in themselves, he insisted that the collection of facts was only part of the historian's work; it was by no means "a substitute for that work." The real task of the historian was to resurrect the past, to marshall the dead facts in which he was steeped and make them live for others.

In a real sense, too, Roosevelt remarked, this task was being made increasingly easy. Whereas the old-time historian had at his disposal few facts, most of which he himself had often had to gather, the modern historian had access to vast collections of facts. These, however, were wasted on him if, for lack of imaginative and literary powers, he failed to breathe life into them; for he could not write a truthful account of the past unless it was at the same time a vivid account. Truth was possible only

17 Joseph B. Bishop, *Theodore Roosevelt and His Time Shown in His Own Letters* (2 vols., New York, 1920), II, 141.

18 See Harrison John Thornton, "Theodore Roosevelt," in William T. Hutchinson, ed., *op. cit.,* pp. 231-33.

if he combined factual knowledge and literary and imaginative talents.

Of all the early presidents of the Association, however, it was William A. Dunning, Roosevelt's successor, who presented the most thoughtful discussion of historical facts. In a sense, this was to be expected. For Dunning had always been wary of rushing into print. "In composition," as Charles E. Merriam has written, "he was very deliberate, choosing his way with extreme caution and only after long consideration of all sides of the situation."[19] For the purposes of his message of 1913, Dunning abandoned the Civil War and Reconstruction, the subjects whose study he had done so much to further;[20] and he referred only incidentally to the development of European political theory, his other major scholarly interest. What he dealt with was "Truth in History," a subject to which he had doubtless given much thought; he was not one to expose himself to charges of lack of restraint or immaturity of judgment.[21]

The historian, Dunning said, must always regret that Pilate never received an answer to his question, "What is Truth?" But at least it was reassuring that the historian did not have to concern himself with the truth of all the facts of the past; he had to concern himself only with the truth of those facts that were related to the social and political development of mankind. The way the primitive Aryan fattened his swine for slaughter, the particular cosmetic that Alcibiades preferred, the species of the maggots that St. Simeon Stylites kept putting back on his sores, the color of Washington's horse at the battle of Monmouth, these were facts of the sort which the historian could ignore.

19 Charles Edward Merriam, "William Archibald Dunning," in Howard W. Odum, ed., *American Masters of Social Science* (New York, 1927), p. 142.

20 *Studies in Southern History and Politics Inscribed to William Archibald Dunning* (New York, 1914), p. v.

21 J. G. de Roulhac Hamilton, "Introduction," in *Truth in History and Other Essays* (New York, 1937), p. xvi.

Despite his own convictions, Dunning did not dare to dismiss the matter dogmatically. He was too much the modest and unpretentious scholar speaking at a time when it appeared that

> no science is sure of its footing until it has proclaimed its special interpretation of history. The economic, the sociological, the metallurgical, the pathologic, the meteorological, the astronomical, the geological, and, for aught I know, the geometrical interpretations are in heated rivalry. It is therefore unsafe to say that the most obscure and least suspected fact of the past will not appear to-morrow as the hinge on which man's whole career has turned. But pending the newest revelation of this sort we are privileged to approach the study of the past under guidance of a series of presumptions, among which is this, that such phenomena as have been mentioned are not of the first importance.

Once the historian decided which facts were important, Dunning thought that he should proceed along three principal lines: he should try to determine what events took place; he should try to determine the chronology of these events and their causal connections. Unfortunately, this third function of the historian had often come to be sacrificed in favor of the first. Neglecting the study of causation, the scientific historian continued to put his main emphasis on the precise determination of the facts. Not that Dunning denied the valuable results of this emphasis. Pursuing facts relentlessly, the scientific historian had exploded many a myth. Insisting on the examination of primary sources and requiring for even a commonplace statement a footnote to an original document, he had made available a mass of new materials. Scorning literary narrative, he had increased enormously the number of monographic studies available. There was, then, no denying his services to history; but neither was there any denying some of his disservices to history. For one thing, he had limited its scope. For another, he had emphasized material at the expense of spiritual and psychic facts. Then, too, he had minimized the investigation of causal relationships.

Worst of all, he had studied the truth about historical facts to the neglect of what people thought to be the truth about those facts.

Dunning had been plunging long and deep enough into the American Civil War and Reconstruction and into European political theory to know "the thrill that comes with the discovery of an unknown or a forgotten fact of the past."[22] He knew that a historical discovery was all the more satisfying when it enabled the gildsman to prove the falseness of long-established notions and to announce that the leading old-time authorities were misinformed. Even so, Dunning, in a passage which for beauty of language has perhaps never been rivalled in a presidential message, had this to suggest:

> Many a fact of history is like the grain of sand that intrudes within the shell of the pearl oyster. Tiny and insignificant, it is quickly lost to sight and knowledge; but about it are deposited the ensphering layers of myth and legend till a glimmering treasure is produced that excites the mightiest passions of men. Under the charm of its beauty, art, religion, civilization, is developed; through the lust to possess it a dynasty is overthrown, an empire falls into ruin. The historian may crush the pearl and bring to light the grain of sand; but he cannot persuade us that the sand made all the intervening history.

Detailing his position, Dunning chose some illustrations from Roman, Hebrew, and English history. Down to the nineteenth century, he pointed out, the lessons of Roman history exerted a powerful influence on the development of Western Europe. Repeatedly, medieval and modern leaders looked to Roman experience to solve their own problems; but the history on which they drew was in large measure derived from Livy and Virgil. In other words, medieval and modern men, when they turned to the Roman past for guidance, were shaped in their thoughts and

22 Dunning's writings are listed in *A Bibliography of the Faculty of Political Science of Columbia University, 1880-1930* (New York, 1931), pp. 58-62.

their actions by a history which, according to recent standards, consisted of a string of unfounded facts. Yet while Niebuhr and his successors succeeded in demolishing these once-accepted facts, they could never undo their influence during the centuries that preceded modern historical scholarship. For example, said Dunning, turning to one of his favorite subjects, it was only necessary to remember the part that the Roman example had played in the writings of Dante, Machiavelli, and Montesquieu.[23] By nineteenth-century standards, these writers were seriously misinformed as to the real facts of the Roman past. From the historical standpoint, however, these real facts exercised no influence during the centuries when the Roman example counted.

Looking for a second illustration, Dunning turned to the Old Testament record of Jewish history, which, he thought, even the crudest economic interpreter would recognize as a major cultural influence in the history of Christendom. Like the Roman example, the Hebrew example furnished precedents for many a secular and spiritual authority during the medieval and early modern centuries. Perhaps the events of those centuries were really caused by the changing value of gold or by the law of diminishing returns; but as far as Gregory VII, Innocent III, Boniface VIII, Charles V, Martin Luther, and many a colonial American were concerned, they were merely acting in harmony with the Biblical revelations of the will and purpose of God. Like the long-standing version of the Roman past, Christendom's long-standing version of the Hebrew past collapsed under the pressure of nineteenth-century criticism. Adam went the way of Romulus. Yet while critics showed that Biblical history was based on flimsy factual foundations, they could not undo the influence of those ill-founded facts during the course of many a preceding century. From the historical standpoint, the actions and thoughts of men were influenced much more by the false facts of Biblical history than by the correct ones.

23 See Dunning's treatment of Machiavelli in *A History of Political Theories, Ancient and Mediaeval* (New York, 1902), chap. XI; see his treatment of Montesquieu in *A History of Political Theories from Luther to Montesquieu* (New York, 1905), chap. XII.

Nor was it only Jewish and Roman history that testified to the influence of false facts. English history offered the illustration of trial by jury, which, through the writings of Fortescue, Coke, Hale, and Blackstone, became so closely linked with Magna Carta that Dunning found it difficult at times to believe that the thirteenth-century document had been drawn up for any other reason than to provide the basis for trial by jury. Nineteenth-century criticism proved that this association lacked any sound factual foundation; but this did not affect the reality of the association for the Englishmen who, through the course of several centuries, believed that Magna Carta did provide the basis for trial by jury. Here was just another instance of the sway of the false fact in history and of the relative insignificance of the true fact.

Dunning did not mean to underrate the phenomenal contributions of nineteenth-century historical scholarship; he considered the scientific historian's reconstruction of man's past just as significant as the scientist's transformation of man's ideas concerning the physical world. Unfortunately, however—and this was at bottom Dunning's complaint—the search for the truth about historical facts had worked to obscure all the other functions of the historian. Delighted with the many new facts at his disposal, even the enlightened gildsman sometimes came to attribute undue importance to them. Unfortunately, moreover, critical historical scholarship worked to encourage the gildsman to feel superior to the hapless generations which antedated the contemporary era. And this was most dangerous. Instead of scorning a past generation for its failure to have achieved an accurate understanding of the history of still earlier generations, Dunning thought that the gildsman would do far better to

recognize frankly that whatever a given age or people believes to be true *is* true for that age and that people. The actual facts as to Adam and Moses and trial by jury and Romulus had no causal relation to the affairs of Europe in the sixteenth century. Erroneous ideas on those topics had very close causal relations to those affairs. For the history of the sixteenth century, therefore, it is the error and not the fact that is important. The business of the historian who studies that century is to ascertain the scope and content of the ideas that constituted the culture of that period. Whether these ideas were true or were false, according to the standards of any other period, has nothing to do with the matter. That they were the ideas which underlay the activities of the men of this time, is all that concerns the work of the historian.

Yet only if he was armed with a feeling of humility could he overcome the tendency to scorn those who lacked the knowledge that he had at his disposal. The nineteenth century had surely seen transformations in the manner and matter of historical writing, transformations whose importance could hardly be exaggerated. The historian, however, ought to be cautious and modest, despite the temptation to rejoice over the scrapping of long-accepted facts. "He must keep in mind that the reversal cannot be made retroactive, so as to affect the thoughts and deeds of the generations who knew not the reality. He must remember, in short, that for very, very much history there is much more importance in the ancient error than in the new-found truth." So it was that Dunning, in effect, offered for discussion a resolution affirming that the influence of new facts had increased, was increasing, and ought to be diminished; and he suggested that, from the point of view of historical understanding, misconceptions of facts were often by far the more important facts, and therefore they deserved the thoughtful attention of the gildsman.

After Dunning's penetrating message of 1913 it was perhaps fitting that for the next decade the presidents rarely discussed the nature of historical facts in their addresses. Even those who did turn to the subject did so only briefly. Andrew C. McLaughlin, for example, had no objection to the gildsman's search for facts. His own writings on American constitutional history tended to be heavily factual in character; and his *History of the American Nation* (1913) bore witness to his respect for cold, hard facts.[24] Nevertheless, McLaughlin made it plain in his message of 1914 on "American History and American Democracy" that while he viewed the search for facts as the gildsman's day to day task, he also viewed that search as a preliminary step towards an understanding of historical tendencies, causes, and interrelationships. He believed, in other words, that the gildsman should not simply catalogue facts. Reflecting perhaps the influence of his position as chairman of the departments of history and of church history at the University of Chicago, he believed that the gildsman should search for "the unifying, the universal, and the eternal."

Five years after McLaughlin, when William R. Thayer addressed the Association, he, too, did not wish to disparage the study of facts. He made it clear that he continued to believe in what he once called "the need of thorough research";[25] but it should be added that his own latter-day writings could not possibly match the standards set by his studies of Italian history, for he had suffered a serious eye injury.[26] Thayer, at all events,made sure, in his address on "Fallacies in History," to proclaim the worthwhileness of any piece of research that established particular historical facts; but he also made sure to announce that ideas were superior to facts, that interpretation was superior to information. Like McLaughlin, he urged the historian not only to catalogue facts but to determine their meaning. Himself an accomplished writer, he also urged the historian to present his facts with literary skill; otherwise he would fail to impress his reader with the meaning of his facts.

This was not the view of Charles M. Andrews, who in 1924 took much the same stand that George Burton Adams, his former colleague at Yale, had taken back in 1908. Substituting for

24 *A History of the American Nation* (New ed., New York, 1913), p. v.

25 Charles Downer Hazen, ed., *The Letters of William Roscoe Thayer* (Boston, 1926), p. 192.

26 *Ibid.*, pp. 356-57.

Woodrow Wilson who had not lived to prepare his presidential message to the Association, Andrews may well have been thinking of his predecessor in some of the remarks which he offered on "These Forty Years." Andrews would have found little humor in the confession that the author of the popular five-volume *History of the American People* (1902) had made when he said: "At one time I tried to write history. I did not know enough to write it, but I knew from experience how hard it was to find an historian out and I trusted I would not be found out."[27] This could hardly have struck Andrews as being humorous. One of the most past-minded gildsmen of his time, he was preeminently a researcher, whose knowledge of the facts and sources of the colonial period had placed him in the front ranks of American historians.

Scoring the frequent emphasis on the literary presentation of historical facts, Andrews suggested in his address that the good historical study was one in which the facts were accurate, one in which the interpretations of the facts grew out of the facts themselves, and one in which form and content were in harmony. Doubtless because he himself had done so much digging, he stressed that the historian should immerse himself so thoroughly in the facts of his period that he would avoid misreading them. As long as he approached his facts from a Whig or a Tory angle, as long as he used them to foster patriotism or to bolster some doctrine, theory, or philosophy, he could hardly avoid doing violence to them. Andrews pointed out that when the historian sang the glories of objectivity, he simply sang the glories of truth for the sake of truth. When he spoke of objective history, he spoke simply of history that was non-partisan in character, history that was written with the impartiality of the observer, not with the bias of the special pleader; for the conclusions in an objective historical account came from the facts themselves—not from the preconceived notions that existed in the historian's mind.

27 Quoted in Louis Martin Sears, "Woodrow Wilson," in William T. Hutchinson, ed., *op. cit.*, p. 112.

Small wonder that Andrews, himself the author of *The Old English Manor* (1892) and of *A History of England* (1903), esteemed Stubbs and Maitland more highly than Froude and Macaulay. Small wonder, too, that he emphasized the relative newness of the "historical state of mind." And the only real contributions to historical knowledge, he declared, were being made by the scholar who had this state of mind. For this scholar was convinced of the value of studying the past for its own sake. Accordingly, he gathered new facts and reexamined old ones, always viewing history not as a string of stories that required telling but as a multitude of problems that required solving. As for the facts of history, he cared little about clothing them in a way to please the public; he had too many more important things on his mind.

Andrews again proclaimed the importance of the gildsman's search for facts when in 1925 he had a second opportunity to deliver a presidential address before the Association. Recognizing that knowledge of the past would always continue to be "in the making," he argued that this did not result primarily from the need that any age felt to rework the past from its own standpoint. Rather it resulted from this: that any generation of historians was likely to uncover new facts, which in turn were likely to make possible a better understanding of the past. It was the frequent appearance of such new facts—and of new interpretations that grew out of them—that made so-called definitive history a myth.

Two years later, Henry Osborn Taylor took the opposite point of view, suggesting that the rewriting of history was due less to the discovery of new facts than to the needs of different generations. One of the foremost students of European intellectual history, Taylor was nevertheless a notoriously vague writer; and the vagueness that characterized portions of his books on ancient, medieval, and early modern thought also characterized portions of his address on "A Layman's View of History." Of this Taylor himself was probably aware, for he was well accus-

tomed to hearing his writings called "difficult".[28] Doubtless he
tried "to make things clear to himself," as the author of his obituary notice in the *American Historical Review* was to remark;[29]
but this did not seem to make the going much easier for his
readers.

Noting that the past would always have a different character
for different generations, Taylor slighted what Andrews had
emphasized, the discovery of new facts, and emphasized what
Andrews had slighted. Just as one historian knew and experienced the present differently from other historians, so, too, Taylor said, one historian knew and experienced the past differently
from other historians; and historians who lived at different
times, sharing the interests and outlook of their particular generation, were sure to discover and stress different facts. The past
not only seemed to be different but actually was different to
different generations, said Taylor, returning to the theme that
he had discussed briefly in *Ancient Ideals* (1896), his first major historical study.[30]

Certainly the historian should present his facts in their topical and causal relationships. But he should concentrate on
"cardinal and potent facts"—those that had "the broadest rational and connective value," those that best served to point up
history as "a linked emergent growth." He must always struggle
for factual precision, for even some slight detail might have considerable causal significance. As a rule, however, Taylor thought
that accuracy concerned the historian less when he dealt with the
larger elements of an account than when he dealt with its details. How, for example, he asked, did the matter of accuracy
apply to the Battle of Salamis or to Caesar's assassination?
Even if the historian had been a contemporary of those events,
even if he had been able to get at "the newspapers of the follow-

28 *A.H.R.*, XLVI (1941), 1014.

29 *Ibid.*, p. 1015.

30 *Ancient Ideals: A Study of Intellectual and Spiritual Growth from
Early Times to the Establishment of Christianity* (2 vols., New York, 1896),
I, v.

ing day," Taylor insisted that he could only have gleaned "obvious details, which buzz about the fact." In short, the reconstruction of a historical event, said Taylor, setting forth a notion that he was later to develop in *Fact, the Romance of Mind* (1932), depended on the knowledge, intelligence, feeling, and intuition of the historian. Using the data at his disposal, he had to draw conclusions concerning the manner in which some event must have happened or probably happened. Having ascertained the facts, he had to face the more difficult problem of joining and interpreting them—something that required not so much accuracy as insight and judgment.

Turning to other aspects of the historical fact, that "awful time-honored figure," Taylor examined it in relation to the human equation and in some of its many meanings. If interpretations of Caesar's death continued to have different meanings for different historians, it was reassuring at least that the event had had a different meaning for each of those who took part in the assassination.

> It was differently intended [said Taylor] and also bore different results, according to the temperament, motives, and situation of each. Indeed it was for each a different fact. No fact can be in and of itself alone. Every fact comes to pass in its relationships and bearings as well as in itself—if indeed there be any clearly marked and delimited *itself*. The causes of Caesar's death had worked up to it through the whole antecedent history of Rome—of mankind, if you will. More immediately it was brought about by the tempers and motives of the conspirators. Neither its causes, its manifold significance, nor its effects could be the same for an ethical intellectual like Brutus and for the sweaty mob about to take the air in Caesar's gardens beyond the Tiber.

The important thing, according to Taylor, was that, like Caesar's death, every historical event was inexhaustible in its relationships and multiple in its meanings; and the different ways in which contemporaries and subsequent generations understood

a fact were parts of the fact itself. This it was that gave history
its unity.

Nor did Taylor overlook some of the divergent ideas as to
what a fact was. Drawing on his considerable knowledge of antiquity and medieval times, he pointed out that ancient Greek
philosphers searched beneath natural phenomena for "a pro-
founder and causally explanatory fact." Obviously, however,
Democritus' atom, Aristotle's substance, and Plato's idea were
all invisible and intangible. Designed to explain the appearance
of things, they were working hypotheses, assumed facts, just
as were the ether and perhaps the nuclei and electrons of more
recent science. Then, said Taylor, there were, in addition to explanatory facts, the physical facts that were viewed symbolically.
The Church Fathers, for instance, considered natural phenomena as "symbols of the spiritual verity which it was their
function to shadow forth"; indeed, some medieval philosophers
viewed the world of nature as an allegory whose reality lay in
its spiritual features. To them, again, it was not so much literal
truth as the deeper truth, the more profound fact, that mattered.
In view of the different notions of what a fact was, Taylor remarked in 1927: "We are haunted by the faith that the surest
and most veritable fact is that which our whole human nature,
passionate, spiritual, and intellectual, might somehow conspire
to substantiate. Fact may not be just as we see it, or scientifically observe it. And perhaps fact is not just as reason argues
it. Assuredly it is not what impulse and emotional conviction
would declare; our intuitions will not suffice. We crave the con-
current verdict—if we could only get it—of all the faculties of
our cognitive and assertive selves."

There was, however, nothing obscure in what James Harvey
Robinson had to say about the nature of historical facts. He had,
indeed, stated his point of view long before his message of 1929.
In his classic collection of *Readings in European History* (1904-
1906) he had made it clear that he was not content simply to

accumulate facts; what he wanted to do was to find out what they meant.[31] In his *New History* (1912), moreover, he had not hesitated to take a number of digs at the gildsman who concentrated too much on details. And in the years after the first World War, as Robinson became "more and more interested in the world outside college walls,"[32] his dissatisfaction with useless historical facts apparently increased. As a social reformer —something, incidentally, that he denied being[33]—he wished the facts of the past to serve the needs of the present.

He complained in his message that the historian, despite his accumulation of vast stores of facts and his worship of facts as revealed in primary sources, had proved to be no wiser than the layman in the heat of the first World War. Yet while Robinson was critical of those who had read the facts of the past in the light of the wartime atmosphere, he was not at all critical of those who would read the facts of the past in the light of the twenties. Advocating the kind of history that linked the past with the morning newspaper, he urged the historian to select those facts from the past that went to explain the present; he should omit many of the facts that were once considered essential but which, in the light of the contemporary era, seemed far from necessary.

Without question, the deftest handling of historical facts since Dunning's time occurred in Carl L. Becker's message of 1931. Like Robinson, Becker had much of the social reformer about him. Long suspicious of the concept of objective facts, he believed that knowledge of the past ought to serve the needs of the contemporary scene; and what he had said of his teacher, Frederick Jackson Turner, he would doubtless have wanted said of himself: that he was "always occupied primarily with the present, and with the past as illuminating the present."[34] Becker, to be sure,

31 *Readings in European History* (2 vols., Boston, 1904-06), I, 6.

32 Harry Elmer Barnes, "James Harvey Robinson," in Howard W. Odum, ed., *op. cit.*, p. 339.

33 *Ibid.*, pp. 393-94.

34 *Everyman His Own Historian: Essays on History and Politics*, p. 224.

ad a remarkable grasp of the facts of both European and Ameri-
an history—something quite unusual among the gildsmen of his
ime. Like Turner, however, he was always on the hunt for
ignificant facts; [35] and what gave facts significance, he thought,
vas their relevance to the current and future needs of society.

   In his presidential message, "Everyman His Own Historian,"
Becker emphasized that history was a creation of the imagination.
This creation Mr. Everyman molded in keeping with his own
ersonal experiences; he adapted it to his own personal needs;
and he adorned it to satisfy his own esthetic standards. Obvi-
usly, there were limits to Mr. Everyman's creation of his own
rand of history. He could not choose to hold just any memories
f things said and done; he quickly discovered that all kinds of
estrictions were imposed by his fellow-men, restrictions which
uickly convinced him of the urgency of remembering certain
acts with considerable exactness. When Mr. Everyman had a
oal bill to pay, he had no difficulty in deciding on the documents
o be consulted and the facts to be selected. Because he was not
reparing a volume on "Some Aspects of the Coal Industry
Objectively Considered," he did not have to worry about gather-
ng all available factual information with a view to permitting it
o speak for itself. Wanting only to pay a bill, he simply had to
hoose the pertinent facts; and wanting nothing to go wrong, he
new well enough, even without benefit of Bernheim's *Lehrbuch,*
hat the facts had to be accurately ascertained. Nor did Mr.
veryman fear that because he was personally involved in the
vent he ran the risk of not getting at the complete truth. Mr.
veryman, indeed, had no such goal in mind. He wanted only to
neet an immediate situation; and what made him a competent
istorian in matters practical was the fact that he was far from
disinterested. He was meeting a situation not with apathy but
vith intelligence.

   Naturally, Becker continued, Mr. Everyman had memories
f things said and done that were not strictly of a practical and

35 *Ibid.,* pp. 230-31.

personal character. His memories consisted also of things tha
were alleged to have been said and done in times and places othe
than his own; and, inevitably, these memories were going to b
both factual and fanciful, accurate and inaccurate. This did no
mean that Mr. Everyman wanted to fool either himself or hi
fellow men. For, though he had a particular fondness for thos
facts that fitted in best with his private interests and emotiona
leanings, he still had "a wholesome respect for cold, hard facts,"
and seldom called into question the extent to which they coul
be coaxed and cajoled. As a rule, he accepted facts as they cam
his way; he lacked both the time and the need to challenge o
substantiate them. Selecting one of his favorite illustrations,[36]
Becker remarked that it was easy enough for Mr. Everyman t
conjure up the stereotype of the signing of the Declaration o
Independence on the fourth of July. This was a vivid image tha
he might hold with impunity to the very end—unless someon
better informed saw reason to point out that the second of Aug
ust, not the fourth of July, was the correct date. As an actuality
of course, the signing of the Declaration of Independence "wa
what it was." As a memory, it was whatever Mr. Everymar
made it. Depending on the way it fitted into his own persona
world, it had various meanings for him.

Not that Becker considered the gildsman very different fron
the informal historian who was Mr. Everyman. For the gilds
man was limited by considerations of time and space; and, like
Mr. Everyman, he patterned his history "at the behest of circum
stance and purpose"—despite all his efforts to the contrary. Al
though Becker recognized that the first duty of the historian wa
to establish the accuracy of his facts, regardless of their meaning
he noted at the same time that it was usual for every age to view
history as an account of actualities from which some meaning
could be drawn. It was usual, moreover, for every age to believ
that because of firm factual foundations its own version o

36 *The Declaration of Independence: A Study in the History of Politica
Ideas* (New York, 1922), pp. 184-85.

the past was valid, whereas previous versions lacked validity by reason of their factual inadequacies. Becker thought, indeed, that this illusion had never achieved such sway as in the recent "age of erudition in which we live, or from which we are perhaps just emerging." Covering part of the same ground as Dunning, he noted the atmosphere in which the scientific historian had been working in recent decades. Tired of being fooled by tempting interpretations that never seemed to hold up, he came to rivet his attention on the close investigation of facts. Mastering the technical aspects of research, he devoted much time and effort to collecting and editing sources. He postponed consideration of the meaning of the medieval period because he first had to determine definitively "whether Charles the Fat was at Ingelheim or Lustnau on July 1, 887," said Becker, quoting from James Harvey Robinson's *New History*.

Becker had no quarrel with the scientific historian, who, recognizing that the establishment of facts was his first responsibility, attempted to avoid factual errors. But he did denounce as a great illusion the notion of the scientific historian that facts, when fully established, would proceed "to speak for themselves." Rather harshly he judged a Fustel de Coulanges who could deny that *he* was speaking and could insist rather that history was speaking through him. It was with some rejoicing that Becker recorded the passing of the point of view of the scientific historian. The younger gildsman was no longer so familiar with his Ranke, and, if he knew Fustel's dictum, he was likely to view it as a statement of perfectionist and futile strivings.

Besides, said Becker, even the most objective gildsman had at least one preconception: the preconception that he had no preconceptions. And even if he could manage to set forth the facts of history without remolding them, he would merely succeed in ridding human life of all meaning.

Left to themselves [Becker declared] the facts do not speak; left to themselves they do not exist, not really, since for all practical purposes there is no fact until some one affirms it.

The least the historian can do with any historical fact is to select and affirm it. To select and affirm even the simplest complex of facts is to give them a certain place in a certain pattern of ideas, and this alone is sufficient to give them a special meaning. However 'hard' or 'cold' they may be, historical facts are after all not material substances which, like bricks or scantlings, possess definite shape and clear, persistent outline. To set forth historical facts is not comparable to dumping a barrow of bricks.

This was much the same point that Charles A. Beard made in 1933, two years after Becker. One of the best-informed gildsmen of his time, Beard had written on medieval England, modern Europe, and contemporary Japan as well as on the United States. And from an early stage in his career he had been thinking seriously about the nature of history. Although he did his doctoral dissertation on *The Office of Justice of the Peace in England in Its Origin and Development* (1904), he quickly became critical of those who neglected the study of the facts of recent history. And he quickly became impatient with those who avoided interpretation in their writings. In *An Economic Interpretation of the Constitution of the United States* (1913), published when he was not quite forty, Beard made it plain that he was not content simply to classify and order historical facts in an impartial way. What interested him was the attempt to explain these facts.[37]

Drawing for the purposes of his presidential message on what was soon to appear as *The Nature of the Social Sciences in Relation to Objectives of Instruction* (1934), Beard pointed out that behind every bit of historical writing there was some thinking person, who had to select and arrange quantities of facts; and their selection and arrangement depended upon a multitude of value judgments. Facts, he insisted, lacked the faculty of self-selection; they lacked the power to move by themselves into some

37 *An Economic Interpretation of the Constitution of the United States* (New York, 1913), pp. 3-4.

fixed pattern in the gildsman's mind. When the sources for a small phase of history were few in number, Beard granted that the scholar might emerge with a product that had a kind of finality. This was true, he thought, of some portions of the works of Fustel de Coulanges. Such completeness, however, was not the completeness of history; it was the completeness of documentation. Beard recognized that there was a type of gildsman who claimed that only "inner necessities" determined the selection and ordering of his facts; but the gildsman who held this view was not likely to acknowledge the same precision and certitude in the products of other scholars—except when the latter had preconceptions that appealed to him.

The important thing, according to Beard, was that recent thinking about history denied Ranke's view that, just as the engineer could describe a machine, so the historian could describe the past as it really was. Pronouncing this view a part of the passing parade of historical thought, Beard suggested that conservative Ranke, who deplored the propagandistic uses to which historical writing had been put in the eighteenth century, saw his ideas and interests best fostered by the kind of historical writing that was coldly factual and seemingly unaffected by the issues of the day.[38] In time, Beard continued, Ranke's view was reenforced by the idea of objectivity that dominated the natural sciences. If objectivity made possible the disclosure of the truth about nature, why could it not also reveal the truth about the past? The logic of the whole argument, Beard remarked, seemed ideal to those whom the approach served.

Reenforced by the vogue of science, Ranke's formula became so entrenched that a critical period in historiography was occasioned by its rejection. The academic historian found himself in an especially difficult position. He could find some kind of escape, if an unsatisfactory one, in silence, in editing, or in the study of some petty aspect of history. Assuming that he was

---

38 Cf. *The Nature of the Social Sciences in Relation to Objectives of Instruction* (New York, 1934), pp. 56-59; and "That Noble Dream," *A.H.R.*, XLI (1935), 77-79.

describing some narrow and isolated segment of the past as it really was, he could confine his study to some minute problem like the fluctuation of cotton prices in the Alabama of the fifties or the variation in the dimensions of wigs in the England of Charles II.[39] Even in such circumstances Beard thought that the historian would be a "strange creature" if he did not wonder why he considered these subjects worthy of study—if he did not wonder why society supported him during his investigations. Beard, then, could not emphasize enough that the gildsman chose and classified historical facts according to the relentless directions of his "frame of reference." His selection of material was unavoidably affected by what he personally viewed as desirable, possible, and necessary.

Beard's conception of "Written History as an Act of Faith" did not win the support of Charles H. McIlwain. An admirer of Maitland and Tout, McIlwain insisted that the gildsman should strive for objectivity and impartiality in his writings. No less important, he insisted that the gildsman should select his facts in the light not of the present but of the past. As a student of English constitutional history, McIlwain understood full well the dangers of the present-minded approach to historical facts; and he pointed to those dangers in his penetrating message of 1936 on "The Historian's Part in a Changing World." Not that he disagreed with all that Beard had said. Like Beard, he recognized that the facts of the past were often reworked in keeping with current interests and problems. But he pointed out that it was one thing to recognize the reality of this practice; it was quite another to regard it as the thing that "ought to be done." Past-minded scholar that he was, McIlwain complained that some gildsmen were so immersed in immediacy that they maintained that all historical facts which were "out-of-date" in their own time deserved to be purged from historical accounts. Other gildsmen, McIlwain continued, were more subtle in their approach. Emphasizing human frailties, they insisted that it was

39 Cf. *The Nature of the Social Sciences,* p. 52.

mpossible for the historian to get at "the complex of innumerble facts and forces" that revealed the life of any segment of he past.

McIlwain condemned the defeatism of this point of view. To dmit that the complexities of the past ruled out the possibility f a perfect historiographical reproduction was not to say that he job should not be undertaken. McIlwain cautioned that overmphasis on the limitations of the historian in his selection and rdering of facts was likely to end in the view that all historical ccounts were "after all little better than fiction, little more than npressionistic pictures." Indeed, if the "act of faith" approach o historical study needed to be refuted by a specific illustration, McIlwain found it in Beard's "own distinguished contributions o history." McIlwain, in a word, was not to be numbered among hose who, along with Becker and Beard, believed that the day f Ranke was past. Even if facts could not be ascertained so bjectively as Ranke had thought, McIlwain was still all in avor of continuing the attempt. Despite the arguments of the ver-skeptical historian, the truth persisted that "some things id actually happen in the past, and that some record of these appenings sometimes survives. And if these things happened, hey had definite historical causes and results of which we often ave some account remaining, even if incomplete."

Nor did McIlwain believe that the historian's function was o square the facts of the past with those of the present. Many f the advances in historical knowledge, he declared, had been aade not because of a rewriting of the past in the light of the presnt but because of a rewriting of the past in the light of the past. Altogether too often, the modernity of the historian's ideas roved to be the greatest obstacle to an understanding of the acts of the past. Not only did these modern ideas frequently ail to fit the facts, but they often made a distorted picture inevible. Seeking to substantiate these points. McIlwain turned to ome of the major revisions that had recently taken place in English institutional historiography. Edward A. Freeman, for instance, author of *The Growth of the English Constitution from the Earliest Times* (1872), had viewed attendance at the Great Council as an enormous privilege, and the reason was that he thought in terms of his own times. The recent scholar on the other hand, ridding himself of present-day notions, regarded such attendance as merely a feudal encumbrance. In other words, the fundamental revision of much of twelfth-century institutional history had nothing to do with "any feeling that earlier historians had neglected the forces of the present in their treatment of the past." What made this revision possible was not a "reading in of modern modes of thought or action but a reading out. It has resulted from no attempt, conscious or unconscious, to rewrite this part of the past in our terms, but rather from a realization, born of careful research into the records of the time, that those records actually tell a story different from the one we have hitherto accepted as history."

Much the same was true of the thirteenth and of the sixteenth centuries. What happened to Magna Carta in the hands of the overly eager historian provided an excellent illustration of the danger of finding the facts of the present in those of the past. No doubt about it, two of the inveterate foes of sound historiography were "retrospective nationalism" and "retrospective constitutionalism." Revised notions of "Tudor absolutism," after all, were based on knowledge not of "modern constitutionalism," but of "reactionary antiquarianism." According to McIlwain, then, the historian should make sure to select and read his facts in the light of the past, not of the present; for facts were going to be misread as long as the present was read into the past.

Max Farrand, who served as president of the Association in 1940, also came to the defense of the study of facts. Editor of *The Records of the Federal Convention of 1787,* Farrand was a careful scholar, whose list of publications was not at all impressive from the quantitative standpoint. His emphasis on meticulousness of scholarship, among other things, kept him from

chieving any considerable output. Highly self-critical, he was
ot one to rush into print.[40]

Discussing "The Quality of Distinction" in his message, Far-
and characterized the business man as a great worshipper of
acts, whose success presupposed accurate records which con-
ained facts that he could not overlook—unless he wanted ulti-
nately to risk failure. For the business man to misrepresent the
acts was for him to risk a trip to court and perhaps a stay in
ail; but what applied to the business man applied only in part
o the historian and to mankind in general. Certainly it was a
ormidable obligation to record and interpret the facts of man's
ast. Just as business success depended on an awareness of "the
acts of experience," so the intelligent conduct of human affairs
epended on accurate information about man's past. But while
he misrepresentation of facts had dire consequences for the
usiness man, it had no such consequences for the historian. Nor
ould Farrand accept "ignorance" as an excuse for such mis-
epresentation. The historian who hazarded interpretations in
pite of the weakness of his knowledge and the strength of his
rejudices deserved to be severely condemned.

From the numerical standpoint, historical facts fell in the same
lass with "drops of water in the ocean or grains of sand on the
eashore"; and it was this that compelled the historian to choose
ome facts rather than others. Yet once the historian made his
election of facts, Farrand suggested, he took leave of the man of
cience or at least moved with him into "the realm of hypothesis
nd theory—that is, into the world of values." For almost all
he records that the historian handled had "already passed
hrough the stage of human interpretation, which means they
ave been subjected to the variables of personal judgment and
aste"; records, in short, lay in a "world of values" that lacked
niversally acceptable systems of measurement.

Just the same, the survival of a historical work depended on
he effectiveness with which the gildsman distinguished between

important and unimportant facts; and this in turn depended c
a variety of factors like knowledge, taste, training, experienc
and character. True, Farrand viewed the power to recogni
quality as dependent on age; but he addressed his remarks to tl
young historian, cautioning him to remember that his know
ledge, ability, and training did not suffice to guarantee the du
ability of his writings. Above all, he should strive through sel
education for the critical power which would enable him to g
rid of private predilections in the process of choosing historic
facts.

Farrand's successor, James Westfall Thompson, also ha
some brief comments to make concerning the gildsman's sele
tion of facts. Doubtless Thompson had reason to be cautious i
discussing facts at all, for he was one of the least trustworth
medievalists of his time. Enormously productive, he had writte
on medieval political, social, economic, and intellectual history
but in his writings he frequently sacrificed accuracy to quantit
His last major work, his *History of Historical Writing* (1942
on which his posthumously delivered presidential message (
1941 was based, contained numerous factual errors. One r
viewer, J. W. Swain, noted that in his account of Josephu
Thompson managed to make at least ten mistakes in his fir
nine lines, and that in his account of Gibbon he made at lea
a dozen mistakes. Swain considered the *History* a shaky refe
ence work; and he recommended that no one "repeat a sing
statement from it without careful verification."[41]

What Thompson had to say about historical facts in his me
sage on "The Age of Mabillon and Montfaucon" was simpl
this: the function of the gildsman was not to compile facts b
to trace the growth of knowledge; and his function was not
follow the development of "all knowledge" but of that knowled
that bore a causal relationship to man's behavior. Because huma
behavior was at bottom determined by human knowledg
Thompson was convinced that the historian would do well

41 *Ibid.,* XLVIII (1943), 292-93.

well on those facts that indicated the relationship between
knowledge and conduct. Such were the facts that related to
"prime movers of human affairs" like law, government, religion,
literature, and art.

Thompson's standard for selecting historical facts was quite
similar to the one that Carlton J. H. Hayes suggested in 1945.
Recently returned from his wartime mission in Spain, Hayes
remarked that it was things cultural that had the profoundest
effect on American relations with the world. Therefore, Hayes,
who had already shifted from a political and social to a political
and cultural emphasis in his own textbooks, urged the gildsman
to give more attention to the facts of linguistic and literary history, of religious and church history, of the history of art and
science, and of intellectual history.[42] The study of such facts
Hayes considered urgent in 1945 because of the continued
strength of American intellectual isolationism, the kind of isolationism that was exploiting the disclosure by the New
York *Times* that there were facts of United States history
which American students had never learned or which they had
forgotten.

Hayes had little confidence in those who were attempting to
overcome the factual deficiencies of American students; he did
not trust the politicians who were enacting state laws requiring
more United States history; he had little faith in the "professional 'educators' " who were refashioning curricula. His
point was that more facts of United States history narrowly
interpreted and fewer facts culled from the rest of history would
scarcely equip Americans with the knowledge they needed for
their position in the world of 1945. Hayes was in favor of more
American history, but not of the kind that started in 1776 or
even in 1492. Back to the ancient Greeks and the early Christians was his slogan; for it was only by going back to ancient

42 *A Political and Cultural History of Modern Europe* (2 vols., New
York, 1932-36), I, vii, II, v.

Greek and early Christian times that Americans could grasp th
basic fact of their history: that their frontier was a frontier
European culture.

Thus in the first sixty years of the Association's histor
roughly one-third of the presidents devoted portions of the
addresses to a discussion of the nature of historical facts. O
those who did, some stressed that fact-worship was likely to b
disastrous to style. Others concentrated on the way in which th
historian should go about selecting his facts; and, as a rule, the
presidents insisted that the needs of the present should play th
decisive role in determining the particular facts that should b
selected or omitted. Few presidents made it a point to emphasi
that the past itself ought to determine which facts were impo
tant and which were unimportant. And few presidents empha
sized that there was need to continue the search for further fact
Yes, according to most of the presidents who dealt with the sub
ject, the fact was not the thing.

CHAPTER VI

THE PHILOSOPHY AND SCIENCE OF HISTORY: EARLY YEARS

The discussion of historical facts was closely connected at nes with the discussion of the philosophy and science of hisry. Some presidents, insisting that the gildsman should not ly collect facts but interpret them and determine their meang, made it a point to endorse the search for tendencies, patterns, d laws in history; and some urged the gildsman to study allied bjects like sociology and economics, subjects that might help disclose these historical tendencies, patterns, and laws. A few esidents broached the subject of the philosophy and science history in order to condemn it. Associating the philosophy history with vague theories and speculations and the science history with oversimplified processes and reckless predictions, ey recommended that the gildsman stick to things as they ally were. Nevertheless, most of the presidents either ignored e subject in their messages or dealt with it incidentally. Both the early and the more recent decades of the Association's story only a small minority devoted the bulk of their addresses a discussion of clues and keys to history.

The first president of the Association, Andrew D. White, was e first to defend the study of the philosophy of history in a esidential message—a fact that Charles Beard pointed out in e thirties when he himself was urging the historian to try to nd out in what direction the world was moving, if it moved all.[1] Nor was it strange that White favored the study of the ilosophy of history. For, in addition to being the president Cornell, he was an active participant in the public life of his mes. Thoroughly present-minded in his approach to the past,

---

1 Charles Austin Beard, "That Noble Dream," *A.H.R.,* XLI (1935), -80, 86-87.

he looked to history for lessons, generalizations, and laws th
would serve the needs of his own day.

The aim of the historian, he said in his message of 188
should be to sum up the past, to work out "a philosophical sy
thesis of human affairs." He even argued that without such
synthesis—one that embraced large areas of space and lor
periods of time—there was little point in the preparation of c
tailed factual studies. Like Buckle, on whose authority he lean
and whom he had long admired, White found that the gre
value of the historical synthesis was that it served to indica

> through what cycles of birth, growth, and decay various r
> tions have passed; what laws of development may be fai
> considered as ascertained, and under these what laws of r
> ligious, moral, intellectual, social, and political health or d
> ease; what developments have been good, aiding in the evol
> tion of that which is best in man and in society; what develc
> ments have been evil, tending to the retrogression of man a:
> society; how various nations have stumbled and fallen ir
> fearful errors, and by what processes they have been broug
> out of those errors; how much the mass of men as a who
> acting upon each other in accordance with the general laws
> development in animate nature, have tended to perfect m
> and society; and how much certain individual minds, whi
> have risen either as the result of thought in their time, or
> spite of it—in defiance of any law which we can formulate
> have contributed toward this evolution.

To White's way of thinking, a writer like Thiers, the histori
of the French Revolutionary and Napoleonic Era, condemn
himself utterly when he denied the philosophical basis of histor
it was this denial, said White, making a point that he wou
again make in his *Autobiography*,[2] that helped to turn Thie
into "the most pernicious special pleader among French h
torians and the greatest architect of ruin among modern Fren
statesmen."

2 *Autobiography*, I, 523-24.

White was convinced that at future meetings of the Association it would be wise to create sections for the discussion of the philosophy of history. Yet, thinking perhaps of his own experiences at the University of Berlin in the 1850's, he cautioned the gildsman to guard against the loose and vague talk that frequently accompanied the discussion of the philosophy of history. Showing the same wariness of abstruseness that he had shown in his own very concrete writings, he urged the gildsman to avoid the "shadowy results" of a Hegel quite as much as a Thiers' denial of the philosophical basis of history.

Just as the concept of law in history appealed to White, so, too, it appealed to his successor, the venerable George Bancroft, the man who, according to Ranke, wrote the best work ever written from the democratic standpoint, the man who, according to Beard, showed "how hard God had worked to establish democracy of a thoroughly reputable variety in America."[3] When Bancroft delivered his very brief presidential message in 1886, he was eighty-six; and this doubtless goes a long way to explain its character. Certainly he did not pretend to have anything new to say. What he did was reassert several views that he had often expressed in the past, the view, for example, that God was visible in history.[4] What accounted, indeed, for the scientific character of historical study, he thought, was the fact that the movements of mankind were controlled by law. "The growth and decay of empire," he said, "the morning lustre of a dynasty and its fall from the sky before noonday; the first turning of a sod for the foundation of a city to the footsteps of a traveller searching for its place which time has hidden, all proceed as it is ordered." Bancroft granted that it was difficult to

3 M. A. DeWolfe Howe, *The Life and Letters of George Bancroft* (2 vols., New York, 1908), II, 183; Malcolm Cowley and Bernard Smith, eds., *Books That Changed Our Minds* (New York, 1939), p. 67; see also Beard's *An Economic Interpretation of the Constitution of the United States* (New York, 1913), pp. 1-2.

4 Howe, *op. cit.*, II, 77, 119, 322; cf. Russel B. Nye, *George Bancroft: Brahmin Rebel* (New York, 1944), pp. 296-97.

detect the presence of law in the behavior of rational human beings because of the "infinite variety of the movements of the human will and of the motives by which it may be swayed." Even so, the task was not hopeless by reason of the fact that the historian dealt with a past that lay "beyond the reach of change." Nor was the task hopeless for the thoughtful statesman, said Bancroft, himself a former secretary of the navy and a former minister to England and to Germany; for, if the statesman had the "spirit of candid inquiry," he would be in a position to "forecast the character of coming events, and form a plan of action with a reasonable confidence in its wisdom."

Bancroft's conception of history as a reflection of the will of God was shared by John Jay, grandson of the Chief Justice. President of the Association in 1890, Jay was preeminently a lawyer, diplomat, and political reformer;[5] he was hardly a historian. Yet while he had done little in the way of historical research and writing to warrant his election to the presidency of the Association, he still had strong convictions concerning the nature of history; and these convictions reflected his own strong religious beliefs. Agreeing with the spiritual approach of Wilhelm von Humboldt,[6] the German philosopher who had figured so prominently in Prussian history during the Napoleonic Era, Jay thought that "beyond the sum of creative forces directly presented by events there remains a powerfully active principle which, though not directly manifest, yet lends impulse and direction to those forces and ideas which according to their nature lie beyond the finite, but still permeate and rule the world's history in all its parts."

Not only that, said Jay. History disclosed something else, too. It disclosed the importance of "the continuing tie" which, in spite of all changes, bound the past and the present. And this

5 A.H.A., *Annual Report, 1894* (Washington, 1895), pp. 57-58.

6 On Humboldt, see Friedrich Engel-Janosi, *The Growth of German Historicism* (Baltimore, 1944), pp. 25-28.

tie needed especially to be stressed in the study of United States history, for the American debt to the world was large, said Jay, himself a former minister to Austria. If, indeed, American history had such "exceptional breadth," it was that the varied nationalities who went into the making of the United States linked the American past with that of so many European countries. Jay subscribed to the conception of the continuity and unity of history that Edward A. Freeman, regius professor of modern history at Oxford, was doing so much to popularize both in English and American historical circles.

These early presidents like Jay, Bancroft, and White turned only briefly to the discussion of the philosophy of history; so that it was not until the Association's decennial celebration that for the first time a president—Henry Adams—explored the subject on a serious scale. Adams managed to avoid delivering his message in person,[7] but he did at least give assurances in his classic letter from Guadalajara that his absenteeism constituted a defect that was "clearly not official, but a condition of the man."

The subject of Adams' letter of 1894 was "The Tendency of History," a subject that he had largely ignored in his nine-volume *History of the United States of America during the Administrations of Jefferson and Madison* (1889-1891), the work which "for clarity, tight construction, and sheer intelligence applied to the exposition of a great theme, had not then, and has not since, been equalled by any American historian."[8] While Adams had largely ignored the science and philosophy of history in his massive masterpiece, he was not to ignore it in his subsequent writings: *Mont-Saint-Michel and Chartres* (1904), *The Education of Henry Adams: An Autobiography* (1907), *The Rule of Phase Applied to History* (1909), and *A Letter to American Teachers of History* (1910). Certainly, however, the

7 Harold Dean Cater, ed., *Henry Adams and His Friends: A Collection of His Unpublished Letters* (Boston, 1947), p. 328.

8 Carl Lotus Becker, "Henry Adams Once More," in *Everyman His Own Historian: Essays on History and Politics* (New York, 1935), p. 166.

vagueness that characterized parts of these later writings—the vagueness which led Carl Becker to remark that "we too often do not know what he wishes to convey"[9]—did not characterize "The Tendency of History."

Adams noted that his generation of historians, reared on Buckle and Darwin, had been encouraged to exploit any hypothesis that seemed to promise the creation of a science of history. By 1894, however, more than thirty years had passed since the appearance in the late fifties of Buckle's first volume and Darwin's *Origin of the Species*. And still no science of history had been achieved; there was still no historical formula that satisfied what Adams would later call in *The Education* "the conditions of the stellar universe."[10] The upshot was that the historian of the nineties had less confidence than the historian of the sixties in the possibility of creating a science of history. Even so, there was hardly a successful historian who had resisted the appeal of the notion, so that fresh analyses, fresh generalizations, and new statements of previously unseen relationships kept growing in number; and so, too, did the peoples, the places, and the ages which the historian sought to include in his works. So much so, that by 1894 Adams pronounced history "encumbered and hampered by its own mass."

While Adams was inclined to doubt the possibility and the probability of formulating a science of history, he saw no abandoning the search. How could science accept the defeat that would be involved in the admission that "man, the most important of its subjects, could not be brought within its range?" And so, the search had continued and would continue. Adams suggested, indeed, that "four out of five" of his serious-minded colleagues had believed at some stage of the game that they were about to hit on a law which governed history as unmistakably as laws governed the physical world. Such was the challenge of Darwinism that

9 "The Education of Henry Adams," *ibid.*, p. 160.

10 *The Education of Henry Adams* (Modern Library, New York, 1931), p. 376.

as the great writers of our time have touched one by one the separate fragments of admitted law by which society betrays its character as a subject for science, not one of them can have failed to feel an instant's hope that he might find the secret which would transform these odds and ends of philosophy into one self-evident, harmonious, and complete system. He has seemed to have it, as the Spanish say, in his inkstand. Scores of times he must have dropped his pen to think how one short step, one sudden inspiration, would show all human knowledge; how, in these thickset forests of history, one corner turned, one faint trail struck, would bring him on the highroad of science. Every professor who has tried to teach the doubtful facts which we now call history must have felt that sooner or later he or another would put order in the chaos and bring light into darkness. Not so much genius or favor was needed as patience and good luck. The law was certainly there, and as certainly was in places actually visible, to be touched and handled, as though it were a law of chemistry or physics. No teacher with a spark of imagination or with an idea of scientific method can have helped dreaming of the immortality that would be achieved by the man who should successfully apply Darwin's method to the facts of human history.

Nevertheless, Adams was preoccupied in 1894 not so much with the creation of a science of history as with the impact of such a creation on existing institutions. Pondering, perhaps not altogether correctly, "the astonishing influence exerted by a mere theorist like Rousseau; by a reasoner like Adam Smith; by a philosopher, beyond contact with material interests, like Darwin," he confessed his inability "to imagine the limits of the shock" that would follow the demonstration of the laws of historical evolution. The historian would take on a position of unprecedented importance in society, ceasing to be viewed as one who carried on "safe and harmless" investigations. Once he established a science of history, he would affect vitally both government and society, leaving no institution and no "prodigious interest" untouched.

Because the church had as one of its basic tenets "the idea of a personal and active providence," it could not accept a science of history, said Adams, writing at a time when the science-religion controversy was a lively subject of discussion. Just as the church could not accept a science of history, neither could the state by reason of its sure opposition to any system that threatened to undermine it. Certainly private property would view with alarm any weakening of its established rights and privileges; and several months after the outbreak of the Pullman strike, Adams, who had little love for trade unions,[11] pointed out that labor would view with alarm a science of history that did not give it aid and comfort. Yet it was impossible to imagine that a science of history would not have much to say concerning the future of church and state and of capital and labor; for it would describe with mathematical precision the course of governmental and societal evolution, bringing bad news to some, perhaps even to all, existing institutions and organizations. If it indicated the triumph of socialism, neither state nor society would permit its foundations to be destroyed. If it pointed to the continuation and intensification of late nineteenth century abuses, it was likely that few people would listen to descriptions of a future characterized by armament races, enormous concentrations of wealth, growing materialism, and deteriorating culture.

The gildsman, however, could not take the science of history lightly and drop it quickly—once he came to understand the dislocations that it would occasion. If a generalization was suggested that brought into causal relationship all the phenomena of mankind's history, the scholar must accept it as a law and teach it as a law. That it undermined existing organizations was irrelevant; for the historian, unlike other members of society, could not disregard it. He had to pursue it wherever it

11 Edward N. Saveth, *American Historians and European Immigrants, 1875-1925* (New York, 1948), p. 73.

led, adopting under pressure, when necessary, Galileo's *E pur si muove*. So thought Henry Adams, one of the few American historians who was to make a serious attempt to formulate a philosophy of history.[12]

As in the years immediately preceding Adams' message, so in the years immediately following it, the philosophy and science of history were neglected in the presidential addresses of the Association. What made this perhaps all the more surprising was the fact that among Adams' early successors were two of the most distinguished clergymen in late nineteenth-century America: Richard S. Storrs and George Park Fisher. Yet while Storrs, the biographer of Bernard of Clairvaux and long-time pastor of the Church of the Pilgrims in Brooklyn, acknowledged the attraction, the fascination, and the "dignity of remoteness" of the philosophy of history, he proceeded to avoid the subject in his message of 1896. And though Fisher, professor of ecclesiastical history at the Yale Divinity School and author of numerous studies on the origins and development of Christianity, announced that he was in favor of rating the philosophy of history at its "full value," he, too, avoided it in his address. He stated his opposition to that philosophy of history which denied an "initiative agency" to historical persons and relegated them "exclusively to the category of effects"; individuals, he insisted, were not automatons, and especially in time of crisis, they displayed a "creative energy" which inspired and guided their fellow men. Apart from these brief observations, however, Fisher steered clear of the philosophy of history in his message of 1898.

The same was true of his successor, James Ford Rhodes. Himself "a storyteller rather than a philosopher,"[13] Rhodes consciously shied away from the discussion of history as a hand-

12 Henry Steele Commager, "Henry Adams," in William T. Hutchinson, ed., *The Marcus W. Jernegan Essays in American Historiography* (Chicago, 1937), p. 195.

13 Raymond Curtis Miller, "James Ford Rhodes," *ibid.*, p. 189.

maid of philosophy and of history as philosophy teaching by example, explaining that to discuss such themes was to arouse
controversy. And controversy he preferred to avoid, believing
like Huxley that it soon tended to "swerve from the great issue
of what is right and what is wrong to the very small question
of who is right and who is wrong." Rhodes, with the modesty
that was generally so characteristic of his utterances, might have
added that his mind was not especially built for the subtleties
of the philosophy of history; at all events, he dropped the subject hurriedly.

Not so Charles Francis Adams. President of the Massachusetts Historical Society and author of that model two-volume
study of local history, *Three Episodes of Massachusetts History*
(1892), Adams headed the Association in 1901; and in his
message he dealt with the general theme that was increasingly
obsessing his brother. Like Henry, he was not content with the
kind of history that was safe and harmless; like Henry, he favored the search for historical laws. He emphasized that the
continuity of history made it possible for the gildsman to anticipate that the future would present no novel features. Reflecting perhaps the influence of his position as one of the leading
railroad experts of his time, he pointed out that the continuity
of history enabled the gildsman to diagnose and measure the factors at work in the present with a view to surmising the nature
and extent of the readjustments that lay ahead. Adams thought
that final historical results embodied "the outcome, not of some
of the antecedent influences, or even of those among them most
preponderating, but of all of them, combined and forever inter-
acting." As a rule, however, he considered moral and historical
factors the most important ones. While he did not deny that
the economic influence was "vital," he viewed it as of less importance than either the moral or the historical influence, declaring that into American slavery and imperialism, for instance,
economic considerations did not enter as "controlling factors."

Good social Darwinist that he was, Adams believed it possible to deduce laws from mankind's experiences; and some of these laws, he thought, needed very much to be drawn for the United States of 1901. Turning to the theme which he had handled quite differently in *Imperialism and the Tracks of Our Forefathers* (1899),[14] he pointed out that Americans ought to understand that their imperialism, far from being a sudden development, was long in preparation and inevitable. It came in response to an "inscrutable law of nature"; it was just another "phase of natural evolution, working itself out, as in the case of Rome twenty-five centuries ago, through the survival and supremacy of the fittest." Not one to shun generalizations, Adams had long insisted that if the gildsman was to make use of the teachings of history, he had to generalize.[15] Drawing, therefore, on Mommsen and Carlyle as authorities, Adams formulated the law that "every great, aggressive and masterful race tends at times irresistibly towards the practical assertion of its supremacy, usually at the cost of those not so well adapted to existing conditions." Even more meaningful to the United States of 1901 was a second law of imperialism, namely, that "the condition of dependency, even for communities of the same blood and race, always exercises an emasculating and deteriorating influence." This, said Adams, was the law that Americans would do well to keep in mind as they assumed the burdens of empire.

In the years immediately following Adams' message, the philosophy and science of history were again neglected in the presidential addresses. Alfred T. Mahan noted simply that it was the continuity of history that was the source of its usefulness. For this continuity enabled the gildsman to draw lessons from the fulfillment of "the plan of Providence" that was called

14 *Imperialism and the Tracks of Our Forefathers* (Boston, 1899), p. 26.

15 Henry Cabot Lodge, "Memorial Address," *Charles Francis Adams, 1835-1915: An Autobiography* (Boston, 1916), pp. xlvii-xlviii.

history, said Mahan, not concealing the religious prepossession that was implicit in much of his writing on naval history.[16]

Mahan's successor, Henry C. Lea, was likewise brief in what he had to say about the philosophy and science of history. He simply expressed his wariness of theories in history, stating that the theory-holding historian did not deserve recognition as a safe guide. So thought the American scholar of whose *History of the Inquisition of the Middle Ages* Lord Acton said that it was "the most important contribution of the new world to the religious history of the old." So thought the American scholar of whom Maitland said: "We trust him thoroughly because he keeps his gaze fixed on the middle ages, and never looks round for opinions to be refuted or quarrels to be picked."[17]

Theories, however, evoked no such response from the next president, Goldwin Smith, the liberal Anglo-Canadian publicist and idol of Andrew D. White. Addressing the Association in 1904 on "The Treatment of History," Smith, who had lost patience with research long before he became an octogenarian, drew liberally on the lectures that he had delivered between 1859 and 1861 as regius professor of modern history at Oxford. History was no science, nor could it be made one, he said, as he had said more than four decades before.[18] To start with, free will ruled out the possibility of establishing a science of history. Besides, valid inductions would require that the phenomena be "completely before us." Man's history, however, had still not reached completion; nor was it known how far from completion it was; and it was not known what phenomena its course might yet reveal. Auguste Comte, said Smith, using one

16 Julius W. Pratt, "Alfred Thayer Mahan," in William T. Hutchinson, ed., *op. cit.,* p. 216.

17 Quoted in Charles Homer Haskins, "Henry Charles Lea," in *Studies in Mediaeval Culture* (Oxford, 1929), pp. 258-59.

18 *Lectures on the Study of History, Delivered in Oxford, 1859-61* (New York, 1866), p. 30.

of his favorite illustrations,[19] had assumed that the positive stage was the final stage in the history of mankind; but there was no telling what "totally new developments" lay ahead, developments which might well make the positive era far from the last in mankind's history.

According to Smith, history was loaded with accidents that often defied theories and calculations. It was by accident that Napoleon became a citizen of France, and such was his hatred of the French that for a time he had even considered joining the British navy. On a number of occasions, moreover, he could have been killed, and his death would have altered "the whole current of history." Examples of this sort, said Smith, could be presented endlessly, and they made impossible the establishment of a science of history. Indeed, the essence of science was prediction, so that a science of history would make events predictable; but Smith had almost no confidence at all in historical forecasts. Had not even the wisest of statesmen made ridiculous prophecies concerning the course of history? Had not Pitt anticipated a long period of peace on the very eve of the French Revolutionary Wars? Had not Palmerston considered German unification a lost cause at the very time that Bismarck was moving into action? If such able statesmen had missed the mark, Smith, who, as one of the intellectual leaders of the Manchester School, had known some of the chief political figures in Victorian England,[20] could see small hope for the mere historian. He doubted that the time would ever come when the historical study would take the form of a scientific treatise.

While Smith denied the possibility of formulating a valid science of history, he did not deny the possibility of formulating a valid philosophy of history. He maintained, as he had long been doing, that the philosophy of history opened up a vast field for rewarding studies that would deal with "the interdependence of events, the connection of causes and effects, the operation of

19 *Ibid.*, p. 56.

20 *Reminiscences* (New York, 1910), chaps. XII, XV.

special influences general or personal, permanent or temporary, the distinction of epochs, the formation of national character, and above all the general progress of humanity." Although the stages outlined by a Comte hardly admitted of "perfect verification," they still threw considerable light on the history of mankind. Hence Smith supported the efforts of the Comtes who suggested historical stages and the Vicos who suggested historical cycles.

Even so, he cautioned that the writer on the philosophy of history was in danger of exaggerating the importance of some particular cause, whose influence he seemed to think he was the first to detect. Buckle sometimes overdid the effects of natural phenomena on the moulding of the national character of peoples. Other writers overstated the influence of the struggle for subsistence and class conflicts on the course of civilization. Smith did not deny that subsistence was basic and that classes, if not sharply drawn classes, were realities. His point was that the complexities of history had so far defied sweeping generalizations.

Smith considered it worthwhile for the gildsman to pursue the philosophy of history. He should continue to try to derive some meaning from mankind's past. Although the recently appearing volumes of the *Cambridge Modern History* did not help much along this line, the effort to find answers to basic questions should go on. After all, unbelievable hardships had accompanied man's struggle to better his social, moral, and spiritual life. Yet were "things tending to a result answerable to the long preparation, the immense effort, and the boundless suffering which the preparation and the effect have involved"? Or, on the other hand, would "the end of all be the physical catastrophe which science tells us must close the existence of the material scene"?

Smith was inclined to credit Vico with having been the first writer "to treat history philosophically"—though, as an afterthought, he admitted that the honor might possibly be claimed by

Aristotle or Bossuet. It was perhaps Smith's grudging acknowledgment of the religious philosophy of history that prompted
Simeon E. Baldwin, associate justice of the Supreme Court
of Connecticut and the professor who had done so much to en-
hance the reputation of the Yale Law School, to emphasize that
religion was still the key to history—and not a key that grew
rusty with the passage of time. A man who "lived constantly
in the mood of high religious conviction," a man who was "as
deeply religious as any of his Puritan ancestors,"[21] Baldwin
suggested in his message of 1906: "Ours is an age of more
reverence for human reason and less reverence for human authority. But as reverence for human authority becomes less, a
conviction deepens that men are subject to a power greater than
themselves. We may call it Nature, or call it God. What we
know is that it speaks by laws—invariable laws. What we feel
is that it is a thing of mystery;—too great to be measured from
earth; too far from man, near though it be at every step, to be
so much as seen in all its outline by his philosophy."

In a none too clear statement of his position, Baldwin stressed
the role of religion as an "inherent, universal, and eternal" historical force; and by religion he simply meant "a reverent consciousness of a power (be it law or spirit) manifest in nature
and stronger than man, and a sense of obligation to answer its
demands." Baldwin thought that it was the complex functioning of just such a force as religion—"vague, impulsive, constant in play, inconstant in intensity"—that accounted for the
historian's inability to make scientific predictions.

Naturally, Baldwin believed that the gildsman should write
in a religious spirit. Even as he dealt with technological discoveries, for example, he should remember that his reader would
view each new advance as "fresh proof of an intelligent creator,
and another step nearer to knowledge of what He is." The historian who did not hold religious beliefs was hardly in a posi-

21 *Records and Addresses in Memory of Simeon E. Baldwin, 1840-1927*
(New Haven, 1928), p. 43; George Edward Woodbine, "Simeon Eben
Baldwin," *Dictionary of American Biography*, I, 546.

tion to understand the influence of religion on others. He could scarcely appreciate that "if mankind is always craving heroes to worship much more it craves a King of Kings, eternal in the heavens. The thought of unity in nature—of a single purpose or power to which all that we see or know or feel is related—is common to most of the great religions. It is also a vital part of them. To those who are possessed by it, it seems 'a clue by which to trace back every event of history to its farthest source. It is distinctly a religious clue." Unfortunately, however, Baldwin led too busy a public life—he was soon to serve as chief justice of the Supreme Court of Errors in Connecticut and then as governor—to apply his key in any serious way to the history he knew best, that of colonial America.

Nor did Baldwin manage to win the support of one of his most distinguished colleagues at Yale, George Burton Adams, who addressed the Association in 1908 on "History and the Philosophy of History." Adams had been trained for the ministry, having taken a B. D. at Yale; but he turned to teaching, and rapidly developed into one of the leading American medievalists. In fact, the seminar he conducted at Yale became one ot the main centers of advanced historical study in the United States. Author of such widely-used volumes as *Civilization during the Middle Ages Especially in Relation to Modern Civilization* (1894), *The Growth of the French Nation* (1896), and *European History: An Outline of Its Development* (1899), Adams had tried to stress in his writings "the movement and direction of historical forces" as well as "the unity and continuous advance of history."[22] Nevertheless, Adams, in addition to writing on general history, also wrote detailed studies of English political and constitutional history, most notably *The History of England from the Norman Conquest to the Death of John* (1905), the one

22 *Civilization during the Middle Ages Especially in Relation to Modern Civilization* (New York, 1894), p. v; *European History: An Outline of Its Development* (New York, 1899), p. vi.

volume, prepared by an American in the important Hunt and Poole series. And it is likely that by reason of his detailed study of the English medieval past he developed a mistrust of keys to history and of ultimate explanations of history, a mistrust that he expressed at length in his presidential message of 1908.

Like Henry Adams and Goldwin Smith, he could understand the appeal of the attempt to formulate "a destined and knowable outcome for the efforts of mankind." He pointed out, however, that in the past the historian had seldom bothered with the riddle of man's existence and the final results of his works. Rather, it was the poet, the philosopher, and the theologian who had practically monopolized the philosophy of history. The historian, indeed, had neglected not only the philosophy of history, with its stress on directions and results, but also the science of history, with its emphasis on processes and laws; and for proof of this neglect it was only necessary to examine the writings of Robert Flint—himself a professor of divinity—on the history of the philosophy of history, writings in which the historian hardly appeared.

How was this avoidance of the philosophy and science of history to be explained? Adams, for his part, suggested that the pre-nineteenth century historian generally fell into one of two groups: the group whose chief aim it was to present "without ulterior design" an account of past happenings; or the group whose chief aim it was to make literature of history. The pre-nineteenth century historian, in other words, sought chiefly to make a contribution to knowledge or to literature, aiming "to tell artlessly, or with all possible art, what happened." The result was that by and large he did not deal with the science and philosophy of history.

Adams would not push his categories too far, acknowledging readily that they would not hold up too well if subjected to close examination. What mattered in any event was that the ideals of Ranke came to exert an increasing influence on the historian, encouraging him to use more careful methods in his study of historical facts; but Ranke's scientific history and the science of history were very different things. The advocate of the science of history, working on the assumption that man's behavior was determined by laws, sought to discover these laws in an effort to establish a science of history that would resemble a science like chemistry. The advocate of Ranke's scientific history, on the other hand, tried to use careful methods of research so as to achieve a more certain knowledge of the past. He did not aim to discover laws that would permit the construction of a science of history; he aimed rather "to ascertain as nearly as possible and to record exactly what happened." Hence the follower of Ranke tended to ignore the philosophy and science of history, leaving this for the poet, the philosopher, and the theologian to explore.

Adams did not wish to oversimplify the cultural milieu in which the early twentieth-century historian worked. Ranke's emphasis on the improvement of methods of research was, after all, only one part of the nineteenth-century legacy. Another part of it was the variety of new subjects that came into their own as systematic bodies of knowledge, subjects which used the same materials that history used, but subjects which were not suspicious of the science and philosophy of history. Adams was tempted to view these new subjects as "offshoots of history"; and history itself he was tempted to view as undergoing the divisions that philosophy had previously undergone. Nevertheless, he felt compelled to resist such views as being incorrect; the new subjects were so harsh in their criticisms of the techniques and aims of traditional history as hardly to suggest the attitude of "dutiful children toward a parent."

Adams distinguished five chief assailants: political science, geography, the economic interpretation of history, sociology, and social psychology. And though all of these were both independent and interdependent, he anticipated that sociology by virtue of "its all-containing and somewhat indefinite nature" would play the role of meditator and synthesizer. Adams, himself primarily a constitutional historian, found the political scientist the mildest of these critics; relatively he was so mild that Adams hesitated to include him, terming him not so much hostile as condescending in his attitude toward the historian. Yet he did include him for the reason that the political scientist tended to assume that the main purpose of the historian was to provide data for political science; and he tended to view political history merely as mankind's attempt "to give objective form" to the principles and laws that he was seeking to formulate.

Somewhat more critical of the historian was the geographer, said Adams, thinking perhaps of Ellsworth Huntington, who had recently joined the faculty at Yale and had already published *The Pulse of Asia* (1907). Indeed, the careless generalizations and exaggerated claims that sometimes figured in the geographer's works showed his determination to exploit the role of climate and environment in an effort to advance a "complete explanation of history." Even more opposed to the traditional historian was the economic interpreter of history. Adams hastened, however, to express his approval of the economic historian—he probably had in mind someone like William J. Ashley, the Englishman who taught economic history at Harvard in the nineties—as distinguished from the strict economic interpreter of history. Wary of a standard formula, the economic historian gave concrete instances of the operation of "influences among the most profound which have shaped human affairs." The economic interpreter of history, on the other hand, was haunted by the notion that economic forces provided everywhere the "final explanation"; if he was a writer like Antonio Labriola, the former professor of philosophy at the University of Rome, he made economics account for all of man's ideas, customs, laws, morals, sciences, and philosophies. Adams was disturbed by the disregard for historical truth that accompanied the blanket application of the economic interpretation: he was not one to view the Reformation simply as an economic revolt of the German people; he was not one to accept the law of diminishing returns or the growth of the division of labor or class conflict as the basic clue to history.

Even more vigorous than the economic interpreter's criticisms of the traditional historian were those of the sociologist, Adams declared. Most suspicious of the sociologist, he addressed these words to the members of the Association: "Let me hasten to relieve your minds of the apprehension that I am going to try to tell you what is the field of the sociologist. He is indeed lord of an uncharted domain, and I have no intention of attempting to supply him with a chart." What Adams emphasized was that the sociologist, one like Franklin H. Giddings of Columbia, aimed at "an ultimate explanation of human history." So, too, said Adams, speaking shortly after the publication of Edward A. Ross's *Social Psychology* (1908), the social psychologist grappled with the science and the philosophy of history, aiming to formulate the laws of psychic forces in order to explain national traits, military conquests, and artistic, literary, and religious developments.

Much as the newer investigators differed among themselves, some conjuring with metaphysics, others repudiating metaphysical links, all joined in invoking the scientific label to characterize their methods, aims, and results. All joined, moreover, in regarding the historian with scorn; and all viewed their own work "as of a higher type, more truly scientific, and more nearly final in character than ours." Detailing his position, Adams pointed to Lamprecht's *Deutsche Geschichte* and Ferrero's *Grandezza e Decadenza di Roma,* two of the foremost products of the recent growth of interest in the science and philosophy of history, works which reflected the departure from Ranke's methods and ideals as well as the new respect for imaginative touches and sweeping statements. Unhappily, said Adams, these were the works that were likely to set the pattern for much of the historiography of the future. For the five-front war on traditional historical scholarship, evident in the growth of interest in the philosophy and science of history, was not a momentary affair but an indication perhaps that the present age was moving from investigation to speculation.

Time was when it had sufficed for the historian to discover the facts and the circumstances that shaped them. Increasingly, however, he found newer investigators in the field, scholars who were concerned not with facts but with ultimate explanations, determining forces, and historical laws—in short, with the philosophy and science of history.

> No matter what disguise may be worn in a given case, [Adams said] no matter what the name may be by which a given group elects to call itself, no matter how small, in the immensity of influences which make the whole, may be the force in which it would find the final explanation of history, the emphatic assertion which they all make is that history is the orderly progression of mankind to a definite end, and that we may know and state the laws which control the actions of men in organized society. This is the one common characteristic of all groups I have described; and it is of each of them the one most prominent characteristic.

What was the historian to do in the face of the advances of these invaders? Was he merely to ignore or deny the value of results achieved in ways other than his own? Adams thought it pointless to underestimate or disregard the historian's assailants. They were not reflections of an intellectual current that would soon disappear; they were here to stay. The historian, therefore, should make the necessary adjustments. Obviously, he should accept any convincing interpretations that the newcomers presented, and he should support every effort to bring old-timers and newcomers together, strengthening the bonds that united all investigators of the past. For the rest, he must discount much of the speculation of the newer scholars. He must stress "the tangled network of influences" that went into the making of history, pointing out the inadequacies of the shortcuts and oversimplifications that figured in the newer studies. Above all, he must continue his search for the facts that the newer investigators—eager for generalizations—found so distasteful.

Not that Adams was so rash as to deny the validity of the notion of a science or a philosophy of history. He was convinced that historical events were determined by forces acting "according to fixed law";[23] he was no less convinced that specific historical facts could be used to bolster up some final explanation of history. All the same, he contended that the historian must continue to concentrate on the establishment of facts, insisting that

> in our field of history, for a long time to come, the man who devotes himself to such labors, who is content with this preliminary work, will make a more useful and a more permanent contribution to the final science, or philosophy of history, than will he who yields to the allurements of speculation and endeavors to discover in the present stage of our knowledge the forces that control society, or to formulate the laws of their action. None of the new battle-cries should sound for us above the call of our first leader, proclaiming the chief duty of the historian to establish *wie es eigentlich gewesen*.

Adams failed to communicate his wariness of the philosophy and science of history to his successor, Albert Bushnell Hart, editor of the *American Nation* series and author of a recent attempt at a synthesis of United States history, *National Ideals Historically Traced, 1607-1907* (1907). Interested not in details but in *Essentials in History,* the title of a textbook series prepared under his supervision, Hart looked to the past for "things that count."[24] And in his presidential message of 1909 he urged the historian to search for things that count. Like Andrew D. White twenty-five years before, he issued a plea for that synthesis of findings which he considered the "final purpose" of historical study.

23 Cf. Max Lerner, "George Burton Adams," *Encyclopaedia of the Social Sciences,* I, 431.

24 *Essentials in American History (From the Discovery to the Present Day)* (New York, 1905), p. 7.

Himself impatient of research, Hart insisted that the establishment of facts was only incidental to the combination of facts, to the arrangement of scattered and seemingly disconnected facts into "harmonious wholes." He was convinced that the study of the past led the historian to the discovery of laws and the formulation of "some of those unsuspected generalizations which explain the whole framework of the universe." Charles Darwin, he said, singling out the individual whom he had once called "the great historical master of our age,"[25] had spent twenty years gathering the facts which enabled him to venture his generalizations. Like Darwin, the gildsman should marshall his facts so as to derive a "universally guiding principle," so as to discern the direction in which a people was tending; but before the historian could make safe generalizations and deduce accurate laws, he needed the help of the philosopher who would determine the laws of the mind. As for prophesies, Hart thought it best to avoid them, for the function of the historian was to treat of the past, not of the future.

Hart had nothing to say about the newer studies, whose emergence George Burton Adams had viewed as a reflection of the growth of interest in the science and philosophy of history. His successor, Frederick Jackson Turner, had much to say about them, and understandably so; for his own investigations of the frontier had led him to a remarkable familiarity with the data of some of these newer studies. Discussing "Social Forces in American History," Turner made sure to emphasize the varied and complex factors that operated in society. He thought that before keys to history could be found, before the ultimate laws of history could be determined, the gildsman had to recognize and study the forces at work in society. Such was the complexity of the past that no single explanation would do—whether it happened to be economic or psychological.

25 *National Ideals Historically Traced, 1607-1907* (New York, 1907), p. xiv.

Such, moreover, was the complexity of the past that the historian, the economist, the political scientist, the psychologist, the sociologist, the geographer, and the student of literature, art, and religion, among others, had no reason to work alone; and as long as each specialist continued to do so, his attempts to arrive at the universal laws of his special science were likely to suffer. The economist, for instance, said Turner, usually formulated his laws on the basis of contemporary conditions. He then proceeded to raid history for "justificatory appendixes to his conclusions." It was not strange, therefore, that the course of history was strewn with economic laws that had broken down; and their breakdown Turner ascribed to the inadequate statistics of the economist, his lack of sufficient historical-mindedness, and his faulty analysis of the transient conditions on which his laws were based.

Turner was critical of the unhistorical-minded economist who used illustrations from the past merely to verify laws that he "deduced from common experience by *a priori* reasoning tested by statistics"; but this critical view of the economist did not prevent Turner from venturing to sacrifice some of his own historical-mindedness. An admirer of "audacious hypotheses,"[26] he endorsed efforts to revamp the past in the light of the insights that the present afforded.

> What continuity and meaning [he said] are furnished by the outcome in present times of the movements of minor political parties and reform agitations! To the historian they have often seemed to be mere curious side eddies, vexatious distractions to the course of his literary craft as it navigated the stream of historical tendency. And yet, by the revelation of the present, what seemed to be side eddies have not seldom proven to be the concealed entrances to the main current, and the course which seemed the central one has led to blind channels and stagnant waters, important in their day, but cut off like ox-

26 Cf. Avery Craven, "Frederick Jackson Turner," in William T. Hutchinson, ed., *op. cit.*, p. 259.

bow lakes from the mighty river of historical progress by the more permanent and compelling forces of the neglected currents.

Turner emphasized that it was not only the past that threw light on the present; it was also the present that threw light on the past, giving it new meaning. Hence the gildsman should examine the contemporary scene not only for its own sake but also for the sake of "new hypotheses, new lines of inquiry, new criteria of the perspective of the remoter past"; and these new viewpoints, Turner insisted, the allied investigator was frequently in a position to suggest.

The allied investigator received no such favorable treatment from William M. Sloane, Turner's successor. Preeminently a Napoleonic specialist, Sloane had had much less occasion than Turner to draw on the findings of the newer studies for the purpose of his own researches. But he obviously associated these newer studies with one of his colleagues at Columbia, James Harvey Robinson, with whom he did not exactly get along; so that the "digs" at the newer studies, embodied in his message of 1911 on "The Substance and Vision of History," were probably designed in part for the benefit of Robinson, whose *New History* was soon to be published.

Like George Burton Adams, Sloane was disturbed by the drift away from Ranke's brand of history. The student with scientific aspirations, he pointed out, had renounced the name of historian and declared his independence from history, proclaiming himself a political scientist, an economist, a sociologist, or some other kind of specialist. Nevertheless, Sloane found the historian only slightly justified in viewing the rise of the newer investigator "with dismay," for his deficiencies were so prominent. The political scientist, for example, he said, without bothering to specify whom he had in mind, usually announced his adherence to inductive methods of research; despite this, he was frequently reckless in determining, stating, and explaining his facts. Even more reckless were the economist and the economic interpreter of history; often their procedure was as utterly theoretical, deductive, and barren as economics itself had been for so long a time, economics which went from dogma to dogma as each generation renounced the fixed laws that the preceding generation had established on the basis of conditions which were already undergoing change. It was, however, the sociologist who received Sloane's harshest treatment; for, after the fashion of George Burton Adams, he criticized the sociologist for attempting to fit the past into the straitjacket of a "predetermined theory" and for attempting to write history with a calm unawareness of the latest scholarly findings.

Perhaps there was no stopping the ruthless oversimplifications of "the rather noisy inventors of systems and doctrines"; but Sloane, like Adams, cautioned that many a historical generalization was premature in the absence of a great deal of preliminary research. Happily, he could detect in some quarters the emergence of some models of self-restraint: a political science that was historical in its approach, an economics that was genetic in its approach, and a sociology that confined itself to "a very small portion of the very small field of true history." Although Sloane again made no references to individual scholars, he may have been thinking of political science as understood by a Dunning, of economics as understood by a Seligman, and of sociology as understood by a Giddings.

Sloane counselled the historian to devote himself with more hope and confidence than ever to the plentiful harvest that still awaited his reaping. More than that, he counselled that if the historian was not only to stop losing leadership but was to regain something of his former position, he and his subject should undergo some modernization. He should recognize that he had only a "finite" mind and that he could not deal "with the infinite," Sloane said, thinking no doubt of Robinson. The gildsman, moreover, should relinquish claims to self-sufficiency and omniscience, and he should develop confidence in the ability of other investigators to track down accurate and useful information. Finally, he should renounce much of his traditional historical terminology and overhaul the words, words, words that figured in his vocabulary.

This process of modernization would present many problems. Fortunately, however, the historian had a powerful ally in the idea of the unity of history, so fruitfully employed by Arnold Heeren in his writings on the ancient world. It may well be that Sloane developed his admiration for Heeren in the period when he was serving as the secretary of George Bancroft, Heeren's translator.[27] In any case, he was convinced that there were no gaps, chasms, or abysses in the ten thousand years for which historical records existed; the continuity of these years was complete if only the historian could find it. He was convinced, moreover, that the idea of the unity of history, with its stress on the horizontal as opposed to the vertical approach to the past, promised to transform much of historical research; and he went out of his way to praise sociology for having pointed up the value of studying the past horizontally as well as chronologically.

Having indicated the need to modernize the study of the past in keeping with Heeren's idea of unity, Sloane proceeded to consider criticisms of history as a science. If anything, he found those criticisms remarkably static. They seemed always to hinge on the claim that the historian could not make predictions; he could establish facts, but he could not establish laws. These claims, Sloane thought, indicated that some of the "rather contemptuous matadors of natural science" were losing sight of the shortcomings of laws in their own domain; and with these shortcomings Sloane had become remarkably familiar as a result of his friendship with some of the most learned scientists on the Columbia campus: Ogden Food and Michael Pupin, the physicists, and Charles Chandler, the chemist. Meteorology, for example, said Sloane, even though it was a department of so exact a science as astronomy, was surely in no great position to stress

27 "George Bancroft—in Society, in Politics, in Letters," *Century Illustrated Monthly Magazine*, New Series, XI (1887), 475.

its ability to predict. And when science approached humans in the form of medicine, the results from the standpoint of prognostication were "amusing," to say the least, Sloane added, speaking perhaps from personal experience. Certainly the meteorologist and the medical man contended that with increased knowledge they would succeed in achieving a greater power to predict; but this was precisely the contention of the historian, whose predictions were easily as accurate as those of the meteorologist and the physician.

Even the novice, Sloane thought, could recognize some of the discarded notions of the sciences. Distinctions between the inorganic and the organic seemed to be going the way of the mineral, vegetable, and animal kingdoms; radiology was difficult to explain on the basis of the holy law of the conservation of energy, and, according to Planck, it made necessary a total reconstruction of kinetic theories as well as theories of energy; relativity was calling forth basic revisions of many a scientific notion; the law of gravitation continued to defy exact mathematical formulation; the Ptolemaic conception continued to explain the universe nearly as satisfactorily as the Copernican conception; and, as a framework, devolution worked as well for some scientists as evolution did for others. Obviously, moreover, instruments like the telescope and the microscope had marked physical limitations.

Sloane was not being critical of science just for the sake of being critical. Science, he thought, had much to teach the historian about the limitation of his field, the definition of his subjects, and the avoidance of the know-it-all phobia. But his point was that even those sciences that claimed to be the most exact achieved "at best but a more or less close approximation to law and prediction, a higher or lower degree of probability." His point was also that the concept of chance, as commonly employed in scientific circles, sounded not at all unlike a " factor beyond finite grasp." Besides, Sloane suggested that once biology was accepted in the ranks of the older sciences the concept of law needed to be redefined; for biology dealt with individuals who made difficult the formulation of universal rules of the sort that figured in chemistry and physics. The acceptance of biology, indeed, meant opening the way for conjectures and hypotheses that were "daring, limitless, vague, metaphysical to a degree never suggested by the humanities." Detailing his position, Sloane turned to the law of natural selection, which for all its usefulness and convenience had no mathematical formulation; on it no predictions could be based. Obviously, appreciable numbers of the unfit did survive and appreciable numbers of the fittest did not. Since alleged natural laws like the survival of the fittest, the attraction of gravitation, and the conservation of energy differed in the extent to which they approximated " the line of absolute uniformity," Sloane drew the inescapable moral that throughout the world of nature the test of prophecy was a relative matter, a matter of probability.

No wonder he saw reason to suspect in 1911 that the remark attributed to Socrates, that man was more subject to investigation than nature, would perhaps come at last into its own. With the movement of physics in the direction of metaphysics, with the drift of chemistry toward industry, and with the orientation of biology along descriptive lines, "all alike declining either generalization or prophecy beyond the present stage," Sloane thought that history and the other humanities would probably make the next big scientific advances; and he thought that it was not hard to find a level on which the test of prophecy would fall within the reach of the historian.[28] Himself no mean student of party government in the United States,[29] Sloane had more faith in the prophetic powers of the practical politician than in those of the weather man: the ward politician, with his remarkable understanding of the stable and unstable aspects of human behavior, often gave startling indications of his ability to predict election returns; and the statesman, Sloane added, making much the same point that George Bancroft had made, was a person who sponsored legislation and formulated

28 Cf. *The Balkans: A Laboratory of History* (New York, 1914), p. viii.
29 *Party Government in the United States of America* (New York, 1914).

policies in keeping with what amounted to historical research—
research which enabled him to foresee results. It was to this research that Sloane ascribed the element of stability in government. And just as the meteorologist would foretell the future
more accurately when he increased his knowledge of the factors
that determined the weather, so, too, the statesman would foretell the future more accurately when he increased his knowledge
of the factors that determined history. Chance played no greater
role in statesmanship than in weather-forecasting or medicine.
Mankind formed a part of nature, and "human natural laws"
were as much a reality as "material natural laws." Indeed, from
Sloane's standpoint, to trace cause and effect relationships was
to establish laws; and this involved not only science but philosophy—the effort to explain why things were what they were.

If it was a question of singling out some individual as the
historian's Newton, Sloane preferred to cast his vote for Hecataeus of Miletus, the Greek of the Persian War period. What
impressed him about Hecataeus was that he grasped what, according to Sloane, was the essential character of history; he understood that history did not involve all the past but only those
portions of it that went to explain the present. Herodotus, as
viewed by Sloane, was educational and not scientific; his work
was especially designed to serve as "a stimulus to posterity."
Thucydides, on the other hand, was preeminently scientific;
his intention was to explain and account for the present. Already, then, in the ancient world, history had revealed its educational, philosophic, and scientific aspects: it could save the
past for the enlightenment of the present; it could account for the
present by way of the past; and it could examine causal relationships in human behavior with a view to establishing laws.

Since in recent times the scientific element in historiography
was assuming increasing importance, Sloane proposed that the
gildsman seek a laboratory in some period of the past; and,
former Latin professor that he was, he suggested that from the
standpoint of the long perspective there was perhaps no better
laboratory than that of antiquity. Through the centuries the

Hebrew language continued to be spoken by a few people; Greek was still a living language; and examples from the Bible and from Greek history continued to serve as vital forces which guided men in their actions. In fact, Sloane, who had established his reputation on the basis of his lengthy life of Napoleon, did not hesitate to put part of the blame for "the last great cataclysm of modern history" on youthful Napoleon's reading of Plutarch's *Lives*. At any rate, he emphasized that all the experiments had been performed in the "laboratory of antiquity." Since hardly a single modern panacea had not had its advocates there, it was only a question of interpreting the economic, political, and cultural developments of the ancient world and of daring to "deduce results more permanent and practical than those of natural science, bewildering as they are." For the "laboratory of antiquity" provided the gildsman with a great opportunity to analyze that interplay of "necessity and liberty," which, according to Sloane, formed the essential stuff of history.

Though Sloane had faith in the establishment of a science of history, he had not succeeded in passing on that faith to William A. Dunning, his colleague at Columbia. This was clear from some of the brief comments that Dunning made in his message of 1913 on "Truth in History." A gildsman who had devoted his scholarly life to the study of European political thought and to the study of the period of the American Civil War and Reconstruction, Dunning was impressed with the complexities of the past;[30] so much so, that he could have small sympathy for the economic, sociological, metallurgical, pathological, meteorological, astronomical, geological, and even geometrical interpreters of history, who ruthlessly oversimplified the past in order to discover "the hinge on which man's whole career has turned." With all these specialized interpreters at

30 Charles Edward Merriam, "William Archibald Dunning," in Howard W. Odum, ed., *American Masters of Social Science* (New York, 1927), pp. 136-37.

work, Dunning conceded that perhaps the most petty and un-suspected fact might yet provide the key to history. Even so, Dunning, who had spent years studying ancient, medieval, and modern political thought, proclaimed himself one of those "de-luded creatures" who continued to believe in the causal influence of ideas and of spiritual and psychic forces. Unmistakably, he declared his lack of confidence in the power of economics and geography to account for social and political systems and phe-nomena. Karl Marx and Ellsworth Huntington, food supply, metal supply, climatic changes, the ups and downs of commerce, the fluctuating value of gold, and the law of diminishing re-turns left him unconvinced; they did not suffice to explain social and political systems and phenomena.

So it was that in the first three decades of the Association's history only four presidents—Henry Adams, Baldwin, George Burton Adams, and Sloane—centered their addresses on the philosophy and science of history. Several other presidents dis-cussed the subject in some detail. But most of the early presi-dents bypassed it or handled it briefly. Some stressed the dis-coverability of historical laws; some, the presence of God in history; some, the unity and continuity of history; some, the possibility of historical predictions, and some, the impossibility of such predictions. A few deplored the oversimplifications that grew out of the search for clues and keys to history. And George Burton Adams, most notably, insisted that much more would have to be known about the past before the meaning of history could be determined.

CHAPTER VII

THE PHILOSOPHY AND SCIENCE OF HISTORY: RECENT YEARS

IN the years from 1914 to 1945 the philosophy and science of history were again neglected in the presidential messages of the Association. Once more it was only a small number of presidents who ventured to deal with the subject in any detail; and several of these dealt with it in order to discredit its pursuit. For a brief time it did seem that Edward P. Cheyney's appeal of 1923 and Charles A. Beard's appeal of a decade later might help to overcome some of the deep-rooted fears of the gild; but the traditional distrust of the speculative and nebulous character of the science and philosophy of history proved to be too strong. Some presidents continued to point up the discoverability of historical laws; some, the unity and continuity of history; some, the possibility of historical predictions; some, the need to study allied subjects which might help to disclose keys and clues to history; and Henry Osborn Taylor, in particular, emphasized the presence of God in history. Nevertheless, most of the presidents either steered clear of the philosophy and science of history or dismissed the subject hurriedly.

When Andrew C. McLaughlin addressed the Association in 1914 on "American History and American Democracy," he made it clear that he had no objection to the study of economics as a key to the past. A specialist in American constitutional history, he had had occasion to use economic interpretations in studies like *The Confederation and the Constitution, 1783-1789* (1905) and *The Courts, the Constitution, and Parties* (1912). Like Dunning, his predecessor, however, he warned of the dangers with which the crude economic interpreter flirted. Speaking the year after the publication of *An Economic Interpretation of the Constitution of the United States,* a work which, according to Beard himself, was "used to justify opinions and projects . . . utterly beyond its necessary implications,"[1] Mc-Laughlin pointed out that the economic interpreter was tempted to read the present into the past, and in the process he discovered not tremendous complexities but the very things that he had intended to discover. McLaughlin believed that the historian must be cautious; otherwise he would find himself enslaved by the same economic man who had enslaved one of his neighbors.

McLaughlin, who was chairman of the departments of history and of church history at the University of Chicago, insisted that history dealt not only with material things but with things of the spirit; and he decried the fears that discouraged the historian from studying the unseen. He found that the scientist who conceived of life in mechanistic terms was "more nearly a ministering spirit" than the historian who merely catalogued events; he found that this scientist was more of a humanist than the historian who dreaded psychology and avoided mores and folkways for fear of becoming involved in sociology. McLaughlin's point was that the gildsman would do well to observe that the scientist had no fear of philosophy and metaphysics; that the chemist had no fear of atoms; that the physicist had no fear of unseen force; and that the astronomer had no fear of infinite space. Science had no fear of seeking "the causative, the unifying, the universal, and the eternal"; but history, unfortunately, was "afraid, industrial, materialistic, satisfied with product, keeping accounts, priding itself on its full storehouses," McLaughlin complained in 1914.

Two years later, when George Lincoln Burr, Cornell's medievalist, addressed the Association, he devoted a large portion of his message to a discussion of the philosophy and science of history. A scholar to whose enormous learning many a distinguished gildsman has testified,[2] Burr was the first president

1 Charles A. Beard, *An Economic Interpretation of the Constitution of the United States* (New ed., New York, 1935), p. viii.

2 See J. Franklin Jameson, "Introduction," in *Persecution and Liberty: Essays in Honor of George Lincoln Burr* (New York, 1931), pp. xvii-xviii.

to show any real familiarity with contemporary German historical thought—the thought of men like Wilhelm Dilthey, Eduard Spranger, and Georg Simmel. It was unfortunate, therefore, that his message was at times so lacking in clarity. In another sense, too, this was unfortunate. For Burr, erudite medievalist though he was, had done little writing during the course of his career, and many a gildsman would have liked to find in his message a real addition to his disappointing paper record.[3]

Drawing for the purpose of "The Freedom of History" on material that he had presented some years before in an essay on "History and Its Neighbors,"[4] Burr suggested that the historian had every reason to rejoice in the progress of the newer studies of society, for they were throwing fresh light on the past and lightening his burdens. With increased effectiveness, therefore, he could undertake the research that would enable him to understand man's efforts and experiences. Burr recognized that there was no ending the demands of laymen, of allied investigators, and even of some historians that a science of history be established; and he pointed out that these demands frequently implied a denial of the value of history as well as a willingness to absorb its methods and even its name. Had not Auguste Comte tried to turn history into sociology? And since Comte's day had not others tried to do much the same thing? Just recently, said Burr in 1916, Frederick J. Teggart, in his *Prolegomena to History,* had claimed the historical label for anthropology.[5] Certainly Burr valued the discussion of the idea of a science of history, but he deplored the inertia that encouraged thinking people not to think; he deplored the inertia which permitted history to rank as art in antiquity, as philosophy in

3 Cf. Roland H. Bainton, *George Lincoln Burr: His Life* (Ithaca, 1943), p. 95.

4 Lois O. Gibbons, ed., *George Lincoln Burr: Selections from His Writings* (Ithaca, 1943), pp. 316-33.

5 See Burr's review of the volume in *Mississippi Valley Historical Review,* III (1917), 521-22.

medieval times, and which was now operating to rank it under the appealing name of science. The classification of history either as art, philosophy, or science, he insisted, was simply a description—not a prescription by any means. Even those whom he styled "the logicians," writers like Benedetto Croce and Antonio Aliotta, found the frontiers between art, science, and philosophy vague indeed. And what mattered, in any case, was that the historian, unlike the philosopher, did not consider it his function to view and interpret human existence in its altogetherness.

Time was when for all practical purposes the historian monopolized the past; and the word *history* came to mean not only the study of the past but the past itself. Yet once the newer students of mind and society adopted the historical method, with its emphasis on the past in its being and in its becoming, they, too, insisted that they were investigating history. More than that, they insisted that there was no longer any need for history as it had been traditionally understood. How, then, could history justify itself? On what grounds could it lay claim not only to its hold on space and time but to its hold on freedom? From some neighbors who saw "some use" in history the gildsman could receive some acknowledgment—though not much —of services rendered. All those who studied human matters, Burr thought, would perhaps recognize history as a "laboratory of politics" and assign to it at least the "lowly task of hewer of wood." Even captious Henri Berr, the founder and editor of the *Revue de synthèse historique,* who sought to replace history with sociology, conceded that history answered some human needs. Certainly, however, Burr found that by far the most encouragement came from the champions of the "new idealism," from German thinkers like Wilhelm Dilthey, Georg Simmel, and Eduard Spranger, scholars who viewed history as basic to the sciences of the mind, which in turn they differentiated from the natural sciences as to aim and method. History itself they considered a science, but one that had methods of its own. And they stressed that history was an end in itself. It offered a way of travelling, of broadening experiences, and of understanding the complexities of life.

As a student of human freedom, Burr suggested that history disclosed one point, the importance of which could hardly be exaggerated, namely that "on the freedom *in* history—and so, perforce on the freedom *of* history—all our other freedom rests." Doubtless it was this kind of playing on words that led William A. Dunning to suspect that he was not quite sure of what Burr had in mind. Burr, at all events, pointed to the example of Ludwig Gumplowicz, the Polish sociologist who ignored freedom to such an extent that man became simply the puppet of a social group which in turn became the puppet of natural laws. Unlike sociology, history retained the individual as a lord of creation and placed constant emphasis on his freedom. According to Burr, then, the method of the sociologist threatened the freedom of history and consequently deserved to be viewed with alarm—the more so because the sociologist was not alone in curtailing man's freedom. He had as allies the anthropologist, the anthropogeographer, and the psychologist, among others. In these circumstances the historian had all the more reason to proclaim the importance of man's freedom; but in the event that he adopted the method of sociology in his effort to construct a science of history, he would join the ranks of those who made man the victim of "the great abstractions" and deprived him of his life as an individual.

Nor did the opposition to the idea of a science of history end with Burr's address. William R. Thayer made sure of that in 1918, the very year that saw the publication of the popular edition of *The Education of Henry Adams,* which Thayer, among many others, had been urging Adams to permit.[6] A biographer who had revealed in his writings on Italian history the subtleties of thought of which he was capable, Thayer emphasized in

6 Charles Downer Hazen, ed., *The Letters of William Roscoe Thayer* (Boston, 1926), pp. 250-51, 266, 271.

his message on the "Vagaries of Historians" that historical writing was seriously threatened by the gildsman's instincts for process and certitude, instincts which encouraged him to believe that he had to explain everything, that he had to make everything fit. As a result, said Thayer, he produced eminently logical and neatly connected studies that often did little justice to the complexities of the past.

Himself a man of strong convictions and of intense likes and dislikes, Thayer was quick to admit that the gildsman could never escape wholly from his cosmic prepossessions, his conceptions of life and the universe. In recent decades, he noted, the cosmic views of all thinking people had increasingly been shaped by evolutionary concepts, which, though they failed to bare the mystery of life, seemed at least to reveal something of the processes of life. And so, the writer of history, always subject in some degree to the currents of his age, proceeded to demonstrate the impact of Darwinian notions on his words and works. But much as Thayer appreciated the contribution of evolutionary ideas to the study of history, he wondered about the extent to which the historian should exploit them. Literary artist and poet that he was, he preferred not to push evolution to the point of obtrusiveness. He preferred to have it serve as a skeletal structure, which, while it determined form and movement, was yet hidden by an outer covering.[7]

Thayer, as a staunch individualist and an expert biographer, doubted the wisdom of applying to the study of human beings the rigid formulae of subjects like chemistry, physics, and astronomy, which dealt with "unthinking and soulless matter." And because the historian lacked the ability to foresee events, something that Thayer had often stressed during the course of his career,[8] he doubted both the correctness and advisability of styling history a science. Although, in some instances, the historian investigated his materials in a manner that resembled

7 Cf. *ibid.*, pp. 34-35.

8 *Ibid.*, p. 68.

the chemist's, there was no basis for concluding that the two types of material were the same or that the adoption of similar methods would make history a science in the sense that chemistry was one. Thayer thought that the less the historian aped the scientist the better off he would be.

Seeking to bolster his position, he turned to an examination of Henry Adams' *Letter to American Teachers of History* (1910).[9] He confessed that the *Letter* confused and baffled him at many a point, containing as it did enough science to meet the demands of the most scientific-minded historian, and far more than enough to go over the heads of most students and writers of history. In spite of some cryptic passages, however, Thayer found the central thesis reasonably understandable. Historical study, according to Adams, should take into account the mathematical and physical laws of man's development. The law of the conservation of energy, for example, should be embodied in historical writing. So, too, Lord Kelvin's law of the dissipation of mechanical energy, which replaced the law of the conservation of energy, deserved to be embodied in historical writing. From this law Adams drew some important deductions, basic among which was the idea that individuals and species were moving in the direction of extinction. Nor did Adams think that the historian should be content merely to understand this law: he ought to trace and illustrate its functioning in his writings. He should view the Peloponnesian War and the American Revolution, for example, not only from the political and military standpoints but also from the standpoint of the dissipation of energy.

Thayer granted that Adams' ideas were stimulating; but the difficulty was that the historian lacked the means by which to compute the extent of dissipation. Besides, what basis was there for favoring Kelvin's law rather than the law of gravitation or that of capillary action or the binomial theorem? Thayer, in short, was no follower of Adams. He could not escape from the

9 Reprinted in *The Degradation of the Democratic Dogma* (New York, 1919), pp. 137-263.

impression that Adams' proposals were designed to poke fun at the gildsman. Were they not utterly impossible of execution? Had Adams himself ever attempted in his own historical writings to engage in the enterprise that he was urging on others? Of course not; his nine masterly volumes on the administrations of Jefferson and Madison, said Thayer, were happily devoid of mathematical flavor and thermodynamical complexity. It was, indeed, a cause for rejoicing that the theory and the practice of Adams' historical writing clashed; that he filled his works with human materials, with sensitive and convincing descriptions, with admirable probings of character, with enriching references to history and literature, with stimulating, if pessimistic and ironic, reflections; and that when he described the interrelationships of people, the clashes of political parties, the plots of rival groups, and the frictions of international diplomacy, he described them not as instances of "abstract laws, but as workings of the human will through concrete human beings."

Thayer, who had corresponded with Adams in connection with the preparation of *The Life and Letters of John Hay* (1915), believed that the *Letter* could be attributed to Adams' craving for ultimate truth. When religion failed him, he turned to science for an answer to his many questions about the cosmos. Not being one to find in evolution a demonstration of the upward and onward character of mankind's march, he came to view cosmic energy in clock-like fashion, and he came to believe that, when at last the energy was dissipated, nothing at all would remain. Yet, according to Thayer, it mattered little that the gildsman drew cheerful or cheerless conclusions from his excursions into cosmology. When he was engaged in the study and writing of history he must combat the intrusion of his cosmic views, whether they happened to be cheerful or cheerless. The gildsman, he said, "should no more convert his history of a period or episode in the life of a people into a proof of Kelvin's law of thermodynamics than into a disproof of quadratic equations. The time may come when human affairs may be described no longer by words and sentences, but by a system of symbols or notation similar to those used in algebra and chemistry. Then it may be possible, as Mr. Adams suggests, to invent a common formula for thermodynamics and history."

Thayer recognized that there were likely to be those who, if they did not try to use history to demonstrate the validity of Kelvin's law, would still insist that history was a science and should be written as one. There were likely to be those, for example, who would try to demonstrate the validity of Vico's suggestions concerning cycles. But how could this be done? How to find "the inevitable sequence of events" that a really scientific proof required? What justification was there for the assumption that progress moved forward regularly?[10] Thayer regarded Vico's law of cycles simply as a "glorified metaphor"; it was no more scientific than the simile of life as a chrysalis and of death as the liberation of the butterfly. In this way Thayer took his stand against the attempt to adjust history to a theory—a stand that was obviously conditioned by his view of the first World War as a product of the German obsession with the theory of the survival of the fittest.

Nor did Thayer remain reticent about the science of history when, by reason of the influenza epidemic which led to the postponement of the meeting of 1918,[11] he had a second opportunity to prepare a presidential message. This time the biographer of Cavour, John Hay, and Roosevelt pressed for the repudiation of the dehumanized kind of history which dealt with men and women as mere abstractions or as chemical materials with fixed reactions. With no less vigor than Burr he deplored the idea that men were simply "soulless machines, pulled hither and thither by mechanical laws in a universe without morals." Yet while he disapproved of the search for a science of history, he approved of the search for the meaning of history. The gilds-

10 The views of Edward Channing and Jean Jules Jusserand concerning progress have been described above in Chapter II.

11 *A.H.R.*, XXIV (1919), 308.

man, he thought, should do more than catalogue facts; he should make sure to search for their meaning.

Among those who upheld the "soulless machine" approach to man, Thayer would doubtless have included Edward P. Cheyney, who headed the Association in 1923. For Cheyney, with a confidence and optimism that were rare in the period of postwar disillusionment, ventured to formulate a science of history. Preeminently a student of social and economic conditions and institutions, he had long been reluctant to attribute any considerable importance to accidental and personal factors in history—a reluctance that he had shown in his *Introduction to the Industrial and Social History of England* (1901), in his *European Background of American History* (1904), in his *Short History of England* (1904), and in his most important scholarly contribution, his *History of England from the Defeat of the Armada to the Death of Elizabeth,* the first volume of which had appeared in 1914. In all these works he had concentrated on what he had once called "the really great movements" in history."[12] And this was what he did again in his presidential message of 1923 on "Law in History."

Contending that petty causes did not bring about the great historical results often ascribed to them, Cheyney believed that accidental and personal factors were less important than a constitutional historian like George Burton Adams or a military historian like Charles Francis Adams thought. Even without the Huns, Roman civilization would have continued to decline; even without the Black Death, social and economic trends would have proceeded in much the same direction; even without black-eyed Anne Boleyn and passionate Henry VIII, England would have gone Protestant; even without the celebrated anti-Spanish and pro-English wind of August, 1588, England would have triumphed over a Spain that had already overreached herself; and even without George Washington, American independence

12 *A Short History of England* (Boston, 1904), p. iii.

would have been achieved.[13] Historical events, Cheyney thought, came "of themselves"; and he favored the rejection of causal explanations that rested on accidental and personal factors. Finding something inevitable about great historical changes, he insisted that they came about in response to "some inexorable necessity" that controlled the course of human events. And he was convinced that in degree as the gildsman studied the past closely, to that degree he would ascribe to accidental and personal factors the insignificance they deserved, to that degree he would emphasize the "great cyclical forces" that operated in the past.

> Human history, like the stars [he declared] has been controlled by immutable, self-existent laws, by what Mr. Gladstone in his sonorous eloquence once described in Parliament as 'those great social forces which move on in their might and majesty, and which the tumult of our debates does not for a moment impede or disturb.' Men have on the whole played the parts assigned to them; they have not written the play. Storms and pestilences and battles and revolutions have been of great significance to participants in them and have seemed so to those who have chronicled their details, but they have really been only ripples and eddies in the great stream. Powerful rulers and gifted leaders have seemed to choose their policies and to carry them out, but their choice and the success with which they have been able to impose their will on their times have alike depended on conditions over which they have had little control.

All this Cheyney found so self-evident that he hardly considered it necessary to point out that the laws governing history did not have to be apparent to exist; nor did he consider it necessary to advance arguments to prove that the course of history was controlled by laws or that the body and mind of man were parts of a complex world that was subject to laws, physical, chemical, biological, psychological, social, and historical. In venturing, however, to guess at six of these historical

13 Cf. Charles Howard McIlwain, *The American Revolution: A Constitutional Interpretation* (New York, 1923), p. x.

laws, Cheyney was the very first to proclaim his humility, his uncertainty, and his incompetence; and it should be added that he had done what he could to find out about the reactions of several natural scientists to what he was attempting to do.

At the head of his list of the laws that governed history Cheyney placed his law of continuity, that "all events, conditions, institutions, personalities, come from immediately preceding events, conditions, institutions, personalities." This continuity enabled the historian to search for the origins of things; it enabled him to trace historical phenomena back to periods of time in which only H. G. Wells and James Harvey Robinson would move with ease; and it enabled him to look into a future in which only Wells would know his way around. Obvious though this law was, Cheyney thought—erroneously no doubt—that it had been only recently accepted and applied by the historian; and it had hardly at all been accepted by the public, which still believed that Gutenberg invented printing, that Luther began the Reformation, that Jefferson composed the Declaration of Independence, that William II started the World War. When judged in the light of the law of continuity, however, these notions showed their superficiality. For everything historical resulted from something that had occurred previously, so that "the immediate, sudden appearance of something, its creation by an individual or a group at some one moment of time, is unknown in history."

Nor would Cheyney classify historical continuity simply as a fact; he would stop at nothing short of the label of law. After all, mere human will was powerless to accomplish any great break in historical continuity. The parliamentarian of 1649 might well declare the abolition of the kingship and of the House of Lords, but in the last analysis historical continuity accounted for the short life of the English republic. The French Revolutionist might well strive to remake society and government, but historical continuity accounted for the restoration of much that was of pre-Revolutionary vintage. And even as the Association was meeting in 1923, Weimar Germany and the Russia of the New Economic Policy were in the process of coming to terms with this law. They were discovering how impossible it was to make any great breach in historical evolution.

The second of Cheyney's laws was one of impermanence, and in its treatment he used material from an old address on "The Agitator in History."[14] The decline and fall of political powers, he said, could not be dismissed merely as historical accidents. The real explanation lay in a law of mutability, to which the key could perhaps be provided by biology and paleontology, with their emphasis on the extinction of those specialized species that failed to adjust to altered conditions. History certainly testified to the frequent operation of this law of decay, demonstrating that the nation that was politically and socially unadaptable could not survive. In the light of this law, conservatism took on a new meaning; instead of preserving the status quo, it worked to wreck it. Personally, Cheyney had come to believe that individualism would give way increasingly to socialism—a point of view that he was to express best in his *Modern English Reform* (1931)—but he did not mention this when he stated the implications of his second law for the United States. He did suggest that hundred per cent Americans were more of a menace to the American way than smaller percentage Americans. The British had renounced some of their older imperial notions, and their Empire survived; Americans had stretched their Constitution beyond the confines of its few thousand words, and it continued to thrive. But what would happen to the United States if it scorned the League of Nations and clung to isolationist doctrines that did not fit into a "world that has been made essentially one by economic and intellectual changes?" The law of impermanence provided the answer, said Cheyney, who, as the author of the *European Background of American History* (1904) had long since stressed "the relation of America to Europe."[15]

14 *Law in History and Other Essays* (New York, 1927), pp. 30-63.

15 *European Background of American History, 1300-1600* (New York, 1904), p. xxviii.

Cheyney's reference to the one-world idea led him logically to the formulation of a third law, which, though it sounded like a pious hope, he proclaimed a law of history. This was the law of interdependence, according to which mankind formed a single unit despite the existence of many nationalities; therefore, any harm done by any part of mankind to any other part was a defeat for all of humanity. Using the recent occupation of the Ruhr to illustrate the functioning of this law, Cheyney showed the same moderation that he had shown in the period of the first World War.[16] France, he declared, could not make up for its losses at German expense without at the same time undermining its own prosperity and that of Europe as a whole; the inexorable law of interdependence, which worked without reference to human desires and controls, would see to that.

Fourth in Cheyney's list came his law of democracy, which guaranteed the ultimate failure of all those who thought and acted along monarchical and aristocratic lines. Drawing on material that he had presented in a public lecture on "Historical Tests of Democracy,"[17] Cheyney noted that there were many factors at work assuring the advance of democracy. Besides, any comparative study of government was bound to demonstrate the superiority of democracy—especially since its meaning was being expanded to embrace spheres other than the political. Cheyney did not deny that proof of the existence of this fourth law had to be largely drawn from the recent past, which betrayed a sprouting not only of democracy but of dictatorship; but he asserted in 1923 that Mussolini, Lenin, and Poincaré were sure to fail, for they were working against a basic historical law.

Closely allied with this law of democracy was Cheyney's law of necessity for free consent. Permanent compulsion, he insisted, defied human nature, and in the long run government by the consent of the governed was the only possibility. For, when consent

16 *A.H.R.*, XLIV (1939), 237.

17 *Law in History and Other Essays*, pp. 90-129.

was lacking, protest, resistance, and rebellion were sure to be the consequences. Of course, Mussolini had proclaimed the failure of freedom, but he merely showed how little he knew of the past. Historically, the great failure was force, not freedom. How long did Bismarck's policies of blood and iron succeed? How long did the terms of the Treaty of Frankfort last? And how long would it take before the provisions of the Treaty of Versailles would be wrecked? Cheyney did not deny that the law of free consent seemed to be more often violated than observed, but these instances of the disregard of the law demonstrated all the more effectively the impermanance of force in history.

Concluding his list, Cheyney set forth a law of moral progress, according to which ethical considerations in human behavior were gaining at the expense of influences of a material kind. In ancient and medieval times, greed for wealth, land, or slaves sufficed to bring on a war, said Cheyney, doubtless disturbing many an ancient historian and medievalist. In modern times, on the other hand, Cheyney thought that "better reasons have been offered, have indeed existed. National independence or security, local liberties, religious or political sympathy, protection of the oppressed, the defense of an ideal—the professed motives for which modern governments and nations have gone to war— belong to a higher group of incentives than those of the wars of antiquity or the Middle Ages." Cheyney granted that these modern motives involved, in part, elements of "camouflage." Yet though economics loomed large in the causation of the first World War, for example, the truth remained that "many higher causes were involved. The people, always more moral than their rulers, would not at any time within the last four centuries have supported their governments in wars merely of plunder, aggression, or revenge."

As in time of war, so in time of peace, moral progress was taking place. Serfdom and slavery belonged to the past; so did flagellation. Women were coming more and more into their own; so were workers and tenants. As a rule, moral influences were becoming increasingly important in the conduct of the affairs of the family, the nation, and humanity at large. Indeed, when international relations did not seem to be faring too well, Cheyney found it consoling "to consider how recently humanity has risen to the realization of its international duties, and yet how sure is its progress toward that realization, for it is a progress governed by law."

Having formulated his six laws, Cheyney took pains to stress the same notion that Henry Adams had stressed in 1894 when he cited Galileo's *E pur si muove*. The gildsman, he said, must accept historical laws, regardless of his personal inclinations. He could no more impede their operation than the scientist could impede the workings of the laws of gravitation, chemical affinity, or organic evolution. Once they were discovered and elaborated, moreover, Cheyney, social reformer that he was, believed that they would serve the cause of human happiness to a much greater degree than physical, psychological, or biological laws. Operating in the past, the present, and the future, they could provide mankind with a much-needed guide to both present and future behavior. "If we knew the laws of history," said Cheyney, "we might reason and act with the same intelligence and precision and anticipation of success with which the engineer acts in conformity with the known laws of physics, or the astronomer with the laws of astronomy, or the cattle breeder with the Mendelian law of inheritance." So it was that Cheyney, himself an amateur geologist and botanist,[18] looked forward to a time when historical laws would form the chief preoccupation of the gild; to a time when meetings of the Association would be devoted to the discussion of laws formulated by talented young gildsmen and to the application of those laws to the problems of society and government. At long last the historian would be prepared to play his role as healer of both national and international ills. At long last he would have every reason to glory in the name of historian.

18 *A.H.R.*, LII (1947), 648.

Charles M. Andrews, the next president to address the Association, also had some encouraging thing to say about what he called in 1924 the "greatest and most important of all historical questions," that of law in history. Andrews himself, however, had paid virtually no attention to the question in his numerous writings on English, European, and American colonial history; he had been too busy accumulating materials. Perhaps, then, it was out of a sense of guilt that Andrews, abandoning the position taken by his former colleague at Yale, George Burton Adams, supported the search for historical laws. Attempting in his address on "These Forty Years" to account for the frequent reluctance of the gildsman to discuss and dispute the question of law in history, he explained that the subject was speculative in nature and remote from day-to-day historical study. But he urged the gildsman to give every encouragement to those who sought to establish a science of history; he should back the efforts of scholars like Cheyney and Frederick Teggart, author of *Prolegomena to History* (1916) and *The Processes of History* (1918).

The student of the science of history, Andrews pointed out, viewed the past in the light of the adjustments that man made to changing conditions and ideas. He emphasized that, as man increased his knowledge of nature, environmental circumstances became less important; and the importance of the individual likewise diminished "as intelligence broadened out more and more among the masses of the population and the collective man overshadowed the individual as a factor in these adjustment processes." Even so, the student of the science of history was forced to grapple with historical persons in order to determine the extent to which they could guide and deflect basic historical forces. As a specialist in the history of the Old British Empire, Andrews suggested that in all ages there were unintelligent conservatives who refused to recognize the impermanence of historical adjustments. Such people, he said, like Cheyney before him, simply prepared the way for resistance, revolt, and revolution, providing the student of the science of history with further demonstrations of some of the underlying laws and forces that governed the past. Certainly the processes of history varied with time and geography, but they were "ceaseless as the tides," and they enabled the scholar "to infer, in some particulars at least and as through a glass darkly, the relation of these adjustments and laws to human conduct in the future, and to predicate in a large and general way the trend of history and the tendencies that are to govern the future movements of human society." Beyond this, Andrews thought that the student of the science of history could not go, first, because he was neither a prophet nor a poet, and, second, because he was always faced with the reality of the historical person's free will.

Andrews' enthusiasm for the study of law in history did not extend to the study of the philosophy of history, an indication perhaps of the influence of George Burton Adams and of his own love of concreteness. The Condorcets and the Hegels, Andrews found, moved about in an unreal world, producing philosophic interpretations of history that were distinguished for their vagueness and unsubstantialness; and the result was that the present-day gildsman had great doubts about those interpretations. What Andrews objected to in treatments of the philosophy of history was the frequent recurrence of expressions like *progress, development,* and the *curve of social evolution.* According to Andrews, it was not at all clear that mankind was "moving steadily forward to a more perfect organization and the attainment of higher ideals"; it was not at all plain that the processes of history worked necessarily for the betterment of mankind, and that they involved a "continuous improvement" in keeping with the growth of man's intelligence and the increase of his knowledge. Loose, if convenient, words like *progress* and *development* defied precise definition; they referred to conditions about which there was little general agreement.

Andrews did not deny that such words, despite their inadequacies, did describe something that had occurred and continued to occur in man's history. Perhaps with Cheyney's sixth law in mind, he suggested that the philanthropic spirit and the urge to serve society had made marked advances in the last half-century; that decent language and manners had become more widespread than before; that the awakening of the social conscience was one of the leading accomplishments of recent times, so that, even though abuses existed, man's awareness of them and his determination to remove them augured well. But Andrews hastened to add that these particular manifestations did not "predicate absolute progress." For progress took place not because man had knowledge but because he was able and willing to apply the knowledge he had. Besides, change as such did not mean that man was becoming better in "such vital and somewhat intangible traits as self-mastery, self-denial, social responsibility, and regard for the generations yet unborn." The curve of social evolution was very broken, indeed; it rose at times and at other times it retrograded. There was no denying that the world was changing; but it was likely that there would always be widely differing views concerning the nature of the changes.

Some of these notions Andrews was able to explore further when he had a second opportunity to deliver a presidential address before the Association. But on this occasion he selected a subject on which he could talk with more authority, a subject on which he could lavish more than just platitudes. Having recently brought out *The Colonial Background of the American Revolution,* he turned, for the purposes of his message of 1925, to the English setting in which the Revolution took place. A gifted researcher, he deplored the frequent explanations of United States history in terms that were "pre-Copernican" in their simplicity, pointing, for example, to the widely-held view that British tyranny caused the American Revolution, a notion that ignored the complexities of the American colonial past. Andrews found it consoling that such oversimplified views were not confined to Americans. Had not Maitland, perhaps the greatest constitutional historian of all times, decried the over-simplifications that plagued English history? Andrews found it reassuring that the recent historian—he doubtless had in mind scholars like Osgood and Beer—approached the colonial era with a keener awareness of many of its underlying factors, realizing that no single explanation sufficed to account for the Revolution.

Andrews did not let pass an opportunity to stress the continuity of history. Revolutions, he declared, were never sudden in origin; they grew out of influences that were long in preparation. They were "the detonations of explosive materials, long accumulating and often long dormant"; they were "the resultants of a vast complex of economic, political, social, and legal forces, which taken collectively are the masters, not the servants, of statesmen and political agitators." Though Andrews regarded the American Revolution primarily as a political and constitutional movement, he was tempted to try his hand at an explanation that was based on what Cheyney had called the law of impermanence. Asserting that the pressure of ideas frequently caused revolutions, he proceeded to reexamine English relations with colonial America in the light of the impact of inheritance and environment on eighteenth-century ideas; and he decided that in the long run opposing mental outlooks proved more of an obstacle to peaceful relations within the Empire than physical separation or divergent historical tendencies.

Mid-eighteenth-century England, he said, making the same point that he had recently made in *The Colonial Background of the American Revolution,* had achieved considerable stability along intellectual, social, and institutional lines; and the formalities, conventions, and artificialities of English life and thought had the effect of closing the self-complacent "English mind" to novelty and change. Even the most thoughtful Englishmen of the eighteenth century viewed the status quo as the best that could possibly be imagined. The upshot was that the England of pre-American Revolutionary days saw little "progress" in gov-

19 *The Colonial Background of the American Revolution: Four Essays in American Colonial History* (New Haven, 1924), pp. 185-87.

ernment, social organization, or the humanitarian point of view. In this society, which worshipped immobility and held on to old defenses in order to hinder the spread of new ideas, traditional privileges and property rights were considered more important than human rights. Governmental and societal relations were viewed as rooted in the fixed order of nature; they were no more to be questioned than the fact that the sun would rise or that trees would bud in the spring.

This lack of adaptability, Andrews thought, was a tremendous factor in the American Revolutionary Era. Even though colonial policy had developed only falteringly in its early stages, it had become systematized by the mid-eighteenth century, so much so that the tendency was to consider colonial policy no less fixed than the constitution itself. Holding to the view that colonies were, by the nature of things, destined for a commercial and political status strictly subordinate to that of the metropolitan country, British authorities sought to maintain old-time mercantilist and political practices unaltered. This disregard of what Cheyney had called the law of impermanence and of what Andrews himself considered "history's most characteristic feature" —change—made likely a conflict with American colonials whose lives were dominated by unending changes. In a real sense, Andrews remarked, the American Revolution, like the nineteenth-century reform movement, was caused by the inflexibility of governing elements who tried to keep existing arrangements frozen at home and abroad. Either reform or revolt was sure to follow such efforts, Andrews declared, adding, like Cheyney before him, that progress could be stopped for a while but not for long.

Just as Andrews commended the search for historical laws, so, too, did his successor, Dana C. Munro. For a medievalist like Munro to take this stand was doubtless surprising. In his writings on the Crusades and in his textbooks he had given no indication of an interest in the search for historical laws. Probably, then, it was his friendship for Cheyney, whose colleague he had been at the University of Pennsylvania, that encouraged him to take the stand that he did. Probably, too, his service as a government expert in the period of the first World War disposed him to look favorably on the search for historical laws, a search that would serve the practical needs of society.

Munro admitted in his presidential message on "War and History" that the gildsman could not predict the future; perhaps his connections with the Creel Press Bureau and the National Board for Historical Service had convinced him of that. Just the same, he believed that the historian could use past and present experience in order to anticipate future probabilities, consoling himself with the thought that only some future generation could demonstrate the falseness of his predictions. Munro was all in favor of drawing lessons from the past to guide the present; he saw in the search for historical laws a means by which to overcome the backwardness of the social sciences in relation to the natural sciences. While the natural sciences were serving to increase national wealth and prolong human life, the sad truth was that the social sciences were serving neither to improve the organization and administration of government nor to make possible a better handling of problems that were being made more complex by the advances of the natural sciences. Hence Munro favored the investigation of historical laws—laws, he was convinced, which would increase the usefulness of the social sciences.

Nor did Henry Osborn Taylor, Munro's successor, neglect the subject of law in history when his turn came to address the Association. One of the outstanding intellectual historians of his time, Taylor had not hesitated in his writings on ancient, medieval, and early modern thought to view the past as a record of God's dealings with men. In his *Freedom of the Mind in History* (1923), he had confessed: "I do not altogether understand history; I cannot explain much that has taken place.

And I feel it safer to assume the constant or occasional participation of unfathomable elements—the animating and inspiring providence of God, the potent waywardness of human genius."[20] Much the same assumptions appeared in his message of 1927 on "A Layman's View of History," though not in such explicit form. Taylor reasserted, moreover, the faith in the unity and continuity of history that he had expressed in many of his past writings—and was again to express in his future writings.[21] He stated, for instance, that the fact of endless movement in the contemporary world suggested the idea that

> a like unbroken movement has brought all things to the present state of heterogeneous correlation as parts of a prodigiously variegated whole. Apparently it is one and the same universal movement that extends throughout our present world and reaches back through time. Within its sweep, past and present become a continuum, and our contemporary happenings are drawn into some real or conceptual unity. We recognize one vibrant current constituting an energizing and effective process. Each event is harnessed to the other, and the present emerges from the past. All seems an organic and possibly intelligent becoming.

Just as past and present defied barriers, so, too, knowledge defied barriers, convenient though they were. The sciences, far from being separate and distinctive, were mere aspects of one another that philosophy attempted to embrace; and all that prevented knowledge from becoming one in practice was the absence of a capable enough mind. Obviously, knowledge of man and of nature in their present-day manifestations was linked with knowledge of man and nature in their past evolution, so that there was no need to draw distinctions between knowledge of the present and knowledge of the past. All political and legal

20 *Freedom of the Mind in History* (London, 1923), p. 38; cf. Harry Elmer Barnes, *A History of Historical Writing* (Norman, 1937), pp. 291-92.

21 See, for example, "Continuities in History," *A.H.R.*, XLIV (1938), 1-19.

institutions, for example, had come into being either by gradual stages or by "notable mutation." Corporation law had many origins, but there was continuity between the corporation law of the present and that of the past, said Taylor, whose very first study had been a widely-used textbook, *A Treatise on the Law of Private Corporations* (1884).

Taylor was not one to adopt the approach of a Maitland; and in his eagerness to break down the barriers that separated past and present he ignored the danger of reading the present into the past. Insisting that the very forms that knowledge took for reasons of convenience gave proof not only of the continuity, but even of the singleness, of past and present, he noted that physiology, for instance, grew gradually, and that the present state of physiological knowledge embraced the whole past of the science. Present-day physics, too, he pointed out, grew out of its past, though more by way of sudden variations. As for philosophy, its past and present were one. Taylor, in a word, upheld the cause of "time-unity" in the approach to any subject, whether it happened to be science, philosophy, religion, literature, art, society, politics, or military institutions. Human life itself he preferred to view as "a universal and dynamic unity in its manifestations, past, present, and to come."

Taylor's successors, James H. Breasted and James Harvey Robinson, likewise preached the cause of historical unity—something, indeed, that they had been doing for years in the popular textbooks on which they collaborated. Yet if their comments on the subject proved to be brief, the explanation was doubtless that they had come to take historical unity and continuity for granted. Breasted was inclined to view the unity of history as perhaps the most fruitful conception of the modern historian. As an Egyptologist, he was naturally interested in furthering the study of early times. Understandably, then, he suggested that the gildsman who applied the idea of the unity of history could push man's past back to geological ages, link his evolution with that of other forms of life, and trace the later stages in "the upward course" of his life. So thought the Egyptologist whose *Ancient Times* (1916) had recently been attacked by William Jennings Bryan and defended by Clarence Darrow at the "Monkey Trial" in Tennessee.[22]

What Robinson had to say about historical unity was also brief. One of the most successful textbook writers of his time, Robinson was enthusiastic about the study of man's career in its entirety; and, as in his best-selling *The Mind in the Making* (1921), he urged that the past be viewed as "one gigantic episode in the history of humanity as a whole." For, if the historian was to demonstrate the intimate connections between the present and the past, he should take into account the "whole sweep of civilization." Accordingly, Robinson repeated the recommendation that he had made long before in his essay on "The New Allies of History," the recommendation that the gildsman pay more attention to the study of man's animal origins. Once again he welcomed animal psychologists as allies, just as he had long been welcoming social scientists in general as allies—despite their interest in the philosophy of history, an interest that had alarmed a gildsman like George Burton Adams.[23]

While Robinson merely mentioned the scientific gildsman's distrust of the philosophy of history, Carl L. Becker tried to account for it. The thoughtful scholar *par excellence,* Becker had indicated his preoccupation with the whys of history in practically everything that he had ever written—from his doctoral dissertation on *The History of Political Parties in the Province of New York, 1760-1776* (1909) to his recently published high-school textbook on *Modern History* (1931). Turning in his message of 1931 to the scientific historian's wariness

22 Charles Breasted, *Pioneer to the Past: The Story of James Henry Breasted, Archaeologist* (New York, 1943), p. 230.

23 Cf. *The New History: Essays Illustrating the Modern Historical Outlook* (New York, 1912), p. 82.

of the philosophy of history—a wariness that had already prompted him in his admirable essay on Turner to remark that he "would not willingly charge a reputable historian with harboring a Philosophy of History"[24]—Becker had this explanation to offer: the scientific gildsman found the past strewn with so many philosophies of history that had been demolished that he came to tire of tempting generalizations. He wished to turn away from interpretations and to concentrate on finding facts.

According to Becker, however, a scientific historian like Fustel de Coulanges

> deliberately renounced philosophy only to submit to it without being aware. His philosophy was just this, that by not taking thought a cubit would be added to his stature. With no other preconception than the will to know, the historian would reflect in his surface and film the 'order of events throughout past times in all places'; so that, in the fullness of time, when innumerable patient expert scholars, by 'exhausting the sources', should have reflected without refracting the truth of all facts, the definitive and impregnable meaning of human experience would emerge of its own accord to enlighten and emancipate mankind. Hoping to find something without looking for it, expecting to obtain final answers to life's riddle by absolutely refusing to ask questions—it was surely the most romantic species of realism yet invented, the oddest attempt ever made to get something for nothing!

This is not to say that Becker himself believed in the possibility of formulating a philosophy of history which would have universal validity. His point was that the historian viewed things in the process of their becoming, but he could arrive only at a tentative understanding of man and his world, because man's world was not yet finished; it was still very much "in the making." Time was the great enemy of the "universally valid philosophy." Just as Becker denied the possibility of formulating

24 *Everyman His Own Historian: Essays on History and Politics* (New York, 1935), p. 207.

a *philosophy* of history that would have universal validity, so, too, he denied the possibility of formulating a *science* of history that would have universal validity. Himself one of the profoundest commentators on Henry Adams—one who was inclined not to estimate "too highly" Adams' ideas on the science of history[25]—Becker thought it impossible to present history "in terms of universally valid mathematical formulas"; he thought it impossible to reduce history to a "verifiable set of statistics." The gildsman knew nothing at all about most historical events. Nor could he even be sure of the small number of those he thought he knew well. Unable to revive historical events, he had no way of subjecting them to direct observation or testing.

Some of these points made by Becker in 1931 were reemphasized two years later in Charles A. Beard's "Written History as an Act of Faith," an address that indicated the remarkable extent to which Beard, despite the heavy demands made on his time by his numerous writings on United States history and politics, had yet been able to keep up with the literature on recent European historical thought. No isolationist—or continentalist—in matters of scholarship, Beard, more than any president since Burr in 1916, showed his familiarity with what European writers were thinking about the nature of history; and the points of view he set forth in his presidential message he was to develop further in such articles and books as "That Noble Dream,"[26] "Currents of Thought in Historiography,"[27] *The Nature of the Social Sciences* (1934), *The Open Door at Home* (1934), and *The Discussion of Human Affairs* (1936).

Beard made it clear that he disapproved of the scientific, artistic, theological, philosophic, and literary labels that were frequently attached to history, for history as actuality had innumerable aspects, of which science, art, theology, philosophy, and literature were simply a few. He also made it clear that he dis-

25 *Ibid.*, p. 163.
26 *A.H.R.*, XLI (1935), 74-87.
27 *Ibid.*, XLII (1937), 460-83.

approved of the Hegels who, despite their small knowledge of
the past, still pretended to detect the deeper meaning of history.
Beard thought that the historian had only one way of handling
the Hegels—just as he had only one way of treating scientists,
artists, theologians, and literary men. All of them he must view
in the light of the ideas and interests of their times.

In many of his writings Beard had shown himself to be "a
great stickler for semantics"; and in his presidential message he
made sure to state the meaning of the Germanic labels by which
he sought to differentiate between several kinds of history—
something that he was to continue to do in subsequent publications.[28] History as actuality, he said, referred to everything
that man had "done, said, felt, and thought" from the time he
began his career on the planet. History as record referred to the
monumental, documentary, and symbolic remains that provided evidence concerning past actualities. Most of all, history
referred to "thought about past actuality, instructed and delimit-
ed by history as record and knowledge—record and knowledge
authenticated by criticism and ordered with the help of the scientific method." Though Beard viewed this as "the final, positive,
inescapable definition," he considered it one that was likely to
distress the gildsman who tended to speak glibly about the formulation of a science of history. He insisted, nevertheless, that this
definition harmonized with the most penetrating of recent thinking about the nature of history—with the findings of men like
Croce, Riezler, Karl Mannheim, Mueller-Armack, and Heussi.
Besides, it harmonized with the obvious reality that the historian
was bound to reflect in his works his national, racial, group, class,
and sectional interests.

According to Beard, then, the historian should recognize that
he was no scientist working "with things open to deterministic
and inexorable treatment"; he should admit that he was "more
or less a guesser in this vale of tears." True, there were several

28 "Grounds for a Reconsideration of Historiography," in Social Science
Research Council, *Theory and Practice in Historical Study: A Report of
the Committee on Historiography* (New York, 1946), p. 5.

escapes for the historian who refused to concede that he was no scientist. He could remain silent; he could retreat to some petty detail of the past; he could take to editing documents. Even so, the need to choose one document rather than another showed the inevitability of subjective intrusions. Hence Beard thought that the gildsman would do well to acknowledge the disintegration of the historiographical order which Ranke and his successors had envisaged. The gildsman should stop his servile aping of the natural scientist and return to his own sphere, that of history as actuality. Declaring his independence from the shackles of natural science, he should view science itself simply as one of the actualities that comprised history; and he should realize that, insofar as science could be accounted for at all, the explanation would depend on history as thought.

What Beard deplored in particular was the gildsman's appropriation of physical and biological conceptions—conceptions which worked to distort thinking about the past and conceptions for which Beard was later to criticize Arnold Toynbee in his review of the first three volumes of *A Study of History*.[29] Borrowings from physics, for example, were based on the causal notion that all occurrences were determined by preceding occurrences; historical events, then, illustrated laws that were discoverable, laws like those of hydraulics. Of course no student of the past—not even Marx—had ever succeeded in arranging deterministically the totality of history, but the supposition that this might be done encouraged the historian to continue to work out ingenious causal connections. When his results fell short of the desired pattern, he blamed not his erroneous assumptions but his deficient data. It did not matter that no single law, like that of gravitation, had been found to encompass all the past. The important thing was to keep searching, for the day of reckoning with historical law would soon come if scientific techniques were pursued tirelessly and if fact-ridden doctoral dissertations were produced on a mass scale.

29 *A.H.R.*, XL (1935), 309.

Not that Beard ignored the implications of a science of history—how above all it would enable an omniscient gildsman to predict the future. Indeed, he suggested that he who formulated a science of history would have the qualities usually attributed to God; and mankind, with its future disclosed, would have only "to await its doom." Nevertheless, Beard found it reassuring that some historians, questioning the bases of "physico-historiography," saw the blunder that was the attempt to order the events of the past in a neat scheme of "historical mechanics." But such was the fascination of science that they merely shifted from the sphere of Newton to that of Darwin. Did not the organismic analogy have great possibilities? So it was that the past came to be viewed in the light of succeeding cultural organisms which arose, grew, competed, and declined; and the historian, free of the pressure of physics, willingly moved on to bear the burdens of biology. Conscious of the complications that entered into the study of the past, he looked for an easy way out, and this he found in the techniques and procedures of the biologist. Though physics had failed to give the answers, perhaps biology might provide the keys that the historian was longing to find.

Soon, however, Beard pointed out, it became plain that the organismic view of history was merely a muddled variation on the determinist theme; for the conception of rising, growing, competing, and declining cultural organisms had significance only when it conformed to some larger hypothesis, theological or deterministic. If the historian persisted in holding to the biological analogy and even made his choice between the mechanists and the vitalists, he was still entrapped in a deterministic framework. In short, the validity of the notion of a science of history depended on whether or not a deterministic sequence could be applied to "the totality of history as actuality."

Beard emphasized that even the natural scientist could find laws only when events were really ordered objectively in deterministic successions; and it was on the basis of some of the events in a particular sequence that the scientist could foretell what would take place when other events in the sequence appeared. Beard did not deny that on occasion the historian discovered something resembling a deterministic sequence; but how long it lasted depended on the duration of "surrounding circumstances" which could not be embraced in a deterministic framework. The sad truth was that the scantiness of the sources made most historical events unknowable. Besides, "the imponderables, immeasurables, and contingencies of history as actuality" differentiated it from the data of physics; so that the events of history defied the use of any such instrument as mathematics.

Beard did not wish to give the impression that recent European historical thought had confined itself to overcoming the oppressive influence that physical and biological conceptions had exerted on the study of the past. Recent thought had also been concerned with the idea that historiography was "merely relative to time and circumstance, a passing shadow, an illusion." Plainly, the advocate of this type of relativity was a self-destroyer, for it in turn was relative; it, too, would pass. And so, said Beard, recent historical thought sought increasingly to turn to "the absolute totality of all historical occurences [sic] past, present, and becoming to the end of all things." This involved a grouping of historical events according to one of three general conceptions:

The first is that history as total actuality is chaos, perhaps with little islands of congruous relativities floating on the surface, and that the human mind cannot bring them objectively into any all-embracing order or subjectively into any consistent system. The second is that history as actuality is a part of some order of nature and revolves in cycles eternally —spring, summer, autumn, and winter, democracy, aristocracy, and monarchy, or their variants, as imagined by Spengler. The third is that history as actuality is moving in some direction away from the low level of primitive beginnings, on an upward gradient toward a more ideal order—as imagined by Condorcet, Adam Smith, Karl Marx, or Herbert Spencer.

What impressed Beard about these three views of history as actuality was that each of them involved an act of faith on the part of the historian. The hypothesis of chaos denied the possibility of ordering events. The cyclical hypothesis permitted an ordering of events provided that all kinds of embarrassing contradictions were omitted. The same was true of the hypothesis of movement. Thus, whether he was aware of it or not, the gildsman, when he studied history, performed "an act of faith, as to order and movement"; even as he wrote he was compelled to act, and acting meant the making of choices that betrayed some conception of the nature of history as actuality. In the last analysis Beard thought that the gildsman's faith rested on the subjective belief that it was possible to arrive at the truth of how history moved.

All this was not to say that Beard viewed the writings of the so-called scientific historian as a "useless" venture nor that he favored the abandonment of scientific techniques. Insisting that the historiography of the last half-century had made possible "achievements of value beyond calculation," he noted that the stress on investigation and verification had worked to dispel the confusion and darkness which had previously beclouded many a phase of history. It was only the scientific method that could enable the historian to arrive at the facts of history. Beard believed, indeed, that the scientific method, as applied to history, had "a value in itself—a value high in the hierarchy of values indispensable to the life of a democracy. The inquiring spirit of science, using the scientific method, is the chief safeguard against the tyranny of authority, bureaucracy, and brute power. It can reveal by investigation necessities and possibilities in any social scene and also offerings with respect to desirabilities to be achieved within the limits of the possible." Still, no matter how valuable and essential the scientific method was to the historian, Beard thought that it ought to be viewed in the light of its inadequacies; it was necessary once and for all to renounce the misleading notion that if long and carefully enough pursued the scientific method would permit the formulation of a science of history which would encompass the totality, or at least some large segment, of history as actuality.

According to Beard, who had long been concerned with "the great case of Mankind vs. Chaos,"[30] the present-day gildsman should make up his mind about the disclosures of recent historical thought. For selfish reasons he could evade those disclosures altogether. Preferably, however, he would expand his knowledge of the past and clarify and enlarge his "frame of reference"—something that he could do by considering carefully the interplay of ideas and interests in history. All this would doubtless occasion many hardships; and, like Henry Adams almost forty years before, Beard warned of the likelihood of opposition from organized religion, the state, capital, and labor. But he himself had faced considerable opposition during the course of his career,[31] and perhaps for this reason he was encouraged to urge the gildsman to try to find out whether the world moved, and, if it did, the direction in which it moved. If the gildsman concluded that it did not move, he could only speak "the pessimism of chaos." If, on the other hand, he concluded that it did move, he had to determine whether the movement was backward or forward. Did it move in the direction of arrangements that had existed in some previous year or century? Or did it move toward capitalist or proletarian dictatorship or collectivist democracy? Speaking at a time when the United States was concluding one year under the New Deal, Russia one year under the second Five-Year Plan, and Germany one year under national socialism, Beard did not conceal his own view of the matter, which he had already expressed in a number of his writings, ranging from his first book, *The Industrial Revolution*

30 *Cross Currents in Europe To-day* (Boston, 1922), p. v.

31 "What Professor Beard Said about the Flag," *New Republic*, VII (1916), 18; "Letter of Resignation from Columbia University," *School and Society*, VI (1917), 446-47.

(1901), to his recently published study of the New Deal, *The Future Comes* (1933). This was the view that the world was moving in the direction of collectivist democracy, a conclusion that Beard based on his study of long-time historical tendencies as well as on his faith in man's invincible spirit.

In the dozen years that followed Beard's address of 1933, the science and philosophy of history were largely ignored by the presidents in their messages to the Association. No doubt Charles H. McIlwain, the authority on ancient and medieval political theory and English constitutional history and one of the most past-minded scholars of his time, expressed the reaction of many a gildsman when, in 1937, he voiced his suspicions of ventures in prophecy that took place in the name of the philosophy of history. True, there were Presidents William E. Dodd, Guy Stanton Ford, and Arthur M. Schlesinger who, like Beard, believed that the tendency of history was in the direction of collectivist democracy. Certainly, however, the great hopes that Cheyney had voiced back in 1923 were not being realized: the search for laws in history was hardly the major preoccupation of the gildsman.

On occasion, a president did return to one of Cheyney's laws. In 1937, the year of the recession, Guy Stanton Ford noted that history was a record of endless changes, but he noted also that this was such an obvious fact that the American of the thirties hardly needed a Spengler to tell him of impermanence; Ford, at any rate, avoided the use of the word *law*. Similarly, when Carlton J. H. Hayes reasserted what to Cheyney had been a law, he too avoided the use of the word. Doubtless influenced by what he had recently seen of the impact of tradition on the conditions of Spanish life, Hayes made an appeal in 1945 for more attention to the continuity of history; and he made this appeal because of the widespread tendency of Americans to view history cataclysmically and to stress the new and unique qualities of things American. Himself the author of a doctoral dissertation on the Germanic invasions, Hayes found it reassuring that the historian, if not the layman, was generally wary of attributing too much importance to cataclysms. He understood that inventions, discoveries, and revolutions simply speeded up processes that had long been under way, leaving much more unchanged than changed. Hayes considered an awareness of the continuity of history indispensable to any understanding of the past. Accordingly, he urged the gildsman to treat skeptically popular ideas about cataclysms like the Russian Revolution, the second World War, and the atomic bomb. For it was likely that, despite them, the Greco-Roman and Judeo-Christian traditions in Western civilization would continue as in the past to exercise their sway. Hayes did not deny that change and progress were factors in history; his textbooks surely proved that. His point, however, was that change and progress could be measured and guided only when they were related to the "constants and continuities in human experience." Hence he could not emphasize enough that the effective teaching of United States history, for example, depended on an awareness of the truth of historical continuity. When, therefore, the gildsman began an American history course in 1776 or 1492, he was handicapped from the start. Unless he began with the ancient Greeks and the early Christians, he could not understand American history; he could not understand the real character of America as a frontier of European culture.

All in all, then, the presidential addresses of the Association in the period from the outbreak of the first World War to the end of the second World War dealt only rarely with the science and philosophy of history. European writers like Benedetto Croce and Oswald Spengler had little influence on the ideas expressed in the addresses; and Arnold Toynbee was not so much as mentioned. Certainly Cheyney wanted the gildsman to try to determine the laws that governed history. And Beard certainly wanted the gildsman to try to determine the direction in which the world moved. Cheyney and Beard, however, to judge by the addresses of their presidential successors, failed to exert much influence on professional historical opinion.

CHAPTER VIII
INDIVIDUALS IN HISTORY

SOMETIMES what the presidents thought about historical laws and the general idea of a science of history was closely connected with what they thought about the importance or the unimportance of the personal factor in history. Some of the presidents who pointed up the influence of individuals denied the possibility of formulating historical laws and a science of history; witness Smith, Burr, and Thayer. On the other hand, some of the presidents who had confidence in the possibility of formulating historical laws and a science of history minimized what Disraeli had called "the influence of the individual character"; witness, above all, Cheyney. This is not to say that the presidents dealt with historical persons only in connection with historical laws. They dealt with them in other connections, too. Some presidents called attention to the need to save particular historical figures from the adulation of zealots and the hostility of iconoclasts; some, to the need to rescue undeservedly forgotten historical persons; some, to the need to judge individuals in the light of their own setting; and others, to the need to judge them by other standards.

Andrew D. White was a great reader of biographies; George L. Burr, one of his closest friends at Cornell, thought that he was perhaps more drawn to biographical literature than to any other kind of writing.[1] Indeed, White was to give considerable attention to the role of individuals in his own post-presidential works: *A History of the Warfare of Science with Theology in Christendom* (1896) and *Seven Great Statesmen in the Warfare of Humanity with Unreason* (1910). It was in this latter work that he went so far as to declare that "it has always seemed to me that Carlyle uttered a pregnant truth when he said that

1 Lois O. Gibbons, ed., *George Lincoln Burr: Selections from His Writings* (Ithaca, 1943), pp. 417-18.

the history of any country is in the biographies of the men who made it."[2] But this was quite different from the point of view that White had expressed back in 1884, the year when he addressed the Association "On the Study of General History and the History of Civilization." For in his message he took the same stand taken by John William Draper, the chemist and physiologist, whose studies of the *History of the Intellectual Development of Europe* and of the *History of the Conflict between Religion and Science* fell within the range of White's own scholarly interests. Like Draper, he insisted that the past should be approached less through the study of any individual man and more through the study of man in general.

White had a neat formula for determining the place of any specific individual in history, a formula that he had already applied in his textbook and booklet writings and one that he was subsequently to apply in his major works. If an individual contributed to "the great lines of historical evolution," he was important historically; if not, not. William Lloyd Garrison, for example, deserved to loom large as a historical figure even though in his own time he edited a small Boston paper that scarcely seemed worth noting; oratorical Rufus Choate hardly deserved to figure at all even though he did much to fill the republic with "mellifluous eloquence." According to White, Metternich and Napoleon III were really less important as historical persons than Stein and Pasteur, for they contributed less to "the great lines of historical evolution." White saw nothing wrong with judging people by standards that were not of their age. Interested in exploiting the didactic value of history, he saw no objection to viewing people in the light of times other than their own.

White's successor, George Bancroft, was a far more prominent historian; with the possible exception of Henry Adams, he was the leading nineteenth-century historian of America.

2 *Seven Great Statesmen in the Warfare of Humanity with Unreason* (New York, 1910), p. ix.

258   HISTORIANS AND THEIR CRAFT

When Bancroft addressed the Association in 1886, he was well into his eighties; and, though he was still showing his ability to engage in historical writing and rewriting,[3] he obviously did not devote much thought to the preparation of his message. In his multi-volume *History,* the last revision of which had recently appeared, Bancroft had given much attention to individuals in American history. But in his short presidential message he made little reference to individuals except to point out that part of the grandeur of the job of the historian grew out of his concern with "men of transcendent genius, such as are vouchsafed to the race at great intervals of centuries." These God-given men of genius, however, Bancroft did not choose to discuss specifically.

William F. Poole, who headed the Association in 1888, had more to say about historical persons than Bancroft; but even what Poole had to say was only incidental to his treatment of "The Early Northwest." Preeminently a librarian and a bibliographer, he had done little in the way of historical writing to justify his election to the presidency of the Association. What historical writing he had done was largely in the fields of colonial and Western history;[4] and it was to the latter field that he turned for the purposes of his message of 1888. Speaking at a time when Frederick Jackson Turner was a doctoral candidate at Johns Hopkins, Poole, himself a mid-Westerner by adoption, complained that for much too long Easterners had been writing American history without taking into account the importance of the West and of Westerners. As a result, George Rogers Clark, for instance, was frequently omitted from treatments of the War of American Independence, said Poole, singling out one of the heroes whose praises he had recently sung in Justin Winsor's *Narrative and Critical History of America.* Clark, according to

3 Russel B. Nye, *George Bancroft: Brahmin Rebel* (New York, 1944), pp. 296-300.

4 See Ray A. Billington, "The Historians of the Northwest Ordinance," in Illinois State Historical Society, *Journal,* XL (1937), 406-07.

Poole, showed intelligence and courage of a sort that was remarkable in the history of warfare; and since his campaigns made it possible for the United States to secure the Mississippi and the Great Lakes for boundaries, he was an individual to whom the historian should give more attention. And there were other figures in Western history whom the historian should stop neglecting, individuals like LaSalle and Father Hennepin, the seventeenth-century writer on North America.

Like Poole, William Wirt Henry came to the defense of neglected historical persons, but persons of a more humble sort. Addressing the Association in 1891, the year that saw the publication of his three-volume family biography of Patrick Henry, his grandfather, Henry turned to his favorite historical subject —the history of Virginia, which he had treated proudly and patriotically in many an address and paper. Seeking to determine "The Causes Which Produced the Virginia of the Revolutionary Period," he made sure to mention the contributions of "men of great capacity." He pointed out, for example, that the members of the Continental Congress of 1774 were a most select group of men; but the important thing was that the localities which chose such men must have ranked "high in the scale of intelligence and purity to have had such men in their midst." Henry granted that now and then the gildsman met with historical figures whose genius and character enabled them "to direct, if not shape, the destinies of their countries." Always, however, he cautioned, the historian should remember that for all their natural gifts these historical figures were themselves the products of their setting; and so, if the historian was to explain their work, he must examine their setting. Descendant though Henry was of one of the most prominent of all Virginians, he expressed in his message his wariness of the great-man approach to history.

In a sense, however, Henry's successor, James Burrill Angell, favored a renewal of this approach. Angell himself had done

little historical research or writing, and he was therefore doubtless limited in the material on which he could draw for the purposes of his message. As president of the University of Michigan
and as a former minister to China, he was, of course, most
familiar with subjects like university administration and international diplomacy; and it was to the latter subject that he
turned in his message of 1893 on "The Inadequate Recognition of Diplomatists by Historians."

Too often, he complained, the scholar ignored important
features of diplomatic transactions, and too often he failed to
give well-deserved recognition to the talented diplomats who
negotiated important treaties. Even when the writer of a general history presented an adequate treatment of the results of
negotiations, he tended to overlook the diplomats whose labors
made possible their completion; in many cases he did not so
much as mention the diplomats. As a result of this negligence on
the part of the historian, who, in the last analysis, made or
unmade historical persons, "no class of public servants of equal
merit" had suffered so unjustly, had gone so unappreciated,
said Angell, putting in a good word for his fellow-diplomats,
past and present. Even a school-child recognized the names of
generals like Wallenstein, Marlborough, Turenne, Condé, Washington, and Greene; but Angell found it highly doubtful that even
a well-informed scholar would be able to name the chief negotiators of the Peace of Westphalia[5] or of many other major
treaties. No question about it, treaty-makers, with the exception
of those who attended the Congress of Vienna, had become forgotten men, whose labors were recognized only in specialized
works. Though George Bancroft and Richard Hildreth stressed
the importance of diplomacy and diplomats, those who wrote
the manuals failed as a rule to follow their example. Even so
splendid a piece of work as the Treaty of Washington of 1871

5 France was represented by Count d'Avaux and Count Servien; Sweden
by Count Oxenstierna and Baron Salvius; the Empire by Count Traut-
mannsdorf and Dr. Volmar; the Papacy by Fabio Chigi, the future Alexander VII; and Venice by Contarini.

had not inspired textbook writers to name the commissioners who settled the Alabama claims.

Why did the historian avoid the contributions of the diplomat and dwell on those of the general? Angell found the reasons understandable, if not justifiable. The battles of the diplomat did not stimulate the imagination and excite the passions the way the battles of the warrior did. The negotiations of the diplomat, moreover, were often so secret in character that by the time the truth did emerge the issues had frequently become stale. Angell, however, reminded the gildsman in 1893 that he was living in an "age of arbitration." And as a student of a subject that could make men "catholic and cosmopolitan" and lift them above "the narrow prejudices and conceits of provincialism," he had tremendous obligations which he could meet in part by publicizing the activities of the peacemaker and the treaty-maker. He could

> emphasize the importance of pacific negotiations as the desirable method of settling international difficulties by giving the deserved place to the histories of diplomatic labors and by asking that historians should place on the heads of great diplomatists the laurels which they merit, and of which they have too long been robbed, and should give them as honorable a position upon their pages as they assign to great admirals and great captains. Let history do what she can to perpetuate the fraternal relations of nations by glorifying the council chamber and the arbitrator at least as much as the field of battle and the warrior.

While Angell called attention to one category of public servants, Senator Hoar of Massachusetts proved to be much more comprehensive in his scope. Disturbed by the iconoclasm that he though was rampant in the nineties, Hoar came to the defense of the schoolbook heroes whose pedestals were being smashed; in part, no doubt, this was because he himself had felt the effects of many an American party battle.[6] Unfortunately, Hoar did not take time out to name names in his message of 1895. Perhaps he had in mind what Charles Francis Adams, the newly chosen editor of the Massachusetts Historical Society, had done to many a Puritan forebear; what Henry Adams had done to Jefferson; what Sydney Gay, his fellow-Republican from Massachusetts, had done to Madison; what William Herndon had done to Lincoln.[7]

Hoar proclaimed "inexorable truth" the chief goal of the historian, and he insisted that the idealization of a country's history and heroes did not necessarily involve distortions and falsifications. Certainly it was not advisable to replace "veritable history" by romantic and fictional accounts of the past; it was not wise to raise the American schoolboy on "pleasant self-delusions." Yet however much Hoar asserted and reasserted that his comments were not to be interpreted as in any way justifying a departure from "absolute verity anywhere," he made it clear that, if a choice had to be made, he preferred an extra dose of historical praise to an extra dose of historical blame.

This defense of the victim of the iconoclast was Hoar's answer to what he termed in 1895 "an unusual fondness of late for overthrowing reputations of dead men." Deploring the revival of obscure slanders, the Senator cautioned the historian to think deeply about the documents he exulted in exhuming and about the reputations he exulted in destroying. Hoar was not one to believe that "a sober and trustworthy history of the United States must only be a chronicle of the discarded and rejected scandals of all past generations; that the men whom their own times deemed most worthy are to be counted unworthy, and that the men whom their own times rejected are now to be ac-

6 *Autobiography of Seventy Years* (2 vols., New York, 1903), II, 271-73.

7 Sydney Howard Gay, *James Madison* (Boston, 1884); William Henry Herndon and Jesse William Weik, *Herndon's Lincoln: The True Story of a Great Life* (3 vols., Chicago, 1889).

cepted." With an eloquence that did not stoop to the citation of specific iconoclasts, Hoar railed against the belittling of United States history and of individual American heroes. He had no use for the base materials which masqueraded as history but which were really written in dilettante fashion and "at the mouth of . . . sewers." Enough from those who were proclaiming that "John Adams was hot-headed, quarrelsome, vain, and egotistical; [that] Jefferson was a poor, impractical philosopher, timid and dissimulating; [that] Madison was a poltroon and coward; [that] Clay was profligate and a gambler; [that] Monroe was feeble and insignificant; [and that Jackson was] an unscrupulous, reckless, fighting frontiersman." Seething with senatorial indignation, Hoar suggested that the iconoclasts who could not discover "ten righteous men in our Sodom or Gomorrah" would do well to "get out of it before the fire from heaven comes down."

The iconoclastic craze had created such an explosive situation by 1895 that Hoar was "astonished" that any American youth could feel any love for his country. Plainly, then, there was much to be done by the patriotic historian who wanted to make himself a useful member of society. He should take action against the advocates of "base history" by demonstrating that these shallow, irreverent minds had erred in their attempts to explain the great currents and the great men of history on the basis of ignoble motives like "greed, selfishness, avarice, ambition, or revenge." The gildsman should expose the iconoclast for what he was. Thriving on ignoble data, he merely betrayed his own deficiencies: lacking greatness and heroism, he could not understand greatness and heroism in others; lacking a sense of honor and of duty, he could not recognize honor and duty as determinants of national and personal behavior. Therefore, the level-headed historian should do his best to debunk the debunkers.

It was with enthusiasm that Hoar reminded the gildsman of the inscription which appeared on the monument of George

Bancroft, one of his own great heroes[8] and one of his close friends:

> He made it the high purpose of a life
> Which nearly spanned a century,
> To trace the origin of his country,
> To show her part in the advancement of man,
> And from the rare resources
> Of his genius, his learning, and his labor,
> To ennoble the story of her birth.[9]

If Bancroft's lofty patriotism had prompted him at times to present some overly reverential descriptions of American history and American statesmen, it was plain that sober time was correcting them. Surely Bancroft did no serious harm. He heaped no indignities on figures of the past merely for the sake of heaping indignities. Bancroft was well worth imitating, because he understood that the "true function" of the historian was to preserve the memory of virtue. And, like Bancroft, if not Tacitus, Senator Hoar thought it best that "the memory and example of evil should perish."

If Richard S. Storrs, the biographer of Bernard of Clairvaux, was animated by none of Hoar's righteous indignation, this Brooklyn clergyman did at least join his predecessor in viewing "with admiring honor" those eminent individuals whose contributions along political, military, scientific, and intellectual lines lent distinction to American annals and helped to establish and embellish American institutions. "The time never will come." said Storrs in 1896, "when such honor to such men will not be appropriate. The impulse to render it belongs to our impelling and governing moral nature; and whenever it shall fail, a loss will be shown in us of that which is essential to noble personal or national welfare." Unlike Hoar, however, Storrs was not con-

8 *Autobiography of Seventy Years,* II, 202-06.

9 Cf. Russel B. Nye, *op. cit.,* p. 302.

cerned primarily with justifying and preserving the reputations of the great men in American history; he was concerned with lesser American lights, who, despite the more powerful radiance of others of their generation, yet managed to illumine the course of United States history.

Deploring the inadequate recognition given these lesser figures, Storrs pointed specifically to "plain men" of the Eleazar Wheelock, Manasseh Cutler, and Marcus Whitman variety. While Wheelock (1711-1779), the Congregational minister, made fewer capital contributions than some .of his contemporaries, there was no overlooking his services as founder of the small charity school for Indian youth that became Dartmouth College; for this institution trained, among others, such luminaries as Webster, Choate, Chase, Stevens, Ticknor, and Sylvanus Thayer, the superintendent of West Point Academy from 1817 to 1833, who of all Dartmouth men left the most "powerful impress" on American history. If Manasseh Cutler (1742-1823), also a Congregational minister, could likewise not measure up to many of his major contemporaries, there was no ignoring what he did for the Old Northwest. Similarly, Marcus Whitman (1802-1847), the missionary and physician, deserved more widespread recognition for his activities in the Northwestern wilderness, said Storrs, several years before the appearence of Edward G. Bourne's article on "The Legend of Marcus Whitman."[10]

Differing from Hoar, whose chief preoccupation was with the manner of treating the galaxy of great Americans, Storrs spoke for those American heroes who had failed to attract much public attention on a national scale. Favoring biographical studies which would publicize the activities and contributions of such forgotten men of American history, he wished to spread an awareness of

> that wide, quiet, unadorned work which has been done for the nation by those in less conspicuous positions—commonly, no doubt, of less signal powers—yet who also have wrought with

10 *A.H.R.*, VI (1901), 276-300.

patience, faithfulness, and consecration of spirit, and sometimes with extraordinary effect, to assure and advance public progress. The consequences of their work have often immensely surpassed expectation; while it is impressive to observe how the work of any one of them has not infrequently interlocked itself with that of another or of others following, till the final effect has been of prodigious extent and value. We see how rich in stalwart life our nation has been, and how manifold and profound have been the sources from which have come its ultimate power. Our gratitude for the past as well as our hope for the future may thus be reenforced.

Speaking in 1896, Storrs felt no need to justify his choice of the topic, "Contributions Made to Our National Development by Plain Men"; but two years later, Storrs' close friend and fellow-clergyman, George Park Fisher, saw reason to apologize for dealing with individuals at all. With the Spanish-American War just recently ended, with American foreign policy a subject of lively discussion, he wondered about the advisability of discussing a subject like "The Function of the Historian as a Judge of Historic Persons." But he decided to discuss it, reasoning that much could be said in favor of a brief respite from current controversies. Besides, though Fisher had written only one biography, that of the chemist, Benjamin Silliman, his former colleague at Yale, individuals had figured prominently in his widely-used textbooks on church history and on general European history. It was easy for him to assume that few gildsmen would deny that the personal traits and actions of individuals formed one of the chief attractions of historical study; and he obviously approved of the good sense that Ephraim Gurney of Harvard had shown when, faced with the necessity of choosing between the philosophy and the history departments, he decided on the latter because he preferred history's people to philosophy's abstractions.

Fisher did not ignore those who ridiculed the effort to call the individuals of the past back to life, but he believed that the

Herbert Spencers, who questioned the wisdom of exploring the life of a Mary of Scotland,[11] overlooked the fact that the past revealed more than merely the development of society, important though that was. Fisher granted that many details which belonged in a biography were out of place in a historical work. He granted, too, that even the most striking individuals were, up to a certain point, the products of their age—but only up to a certain point. There was, in other words, no minimizing the fact that

an initiative agency belongs to the leaders of men. It is an extreme theory that relegates them exclusively to the category of effects. Human beings are not automatons. Especially are signal epochs in history, turning points, marked by a rallying about persons. From them goes forth a creative energy, inspiring and guiding their fellows. Let sociology, the philosophy of history, be rated at its full value. In the drama of human affairs there is an endless appeal to psychological curiosity, a constant stimulus to poetic feeling. And so even such a tragedy as that in which Mary of Scotland bore a part will always enlist human sympathy, and impel to researches having for their object to solve the questions in doubt. It is a dry-as-dust theory that would drive out these inquiries from the domain of history.

According to Fisher, the gildsman was a member of a high court of appeals for historical figures. Naturally, this brought responsibilities, whose enormity could be appreciated only in the light of the split decisions of past historians. After all, the Cromwell whom Clarendon described turned out to be quite different from Carlyle's hero; and Froude's Henry VIII bore little resemblance to Macaulay's. All this might well be discouraging; but Fisher thought that the present-day gildsman had certain advantages over his predecessors, advantages which made less likely some of the flagrant misjudgments of the past. For one thing, he had many more sources at his disposal. Generally,

11 Herbert Spencer, *Education: Intellectual, Moral and Physical* (New York, 1860), p. 83.

moreover, he had a greater spirit of fair play and a greater sense of responsibility to do everything possible to find out the truth. Laziness would not deter him, as it had David Hume back in the eighteenth century, from "rising from his chair to consult the authorities on his shelves, if not literally within reach," said Fisher, showing little awareness of the effects of Hume's physical infirmities on his historical writing.

Since the present-day historian had so many advantages over earlier writers, he had all the more reason to guard against a number of "misleading influences"—influences against which, it should be added, Fisher himself had generally succeeded in guarding even in the treatment of such a delicate subject as the Reformation. To start with, the gildsman should be alive to the distortions that grew out of both hero worship and iconoclasm If, nevertheless, a choice had to arise, Fisher sided with Senator Hoar: even extravagant hero worship was more to be condoned than the sensationalism of iconoclasm. There was no point in searching for flaws in a Washington's character, said Fisher, himself the author of a standard introduction to *The Colonial Era* (1892). Every nation needed at least one sacred hero who was "justly enshrined in popular veneration."

Just as the gildsman should guard against the perils of hero worship and idol-smashing, so, too, he should guard against having a limited supply of colors on his palette; Macaulay's use of a saintly white and a savage black did not suit the dispassionate student. The historian should also avoid a Froude's passion for paradox. Especially when he dealt with a subject that had been covered by numerous predecessors, he was tempted to say something original even though the evidence did not justify the new viewpoint. It was this striving for novelty, this search for "revolutionary hypotheses," that accounted frequently for the attempt to clear the reputations of justly condemned individuals; and everyone, it seemed, not excluding Henry VIII, managed in time to find a biographer who would serve as a friendly character witness. The dispassionate historian, however, should shun sensationalism; he should resist the temptation to be hailed as a "discoverer" in his field. Finally, he should make sure not to undertake a study for which he was not suited temperamentally, for diligence and good intentions did not suffice in the absence of these qualifications of temperament. Drawing on the literature of religious history, with which he was so familiar, Fisher pointed out that it was for lack of "imaginative sympathy" that Robert Southey's account of John Wesley and Milman's treatment of Hildebrand and of Louis IX failed. Fisher shared Senator Hoar's view that to do justice to a historical figure the gildsman must partake of his qualities.

While Fisher went along with Hoar on this point, he disagreed on another; for, in 1898, just three years after the Senator's address, he announced that he detected in historical works a "better tone," and this he attributed to the lessened influence of personal and party bias. On the decline was the practice of labeling political and religious heretics "with epithets appropriate to thieves and robbers"; and the wise maxim, *Audi alteram partem*, whose glories Fisher had proclaimed in the past,[12] he found was coming more and more into its own. But it was one thing for the historian to listen to all points of view; it was another for him to decide that he was to hand down no decisions at all, that he was to confine himself merely to the presentation of the available evidence. A clergyman and professor of church history, Fisher believed that the morally earnest historian could "hardly fasten such a padlock on his lips"; he could not stifle his own verdict; he could not conceal his personal reactions to vile acts. Arnold of Rugby had the right spirit, for, when he discussed historical subjects about which he felt deeply, he was not averse to becoming "livid with rage."

Yet by what moral standards was the gildsman to judge the historical person? Fisher was sympathetic to the point of view set forth in Lord Acton's recent inaugural lecture on the study of history, that historical persons and acts should be judged on the basis of absolute rules of conduct. At the same time, he was

12 *The Colonial Era* (New York, 1892), p. ix.

sympathetic to the opposite view, that historical persons should
be judged in the light of the standards of their own times.
Fisher found much to be said for both parties to the dispute.
The historian ought to try to keep ethical standards high, but
he should also understand that some ethical conceptions changed
through the ages. While some acts were "always and everywhere
known to be wrong," others were not. Fisher recalled Xeno-
phon's account of a visit that Socrates and some of his followers
paid to Theodota, the Athenian courtesan, during the course
of which Socrates gave the courtesan some pointers concerning
the conduct of her business.

> Suppose [said Fisher] a teacher of moral philosophy in one
> of our universities—for Socrates was a teacher of ethics—
> were to copy his example as thus related, and related, be it
> observed, without the least censure, by one of his disciples.
> Shall we then denounce Socrates, one of the noblest men of
> all time, and a martyr, if there ever was one? I have heard
> a theologian speak harshly of him on the ground of this record
> in the Memorabilia. But the good man forgot that on the
> roll of heroes and saints, in that splendid passage of Holy
> Writ, the eleventh chapter of the Epistle to the Hebrews,
> there stands the name of Rahab, the harlot.

In this way Fisher defended the conception of historical relativity. He believed it unjust, for example, to hold Caesar and
Napoleon equally responsible for their treatment of prisoners
of war. On the other hand, he introduced no notion of relativity for Bismarck's manipulation of the Ems dispatch, an act
that deserved to be universally condemned. Even so, Fisher
suggested that, with the passage of time, it was the controlling
aims of any historical person that would determine subsequent
estimates of his "personal worth." With the passage of time,
many embarrassing details would be overlooked, and even condoned—provided that, when some critical situation arose, an
individual placed himself bravely and unselfishly on the "right

side." The essential point, at all events, was that the historian must always keep in mind the demands of his "high office" as a judge of historical persons. To clear the worthy of undeserved blame and to strip the unworthy of undeserved praise, these were major responsibilities. Yes, thought Fisher, Tacitus was right when he said that the historian should record virtuous deeds and "make the reprobation of posterity a terror to evil words and acts."

This approach of Tacitus likewise called forth the approval of Fisher's successor, James Ford Rhodes, the historian of the United States from the Compromise of 1850. Rhodes, indeed, was at his best when it was a question of assessing individuals and their motives; and while his hostile comments on figures like Andrew Johnson, John Brown, and Stephen Douglas have been widely criticized, his treatment of scores of other individuals has held up remarkably well.[13] Certainly he made it plain in his message of 1899 that he preferred to dwell on worthy people and acts rather than on unworthy ones. A brother-in-law of Mark Hanna—and a former coal and iron magnate in his own right—he thought that the historian could never weary of references to the captains of industry whose ability and vigor made possible American industrial development. Much more important, Rhodes, who had not hesitated to inject his patriotism into his writings, pointed out that the historian could never say enough about Washington and Lincoln and those who followed their lead; he could rest assured that a country with men of their caliber was "indeed one to awaken envy." Rhodes indicated in his message that he placed a high estimate on the role of individuals in American history. And he showed something of the same fondness for might-have-beens that he had shown in his *History*, pondering, in the case of Garfield, for example, "the opportunities destroyed by the assassin's bullet."

13 Raymond Curtis Miller, "James Ford Rhodes," in William T. Hutchinson, ed., *The Marcus W. Jernegan Essays in American Historiography* (Chicago, 1937), pp. 184-86.

This was not the reaction of Charles Francis Adams, who, as a believer in historical laws, was inclined to call into question the event-making powers of historical persons. Addressing the Association shortly after the assassination of McKinley, Adams, descendant though he was of a long line of statesmen, noted "how much less momentous the average presidential choice becomes, the further we get away from it"; so that, from the standpoint of national and world affairs, things would have been no different even if Garfield had failed to be elected in the first place. Impressed with long-time trends, Adams could brush individuals aside, though he himself was the biographer of his father and of Richard Henry Dana.

Rhodes and Charles Francis Adams dealt only incidentally with historical persons; and in their addresses neither of them took sides in the Actonite controversy. Henry C. Lea, on the other hand, devoted the bulk of his message to a critical analysis of the Actonite position. Heading the Association in 1903, the year after Acton's death, he registered his dissent from the Cambridge scholar's view of "Ethical Values in History"; and, as the author of numerous volumes on Roman Catholic ecclesiastical institutions and of "the most considerable product of any American historian in the European field,"[14] he was eminently qualified to express a point of view.

Lea was opposed to Acton's presupposition of an ethical code that was applicable to all times, places, and peoples. He was likewise opposed to Acton's flattering presupposition that the historian had an absolute knowledge of right and wrong which enabled him to hand down conclusive judgments on historical persons. These presuppositions were based on grand illusions, Lea insisted; even a slight familiarity with the history of ethics sufficed to drive home the shifting character of ethical conceptions. Perhaps there was such a thing as a universal and eternal moral code by which people of different periods and on different

14 *A.H.R.*, XXVIII (1923), 221; Charles Homer Haskins, *Studies in Mediaeval Culture* (Oxford, 1929), pp. 256-62.

levels of civilization could be judged; but the fact was, said Lea, that the history of mankind failed to disclose it. Therefore, since distinctions between right and wrong varied from age to age under the impact of factors like race, civilization, and environment, the historian should not try, convict, or acquit the people of one age by his own standards of right and wrong or by those of his own time. He should not condemn Louis IX because of his attitude toward heretics, nor Justice Hale for his attitude toward witches. He should judge the people of any age only by their own standards, those they set or accepted.

Lea was thus the first president to take a strong stand in favor of historical relativity. That he did so was all the more remarkable in view of his keen interest in the affairs of his own time; he was, after all, not only a historian but a "publisher, capitalist, scientist, man of letters, and political reformer."[15] His concern with the present, however, did not undermine his pastmindedness; for he believed that it was only by viewing historical persons as representatives of the ideas and aims of their age that the historian could recreate the past scientifically. He believed, moreover, that the historian would not be so quick to condemn if he immersed himself thoroughly in an age, learning to view events from the standpoint of the men whose conduct he was describing. When, instead of taking a relativistic view of the past, the historian read moral conceptions into his judgement of bygone men and institutions, he introduced an element of subjectivity that was sure to destroy the accuracy of his picture of the past. Lea's counsel, therefore, was that the historian should view "righteous indignation" as a luxury that only a reader could afford. For the historian was neither an advocate nor a prosecutor; he was a judge, and a judge who dared not "try a case by a code unknown to the defendant." Lea could not agree with Acton or with Fisher, who had argued that moral earnestness required the historian to abandon the padlock principle. To do this, Lea insisted, meant inevitably to

15 Edward Sculley Bradley, *Henry Charles Lea: A Biography* (Philadelphia, 1931), p. 3.

read the present into a past that was not at all likely to be of the same mind as the present.

Lea recognized that Acton's formula, with its disregard of the temporary and variable character of morals, had many attractions. It could serve to "give point and piquancy to a narrative, to stimulate the interest of the casual reader by heightening lights and deepening shadows, and to subserve the purpose of propagating the opinions of the writer." But Lea cautioned that the gildsman who applied Acton's defective formula would make of history little more than "a Sunday-school tale for children of larger growth"; and he did not want the historian to make such a tale of history. Rather, he wanted the historian to make a serious effort to determine the truth about the past and to present it "without fear or favor."

Applying his conception of historical relativity to the career of Philip II, Lea was able to draw on his knowledge of a country whose history he had done—and was yet to do—so much to illumine. Philip was hardly an attractive person, said Lea; but neither was he the monster that appeared in the pages of Motley's *Rise of the Dutch Republic*. Lea did not seek to minimize the lurid aspects of Philip's career; he did not overlook his many shortcomings. But he thought that there was another side to the story that made less Motleyan Philip's misdeeds. Philip, said Lea, using the approach that he was to apply in his *History of the Inquisition of Spain* (1906-1907), was "the misguided agent of a false standard of duty, and conscientiously believed himself to be rendering the highest service to God and to man"; and, almost without exception, the acts for which Motley condemned him were the very acts that had as their object the extinction of heresy and the enforcement of religious unity. Philip did not use religion as a pretext. He viewed the heretic as worse than a murderer or a highwayman; he viewed him as a slayer of souls. Therefore, when he persecuted the heretic, he performed his supreme duty; he served as God's instrument in the defense of the true religion.

Along with these religious convictions went Philip's political convictions; and these rested on the idea that unity of faith was necessary for domestic peace. If, then, Philip was to be correctly understood, he must be viewed as a product of the political and religious forces of his time. To view him thus was not to "approve, tacitly or overtly, the influences which made him what he was—what, in fact, he could not help being." To give Philip the "colorless treatment" that Lea favored was not to repudiate the morals that the study of history conveyed. Far from it. As Lea put it:

> To depict a man like Philip as a monster of iniquity, delighting in human misery, may gratify prejudice and may lend superficial life and vigor to narrative, but it teaches in reality no lesson. To represent him truthfully as the inevitable product of a distorted ethical conception is to trace effects to causes and to point out the way to improvement. This is not only the scientific method applied to history, but it ennobles the historian's labors by rendering them contributory to that progress which adds to the sum of human happiness and fits mankind for a higher standard of existence. The study of the past in this spirit may perhaps render us more impatient of the present, and yet more hopeful of the future.

Understandably, Lea's statement of the case for historical relativity and past-mindedness failed to gain the support of his successor, Goldwin Smith, the Anglo-Canadian publicist. Smith was less a historian than a student of current events;[16] but his stand on historical relativity was hardly less strong than his stand on imperialism, which he opposed, protective tariffs, which he opposed, and Irish home rule, which he opposed. Accustomed to the use of history as a weapon in many a controversy, Smith could not judge individuals in the light of their own times and without recourse to moralizations. To do this, he said, was to

16 Cf. Edward Potts Cheney, "Goldwin Smith," *Encyclopaedia of the Social Sciences,* XIV, 115-16.

divide history into "a series of moral zones with which our judgments of action and character ought to vary"; and such a division would imperil "morality itself, as it would destroy the identity of the moral law." So it was that Smith came to the defense of his friend, Lord Acton.

Yet he would not throw out Lea's conception of historical relativity altogether. After all, Smith had once been regius professor of modern history at Oxford, and he had taught English and constitutional history at Cornell. Perhaps, then, it was his academic background that prompted him to concede that in the attempt to judge the character and behavior of a historical person "just allowance" should be made for "the general beliefs and prevailing influences of the time." Beyond this, he would not go. The upshot was that, when he proceeded to characterize Philip II, Smith, as a good nineteenth-century liberal, sided with Motley —something that he had made plain decades before at Oxford.[17]

> The age of Philip II and the Spanish Inquisition [he said] was an age of murderous persecution. What made it so? The conduct of Philip II and the inquisitors, which itself was influenced not solely by hatred of misbelief but by criminal propensities of a grosser kind: the despot's lust of unlimited power, the hierarch's lust of ascendancy and wealth. Philip II was not only a persecutor, he was a murderer and adulterer. He hired assassins to take the life of his noble enemy William the Silent. It is by no means certain that the propensity to religious murder was universal or even general among the people of that day.

Nor was Philip II the only historical figure whom Smith had occasion to use for illustrative purposes. Napoleon and Gustavus Adolphus also appeared in his address—but for a very different reason. On their careers Smith drew in order to point up the influence of historical accidents which, by altering "the whole current of history," ruled out the establishment of a valid science

17 *Lectures on the Study of History, Delivered in Oxford, 1859-61* (New York, 1866), p. 81.

of history. What if Napoleon had not become a French citizen? What if he had enlisted in the British navy, as he at one time planned to do? What if he had been assassinated at some early stage in his career? Similarly, what if Gustavus Adolphus had not died at Lützen? Smith granted that Napoleon and Gustavus Adolphus were influenced by the "predisposing forces" of their age; but he regarded them and other great men as fatal to the establishment of a science of history, one which would make possible the prediction of future developments.

Doubtless it was Smith's association with leading public figures in England, the United States, and Canada that encouraged him to stress the historical importance of individuals. Certainly, however, he was no upholder of the great man approach to the past. Much as he admired Carlyle as a stylist, he questioned the validity of the basic view expressed in *On Heroes, Hero-Worship, and the Heroic in History* (1840), the view that history was at bottom an account of the activities of the great men in the world. "Great men," Smith argued, "were not creators, but the consummate products of their generation, giving its tendencies the fullest expression, and reacting upon it by the force of their genius. But they were its offspring, not its creators." Singling out some of the individuals who figured in Carlyle's lectures on the hero as divinity, as prophet, as poet, as priest, as man of letters, and as king, Smith had these questions to ask: "What would Odin, if there was such a man, have been without Norse tendencies and beliefs? What would Mahomet have been without Arabian tribalism, Judaism, and Christianity? What would Luther have been without the ferment of spiritual insurrection against Rome which had long before produced Wycliffe? What would Shakespeare have been without the Elizabethan era, Voltaire without his century, Napoleon without the Revolution and the outbreak of military adventure which ensued"? Smith considered historical persons the products of their times, but he was unwilling to judge them in the light of their times.

If Lea's address called forth Smith's response, Smith's address called forth no response from his immediate successors among the presidents of the Association. Even when, in 1907, J. Franklin Jameson resumed the discussion of individuals in history he did so only in the form of an aside. Jameson himself was a leading hero in the history of the Association; he was indeed "its most continuously active and devoted member,"[18] the gildsman who had already played—and was to continue until 1937 to play—such an important role as an organizer and promoter of historical activities.

Discussing briefly the idea of national character, one of the most popular ideas at Johns Hopkins when he took his doctorate there in the early eighties, Jameson attempted to draw a connection between a country's national character and its heroes. For example, he said, the chief saints of a nation were those who harmonized most with the traits of the nation itself. St. Louis embodied French chivalry, and Joan of Arc "typified the high spirit of the French nation, its military instinct, its imaginative heroism, its enthusiasm for ideals, its ardor of self-sacrifice." Moreover, said Jameson:

> In St. Elizabeth of Thuringia we see the type of German domestic and practical piety; in St. Ignatius and St. Francis Xavier the independence, the reticence, and the organizing power of the Basque. St. Francis of Assisi, with his sensitive poetic imagination, fresh, simple and childlike, sympathetic with the poor, joyful in all renunciations, could be no other than the best-beloved saint of the Italians. St. Teresa, ecstatic in her mystical union with God, yet gay and natural and gifted in practical reforms and other dealings with this world, is as distinctly the Spaniard as the impulsive, passionate, warm-hearted Columba is the genuine Irish Celt, while in St. Cuthbert, buoyant, energetic, the strong walker, the lover of the country and of boyish sports, we see the genuine Northumbrian.

18 Robert Livingston Schuyler, "John Franklin Jameson," *A.H.R.*, XLIII (1938), 244.

Unlike Jameson, Albert Bushnell Hart had much to say about historical persons. One of the major figures in Harvard yard, Hart knew what it was to worship and to be worshipped; and doubtless it was his own colorful personality that went a long way to explain his interest in other colorful characters. This interest Hart had shown in any number of his writings. In the "Introduction" which he, as editor, wrote to *The American Nation,* he pointed out that the series was designed "to select and characterize the personalities who have stood forth as leaders and as seers."[19] Similarly, in his *Manual of American History, Diplomacy, and Government for Class Use* (1908), he pointed out that a historical work was incomplete unless the reader could "feel the personality of those who have most affected the course of events," unless the reader understood "the marvelous effect of leadership."[20] Hence it was not surprising that in his message of 1909 on "Imagination in History" Hart insisted that the dynamic influence of great men upset the calculations of the historian.

Yet it was surprising that Hart, who had expressed his faith in the search for historical laws, should have criticized attempts to push too far analogies between history and the natural sciences. He thought it unwise for the historian to adopt some of the favorite words in the scientist's vocabulary, words like research and investigation. His point was that history could not be treated like atomic weights and insurance losses, that history did not lend itself to preparation in a laboratory where accidental factors could be eliminated and particular phenomena isolated for purposes of examination. Hart believed that the gildsman could never really escape from the conclusion that the ultimate historical material was mind. And since all historical facts were related to personalities, the gildsman could not avoid the con-

19 "Editor's Introduction to the Series," in Edward Potts Cheyney, *European Background of American History, 1300-1600* (New York, 1904), p. xvii.

20 *Manual of American History, Diplomacy, and Government for Class Use* (Cambridge, 1908), p. 41.

sideration of human nature, conduct, and standards. Quickly enough, he discovered that the attempt to understand human character formed the starting-point of his study. Having to deal with the complexities of human nature, he learned to try, at least, to "decipher triple and quadruple palimpsests of human character." He learned to try to understand the behavior of individuals who frequently had failed to understand themselves. Hart found indeed that the study of motives formed "the most interesting if the most elusive part of history."

Unlike the natural scientist, the historian often had to grapple with unusual individuals. The geographer did not have to alter his theory concerning the building of mountains because of the sudden emergence of some abnormally high peaks. Nor did the botanist find "a Napoleon of the forests" to embarrass him. The historian, on the other hand, was constantly faced with the need to study extraordinary figures, and this study Hart considered worthwhile. Like Henry C. Lea before him, Hart thought that figures of the past should be judged by the standards of their own times. Don John of Austria should not be denounced for seizing the possessions of his enemies at sea, and Lord Mansfield should not be attacked for condemning sheep-stealers to death; nor should James I be criticized for never having developed the habit of washing.

Like Fisher, if not Hoar, Hart detected a "visible reaction" against the practice of attacking traditional heroes. As for the villains of history, they seemed to be benefiting by the whitewash brush. Men like Benedict Arnold and Aaron Burr were inspiring apologists to do for them what Horace Walpole had done for Richard III and Froude for Henry VIII, said Hart, thinking probably of Isaac Jenkinson's *Aaron Burr* (1902) and of Charles Burr Todd's *The True Aaron Burr* (1902) and *The Real Benedict Arnold* (1903). Yet what mattered was that, whether a great man was hailed as a saint or condemned as a villain, he continued to defy any neat categories that the historian might devise. Louis XIV, for example, said Hart, venturing into a field about which he knew little, delayed for two hundred years "the adjustment of Europe." Napoleon, on the other hand, made up for those two centuries of delay in a decade.[21] It was perhaps true that historically no person was indispensable, but Hart saw reason to believe that if not for Luther the German Reformation would have failed; if not for Washington the American colonies might have remained within the British Empire for another fifty years; and if not for Lincoln the rivalry between North and South would have continued indefinitely. In Hart's words: "Great men perhaps do not make history; they are never greater than the country through which they work, but they concentrate history, reflect it, exemplify it, alter it. Great men have some power to accomplish things; they are spokesmen of national purpose; they at least suppose themselves to be re-making the world, and no strictly scientific statement can account for great men or measure their influence." So thought the Harvard professor who was to devote the last years of what proved to be a very long life to promoting the study of George Washington and Theodore Roosevelt.[22]

Hart's immediate successors paid only scant attention in their messages to the role of individuals in history. Frederick Jackson Turner simply proclaimed it part of the function of the historian to indicate how leaders were shaped by their time and their geographical setting and how they exercised an influence that grew out of their own originality and creativity. For the rest, Turner did not deal with historical persons. Nor was this surprising, for he was attracted above all by the study of social forces.

Yet it was surprising that the next two presidents, William M. Sloane, the biographer of Napoleon, and Theodore Roosevelt, the biographer of Gouverneur Morris, Benton, and Oliver Cromwell, should have given such slight attention to the role of the hero in history. Sloane did make it a point to include a reference

21 Cf. Edward Eggleston's remarks in A.H.A., *Annual Report, 1900* (Washington, 1901), I, 40-41.

22 *A.H.R.*, XLIV (1943), 193.

to Napoleon to the effect that "the last great cataclysm" in history—he spoke in 1911—was due partly to Napoleon's reading of Plutarch's *Lives*. And Roosevelt stated in 1912 that the gildsman should use his imaginative and literary powers so that figures of the past might live again in his pages. As a moralist, moreover—the man of good and bad trusts, the historian of good and bad people—Roosevelt deplored the view that impartiality required the virtuous and the wicked to be treated on an equal basis. He granted that the historian of the United States would have to describe much that was "unpleasant"; but it was clear that a nation whose heroes were Washington and Lincoln must have high standards indeed.

It was only briefly, too, that Roosevelt's immediate successors addressed themselves to the role of individuals in history. In 1913, William A. Dunning announced his unwillingness to accept any interpretation that discarded the personal factor, declaring that the ideas of individual men exercised a potent causal influence. In 1914, Andrew C. McLaughlin proclaimed the frontiersman "the very genius of American history," insisting that the scholar who wished to understand the American past should focus his attention on this central figure. In 1915, H. Morse Stephens proclaimed the nineteenth-century historian an important historical person, one who played a major part in arousing consciousness of nationality. And in 1916, George L. Burr announced that he prized historical study because in it alone the life of the individual survived. In view of the inroads that allied investigators were making on man's freedom and of the little thought they gave to the individual, Burr rejoiced that the historian retained man as a lord of creation and did not make him a mere victim of impersonal forces and great abstractions.

While historical persons were dealt with only briefly by Hart's early successors, they did come into their own once more in the message of Worthington C. Ford, the editor of the Massa-

chusetts Historical Society and the editor of the writings of
George Washington and John Quincy Adams. President of the
Association in 1917, Ford was impressed by the wide variety
of topics which his predecessors had explored, and therefore
he made a conscious attempt to inject a new note into his address. One of the most prolific editors in the whole history of
American historiography,[23] he turned to a subject that he was
well equipped to handle: "The Editorial Function in United
States History." And in the course of his discussion he had
much to say about the treatment of historical figures.

Ford remarked that the European brand of political autobiography had not achieved any real prominence in the United
States until the latter part of the nineteenth century; for a long
time there were few Americans who would and could describe
their own careers. This reticence Ford found all the more strange
in a country where every citizen insisted on his freedom of expression, and where the freedom of the press made possible "the
glorification of the seamy and the sordid as freely as of the great
and the admirable." Even when biographical materials did
exist, Ford pointed out that the desire of relatives to do their
own editing long made the going rough for would be American
editors; scions sufficed or thought they did. Even so, editors
proceeded to make their entrance: Ebenezer Hazard, in his
Historical Collections (1792-1794), and Thomas B. Wait, in
his *State Papers* (1815), showed a real understanding of the
editorial function. They had the right spirit; they stuck to their
texts, avoiding alterations of language or of purpose.

Unfortunately, their correct view of the editorial function did
not last long. After a good start, editing soon saw some of its
main commandments violated; and this deterioration was best
exemplified in the works of Jared Sparks. Beyond doubt, Sparks
was a pioneer among editors, said Ford, whose own indebtedness to him was so considerable at times that he was to be ac-

23 *Ibid.*, XLVI (1941), 1013.

cused of having plagiarized the master.[24] Yet for all his prodigious undertakings—his editions of the writings of Washington, Franklin, and Gouverneur Morris—Sparks deserved to be
severely criticized. For subsequent scholars had had to redo
his work, not because new documents had been uncovered, but
because Sparks had taken considerable liberties with his texts.
Of intentional misrepresentation Ford did not wish to accuse
him and those whose methodology he fathered. It was just
that Sparks and his disciples were conscious of the living presence of some of the figures whose activities were described in
the documents they edited. Why, then, revive unpleasantness
and partisanship? Why expose the weakness of individuals who
bulked large as heroes? Some of them, after all, were incapable
of defending themselves. Worn out by political strife, they asked
only to live out their lives. Others were still office-holders. Better,
then, not to raise past controversies; newspapers and pamphlets
offered enough of personal abuse. In the circumstances, Ford noted that careful editing could come into its own only slowly. The
old obstacle, moreover, remained: the reluctance of some descendants to permit the records of their ancestors to be examined
by scientific editors. Therefore, when old scandals were revived
from time to time and circulated in the juiciest of prose, Ford
believed that these descendents, who sabotaged rather than encouraged the efforts of editors, were really the guilty ones.

Ford suggested that it was perhaps the unsuccessful character
of many a nineteenth-century venture in biography and editing
that smoothed the way for the later host of political autobio-
graphies like that of Senator Hoar, the former president of the
Association. Ford recorded his unmistakable opposition to such
works. He wondered indeed why it was that a man wrote an
autobiography. Was it that he feared what an editor or a biographer might find? Was it that he wished while still alive to
advertise himself so that he might enjoy the praise of his con-

24 W. Stull Holt, ed., *Historical Scholarship in the United States, 1876-
1901: As Revealed in the Correspondence of Herbert B. Adams* (Baltimore,
1938), p. 177.

temporaries? What irritated Ford was that the autobiographer, if he spoke of many things, often managed to steer clear of the very things that mattered most to the historian. Worse, there were those who, after having prepared an autobiography, proceeded to destroy the original documents on which it was allegedly based. This Ford considered "a crime against history, and an unavailing plea in abatement against further consideration."

If, in matters of form and content, political autobiography was lagging behind history, the reason was not far to seek: the political autobiographer was likely to be childish, simple-minded, and unreliable. As a rule, he was likely to overstate his own importance and emphasize the *Magna* in the *Magna pars fui*. Certainly Ford failed to appreciate one major value of an autobiography: that while it did not perhaps present the truth, it did at least indicate what the autobiographer wished to be viewed as the truth. Ford considered autobiography a coarse form of vanity; and for a person to prepare such a work was for him to confess that he found it advisable to justify his behavior.

According to Ford, the author of a political autobiography was not likely to further the search for truth. This the editor and the biographer would have to do. Of the two, Ford pointed out that the biographer had the greater opportunities. In his treatment he could highlight dramatic and picturesque details; and he could color his account with his own point of view, said Ford, himself the biographer of George Washington (1900). The editor, on the other hand, was more restricted. Verbal traditions and the remembrances of contemporaries mattered little to him. His function was simply to present his material completely and without change. Obviously, he should not lack sympathy for the individuals who figured in the records; but, then again, no one could immerse himself in historical documents without imbibing something of the spirit that motivated the men in the documents. Ford emphasized that the editor ought to make every effort to see through the eyes of these men, and he should try to reenact their deeds. In deciding, however, to withhold information, he must depend on the dictates of his "sense of decency." For the rest, he could confidently submit his materials for history to judge. For Ford believed that it was good "to humanize Washington, to have the means of tracing the tortuous policy of Jefferson, to measure the ability and ambitions of Hamilton, to comprehend the rash but honest conduct of the Adamses, and to wonder at the little greatness of Monroe."

While Ford viewed historical persons from the standpoint of an editor, his successor, William R. Thayer, viewed them from the standpoint of a biographer. And this Thayer was in an excellent position to do, for his masterly two-volume life of Cavour (1911) had shown how skilled he was in the art of biography. First of all, however, Thayer had some strong views to express about instincts, two of which he considered particularly destructive of sound historical study: the instincts for process and certitude. These instincts had never before achieved their recent intensity, Thayer thought in 1918, and they promised to subvert genuine historical study, making as they did for a false precision and an unjustified cocksureness. Himself a former literary and dramatic critic on the Philadelphia *Evening Bulletin*,[25] Thayer pointed, for instance, to the treatment of individual authors in the usual history of literature. Whether he had in mind the recently published *Cambridge History of American Literature*, he did not indicate; but he emphasized that in the usual history of literature

> the sequence of cause and effect rolls on as smoothly as does the leather belt which turns the wheels in a factory. There are no gaps, no doubts, no hesitation. Take the history of American literature, for example, and see how simply Washington Irving is 'accounted for', and then how naturally William Cullen Bryant followed him, and when you come to the

25 Charles Downer Hazen, ed., *The Letters of William Roscoe Thayer* (Boston, 1926), pp. 26-27.

New England School, how Emerson, and Hawthorne, and Longfellow, and Whittier, and Holmes, are beautifully related to each other in a fatal rack-and-pinion combination. There is an implied causal connection, and everything is so perfectly adjusted that you begin to infer that nature amuses herself by playing an unending ball-and-socket game.

As far as Thayer was concerned, the establishment of direct causal ties among these authors involved a falsification of the facts. As contemporaries, the writers in question doubtless influenced one another superficially. By and large, however, Thayer contended that Emerson could have developed the way he did even if Holmes and Hawthorne had never been born; and "not one of them was important, much less indispensable, to the development of the others." Thayer would not endorse the writing of literary history without regard for the essential independence of individual authors. He granted that those who wrote the traditional brand of literary history did not intend to do harm; their machine-like precision and their recondite evolutionary interconnections simply showed that they had been victimized by the instincts for process and for certitude.

Long before his presidential address Thayer had emphasized the historical importance of individuals. He had done so in his *Dawn of Italian Independence* (1892); in his *Throne-Makers and Portraits* (1899) he had criticized those who belittled the influence of individuals; and in *A Short History of Venice* (1905) he had "taken care" to describe many of the great men who shaped the course of Venetian development.[26] Therefore, it was not surprising that in his message on "Vagaries of Historians" he expressed the view that biography was to history what portraiture was to painting; nor that he sang the praises of historical personalities, "the most fluid and elusive of essences." Deploring the mechanical treatment of these personalities, he criticized the historian who standardized them and made them fit into some neat scheme—"as if they were pieces of metal, moulded

26 *Throne-Makers and Portraits* (Boston, 1899), pp. v-vi; *A Short History of Venice* (New York, 1905), p. ix.

into interlocking parts of a soulless machine." The historian,
Thayer thought, should stop trying to fit the individuals of the
past into cleverly devised patterns. Instead, he should try to
humanize them; and, mindful that telescopes and microscopes
were of no use in the study of human actions and motivations,
he should try to release history from scientific clamps.

> In so doing [Thayer said] the historian will abdicate no high
> and hard-won office; on the contrary, he will rise to the full
> glory of his mission. If he must have some watchword to
> guide him, let that watchword be 'Man the Measure'—*man,*
> not the laws which apply to the animal kingdom, or to un-
> thinking and soulless matter. Human nature is the substance
> in which the historian must work. He must try to discover
> how the human will—that force more mysterious than elec-
> tricity—shapes and directs the deeds of men.

In a general way Thayer thought that he could distinguish
three groups of historians: one that stressed external deeds and
events; a second that stressed inner motivations; a third which,
on the basis of outward acts, sought to interpret inner motives.
Thayer did not wish these categories to be viewed in any rigid
sense. Obviously, however, the historian who was content with
surface manifestations had a relatively simple task. Far more
difficult and fruitful was the work of the historian who tried to
treat of motives, for these were frequently unrecorded and could
be determined or divined only by the specially gifted. Yet this
ability to divine was indispensable to him who would derive
the greatest benefit from the study of the past. For with this
ability he could explore the role of the human will in history.
Thayer granted that the gildsman who dealt with long stretches
of time was not likely to recognize the role of will in history;
he was more likely to recognize the role of material law in history, for will seemed to emerge only with the emergence of individuals who led and influenced the masses. Yet if Athenian
history had more significance and interest than Assyrian or
Egyptian history, it was this emergence of individuals that ac-

counted for the difference. Similarly, Thayer thought that much of the fascination of modern history stemmed from the multitude of absorbing individuals who lived in recent centuries.

It was not only the complex motivations of these individuals that made the task of the historian difficult. Chance, too, introduced all kinds of complications. If Woodrow Wilson or Lloyd George, for example, were to die immediately, said Thayer in 1918, the course of history would doubtless be affected; but the nature and the extent of these effects the gildsman was powerless to foresee. And chance worked in another way to complicate the task of the historian. Rameses II, for example, counted for less historically than Napoleon, and the explanation was in part that the historian knew vastly more about the one than about the other.

Though Thayer would not reduce historical persons to a minor rank, he was sufficiently familiar with the historical literature of his time to detect the tendency in some quarters to see in history merely the interplay of impersonal and abstract laws; he was familiar, for instance, with the writings of Henry Adams. Thayer, however, could only reiterate his own guide to the study of history, Man the Measure, a watchword that expressed for him the nobility of the historian's calling. For, unlike the man of letters, the historian had his plot and characters ready-made. He had simply to present them truthfully and vividly, never forgetting that "*life* is the one indispensable God-given essence."

When, because of the postponement of the meeting of 1918, Thayer had a second opportunity to prepare a presidential message, he again emphasized the importance of individuals in history; and in the process he displayed some of the same anti-Germanism that had colored practically everything he had written since the outbreak of the first World War. The German historian, he said, deserved to be condemned, for he dehumanized a subject that was preeminently human, one that dealt entirely with human emotions, acts, and motivations, one that was eminently concrete because human beings were not abstractions.

The German historian did not understand the real nature of history, for he handled human beings like chemical materials which had fixed reactions in given circumstances. No doubt Thayer was doing an injustice to writers like Mommsen, Sybel, and Treitschke; his generalizations about them would seem to indicate that he had not read their works very carefully.[27] Be that as it may, he found the German way of writing history utterly inadequate. Man, he insisted, was not a soulless machine which operated according to physical laws in a cosmos without ethics.

Thayer failed to win the backing of Edward P. Cheyney, who, in his address of 1923, proceeded for all practical purposes to make of historical figures what Thayer would have called soulless machines. Nor was this unusual for Cheyney. Many times before his message on "Law in History" he had belittled the historical importance of great men. He had done this in his *Introduction to the Industrial and Social History of England* (1901), in his *European Background of American History* (1904), and in his most important scholarly work, his *History of England from the Defeat of the Armada to the Death of Elizabeth,* only one volume of which had so far appeared. Cheyney had also shown his unwillingness to ascribe more than slight influence to historical figures in a number of addresses and articles, most notably perhaps in "The Tide of History" (1913), an address on which he drew liberally for his presidential message of a decade later.[28]

Viewing history as the result neither of will nor of chance but of law, Cheyney suggested that even if Henry VIII had had no marital troubles, even if he had never cast covetous eyes on Anne Boleyn, even if he had never become king, even if he had never been born, England would have undergone the Reforma-

27 Cf. Hazen, ed., *op. cit.,* p. 80.

28 "The Tide of History," in *Law in History and Other Essays* (New York, 1927), pp. 64-89.

tion. Furthermore, even if Washington had not been so capable a leader, even if he had not been commander-in-chief of the revolutionary armies, American independence would have been achieved. In taking these flings at history-as-it-might-have-been, Cheyney sought to drive home the point that to attribute major historical influence to figures of the past was to take the superficial and easy way out of the complexities of historical causation. The historian could avoid all kinds of difficulties if he had some convenient historical person on whom to hoist great causal powers, said Cheyney, thinking probably of writers like Carlyle and Froude.[29]

Cheyney was sure that the more the historian studied the past the more he would discover the slight extent to which individuals exercised a causal influence. The more he explored the past the more he would find that historical laws had a profound bearing on the freedom of individuals to choose and act. Just as physical laws imposed limitations on the activities of the engineer, the navigator, and the aviator; just as chemical laws imposed limitations on the activities of the metallurgist, the dyemaker, and the synthetic chemist; just as psychological laws imposed limitations on the activities of the scientist, the philosopher, and the historian; so historical laws, while they left man far from powerless, yet formed the framework within which he must think and act.

Cheyney recognized that there were those who would object to his analogical use of "laws of external nature," that there were those who would emphasize that history involved the human will. Countering, however, that the freedom of the will had been much overrated, Cheyney insisted that man by and large played the part to which he was assigned in the human drama; he was definitely not the author of the play.

A man [said Cheyney] can live only in a certain period, neither in any earlier or later time. Ordinarily he can live only

29 See his article on Froude in the *Encyclopaedia of the Social Sciences,* VI, 506.

in one particular country and in the midst of one set of social
and political conditions. He can possess only his own heredity.
His physical and mental nature are drawn entirely from his
ancestors. He has no capacities or proclivities that have not
come to him through his inheritance. He is controlled at every
turn by the natural laws of the world in which he dwells. And
yet we feel free to act much as we choose. If our action is
not entirely free it simulates freedom. We are so used to
our limitations that it is only exceptionally we feel them. In-
dividually we find a wide field of activity within the limits
that condition and to a great degree control our action. We
are free to act, subject to irresistible law in the background.
We have only a margin of freedom but that margin is wide
enough for judgment, effort, self-sacrifice, heroism; for fool-
ishness and wisdom, for weakness and strength.

What was true of man as an individual was no less true of
him as a historical creature. In other words, even though historical events were controlled by laws, man could in a slight way
deflect the course of those events, giving to general tendencies
a particular mold. The important thing was that when man acted
in conformity with historical laws, he acted effectively; when
he cooperated with the great historical forces, he exercised an
influence that was historically constructive. When he acted in
violation of the laws of history, he acted destructively and exercised only a temporary influence, one that was sure to be re-
versed. Man always had freedom of action; but the consequences
of his exercise of this freedom depended on the extent to which
his acts conformed with historical laws. In degree, then, as the
historical person worked in harmony with the laws of continuity, impermanence, interdependence, democracy, free consent,
and moral progress, to that degree he would exercise a constructive influence on his times.

Cheyney's successor, Charles M. Andrews, also objected in
effect to Thayer's approach to historical personalities; and, like
Cheyney, Andrews had been objecting to this type of approach

for a long time. Though by 1924 Andrews was known mainly as a colonial historian, he had done considerable work in the fields of English and general European history; and in his books on *The Old English Manor* (1892), *The Historical Development of Modern Europe from the Congress of Vienna to the Present Time* (1896-1898), *Contemporary Europe, Asia and Africa* (1902), and *A History of England* (1903), as well as in his volumes on American colonial history, he had emphasized institutions and people and had shown his distrust of those who would maximize the importance of the hero in history.

When, therefore, in his message of 1924, he undertook to summarize some of the main currents in American historiography in "These Forty Years" since the founding of the Association, it was no surprise that he rejoiced in the tendency of the modern historian to abandon the study of the picturesque and dramatic aspects of the past in favor of the study of ideas and conditions. The gildsman, said Andrews, would not venture to assert that the chief aim of historical study was descriptive, narrative, or biographical; on the contrary, he would call into question the worth of biographical history. No doubt the almost shameless lengths to which some Victorians had pushed their hero-worship had helped to prepare the way for this recent reaction; but Andrews believed that Carlyle deserved to be criticized for his inordinate exaltation of the dramatic and the heroic, for his inability to view humanity apart from individuals, and for his failure to understand the collective life and purpose of a people. Andrews might have added that Carlyle had urged the study not only of great men but of the fathers that begat us, as Eileen Power had recently pointed out in her *Medieval People* (1924).[30] Andrews, at any rate, found it an indication of growing maturity that the contemporary historian dealt less with isolated individuals and events and more with the growth and interplay of ideas and institutions and with the bearing of eco-

30 Eileen Power, *Medieval People* (London, 1924), pp. 1-2.

nomics on society and politics. And just as he placed less stress on the personal element in history, so, too, he placed less stress on personal liberty in history, acknowledging that social existence required that man renounce some elements of his freedom to act.

Nor was this all that the contemporary historian acknowledged. He recognized, too, that every individual was dominated by his surroundings, even as he admitted that the individual's free will could "never be reduced to the control of historical law." He recognized that no individual could be viewed as a free agent, that no individual could be understood apart from the intellectual, moral, and social currents of his age. Not that the contemporary historian denied the interest and importance of the individual. He simply insisted that the individual's relationship to the "collective mind" was of greater significance than his individual behavior; and so, the contemporary historian was less interested in what the individual man thought and did than in what large numbers of men thought and did, for the future depended on the views of the majority of men, said Andrews, reflecting, no doubt, the influence of Cheyney's laws of democracy and free consent.

While the present-day gildsman demanded more of history, so, in turn, history demanded more of him. He must become altogether absorbed in the period with which he dealt, so that he could do justice to the individuals and institutions of the past. He must liberate himself from the prepossessions, ideas, and even the language of his time, so that he would not be like seventeenth-century French writers who tended to bedeck Frankish chieftains in the garments of Louis XIV. History demanded, furthermore, that the gildsman forget about being a moralist; he must realize that it was no part of his function to provide his reader with ethical yardsticks for the judgment of the individuals and events of the past. Illustrating this point, Andrews referred to his predecessor by twenty years, Goldwin Smith, with whose writings he was no doubt familiar from the time when his own major interest was English domestic history. Smith, Andrews pointed out, was fond of historical moralizing; it was characteristic of him to see in history the story of the activities of corrupt, superstitious, rapacious, and inefficient individuals. Nor had Smith's approach disappeared altogether. Unfortunately, some writers still viewed history as an account of the activities of sinful men, Andrews complained, without making clear which historians he had in mind; some still held that the study of history was worthwhile only to the extent that it provided examples for the teaching of ethical principles; some still insisted on assigning to the individuals of the past their "full quota of moral responsibility"; and some continued to consider it the function of the historian "to instruct statesmen and governments of the past in what ought to have been their duty." Possibly Andrews was thinking in 1924 of some of the literature concerning the origins of the first World War. At all events, he pointed out that to moralize on the basis of history was to exclude the time test and to apply modern and subjective criteria to the individuals and peoples of former times. Besides, historical study was not designed to condemn and revile the individuals and institutions of the past; it was designed to interpret and understand them in the light of their own setting. Andrews, in a word, stood solidly on the side of historical relativity— on the side of historians like Lea and Maitland.

In the twenty years or so after 1924 historical persons were by and large slighted in the presidential message delivered before the Association. In the very years when the "new biography" was achieving some of its greatest triumphs, the subject of individuals in history entered only incidentally into the addresses of Andrews' successors. Henry Osborn Taylor, for example, many of whose studies of ancient, medieval, and early modern thought were organized around individuals, took time out to say simply that, unlike the scientist, the historian found men in the center of his world. James Harvey Robinson's comments on individuals in history were also brief. Addressing the Association in 1929, by which time revisionist war historiography had come into its own, Robinson recalled that the first World War had not brought out the best in the gildsman; but he was reassured by the thought that war-time intolerance had taught the gildsman much. It had taught him the lesson of genuine tolerance; and this was reflected in the way he approached historical figures. Naturally, said Robinson, the historian must be on guard if he wished to cast "reflections on standardized patriots and glorious deeds." Yet Robinson was happy to record that the historian was tending to follow the leadership of those novelists and dramatists who considered description and narration rather than applause and blame their proper function. He tended to view historical figures not as creatures of vice or virtue but as "poor devils of various temperaments in bewildering situations, groping their way through the maze of life."

It was essentially this same tendency in historical writing that was noted by Robinson's successor, colonial historian Evarts B. Greene, who addressed the Association in 1930, the year of the tercentennial celebration of the founding of the Massachusetts Bay Commonwealth. Greene, who had only recently published *A New-Englander in Japan: Daniel Crosby Greene*, an account of his father's missionary activities, emphasized that filiopietism had had its day; and he rejoiced that the filiopietistic tendencies which Charles Francis Adams had bemoaned in his writings on Massachusetts history were much less in evidence. Hence Greene thought that the time had come to reappraise what New Englanders had contributed to the making of American history. Yet though individuals entered only slightly into Greene's address on "Persistent Problems of Church and State," the Columbia professor did single out William Penn for having done more to secularize the American state than probably any other person.

Carl Becker, on the other hand, singled out no particular historical person. Instead, Becker, one of the most highly respected

American historians of his time, concentrated on Mr. Everyman; and he took the stand in 1931 that Mr. Everyman not only influenced historical writing but that in the long run he determined its emphasis. Much of this was no doubt wishful thinking on Becker's part; certainly he would have found it difficult to footnote. At any rate, he argued that ultimately it was Mr. Everyman's demands that decided the type of history—political or economic, for example—that the historian would write. As for the historian himself, he could be understood only as a product of his times, said Becker, whose presidential address clearly reflected his own concern with the impact of the Depression on the welfare of Mr. Everyman.

Like Becker, Charles A. Beard also emerged as an advocate of historical relativity. This, in a sense, was surprising, for more than most of the leading historians of his time, Beard was preoccupied with the present and with the future. Yet even these preoccupations did not prevent him from taking the stand that if any historical person—and that included the historian himself— was to be understood, he must be viewed in the light of his setting; he must be viewed in his relationship to the ideas and interests of his age.

On this point, Charles H. McIlwain agreed with Beard, and understandably so. A scholar who had specialized in the study of political thought and of English constitutional development, McIlwain could insist that the cause of truth required that the historical person be regarded "as a man of his own time rather than of a later time." A devotee of the type of scholarship associated with English constitutional historians like Maitland and Tout, McIlwain could insist, moreover, that the historical person—a Simon de Montfort or an Edward I—did not suffer when he was viewed in the light of his own setting; he suffered when he figured in a romantic biography or history that exploited his life for some "present purpose." McIlwain did not see St. Thomas Aquinas as a "modern Whig," Cardinal Bellarmine as a modern democrat, and Sir John Eliot and Sir Matthew

Hale as "parliamentary Austinians." Obviously, McIlwain could hardly have approved of many of the biographies that had hit the best-seller lists in recent years, books like Emil Ludwig's *Napoleon*, André Maurois' *Disraeli* and *Byron*, Francis Hackett's *Henry the Eighth* and *Francis the First*, Lytton Strachey's *Elizabeth and Essex*, and Stefan Zweig's *Marie Antoinette* and *Mary Queen of Scotland*.[31]

Nor was McIlwain alone in complaining that too many recent biographies were filled with too much "historical romance." Guy Stanton Ford, the leading American authority on Baron vom Stein, and Max Farrand, a leading authority on the Founding Fathers, had much the same complaint. Some of the "most widely read" of recent books about individuals and events in American history lacked balance and historicity, Ford said in 1937, thinking perhaps of books like Means and Thacker's *The Strange Death of President Harding* and Emil Ludwig's *Lincoln*. When, three years later, Max Farrand raised much the same objection to some of the historical biographies that were reaching bestseller status, he found consolation in the thought that, although these works lacked distinction, they did at least arouse popular interest in the past.

Even so, the subject of individuals in history entered only slightly into the presidential addresses that were delivered before the Association in the thirties and early forties. Different presidents had specific historical figures to whom they attributed varying degrees of causal influence; Bolton had, among others, his Napoleon and his Bolívar; Dodd his Earl of Clarendon; Rostovtzeff his Alexander; Guy Stanton Ford his Franklin; Paxson his Woodrow Wilson; Ferguson his Solon, his Cleisthenes, his Themistocles, his Pericles, and above all his Athenian Mr. Everyman; James Westfall Thompson had his giants of historical scholarship, his Mabillon and his Montfaucon;

31 Alice Payne Hackett, *Fifty Years of Best Sellers, 1895-1945* (New York, 1945), pp. 55-71.

Schlesinger his American Mr. Everyman; Miss Neilson her William the Conqueror; Westermann his Delphic priests; and Hayes his Franklin D. Roosevelt. On the whole, however, the historical importance of great men was given little attention in the presidential addresses of the thirties and early forties. In years when "interest in the words and acts of outstanding individuals [had] flared up to a point never reached before,"[32] when dictators and democratic leaders figured so prominently in domestic and world affairs, and when the fate of nations seemed to hang on the decisions of a single person, the presidents of the Association did not read the present importance of individuals into their treatments of the past.

32 Sidney Hook, *The Hero in History: A Study in Limitation and Possibility* (New York, 1943), p. 3.

CHAPTER IX
THE CONTENT OF HISTORY: EARLY YEARS

So far this book has dealt with subjects on which particular presidents held conflicting views. They differed widely in their conceptions of the immediate usefulness of history; of history as literature; of facts in history; of the philosophy and science of history; and of the role of individuals in history. On at least one subject, however, the last with which this book is concerned, there was no real disagreement. No president denied the richness of the content of history. No president opposed a broad view of the past. Long before James Harvey Robinson and his New History, many a president made it plain that the study of the past was more than the study of politics and of war.

Andrew D. White was a strong supporter of the history of civilization. Though his major works were written in the years after he headed the Association, he had already brought out a number of pieces that showed his interest in economic and cultural developments: *Paper-Money Inflation in France* (1876) and *The Warfare of Science* (1876). Even so, White did not proclaim the "supreme worth" of the study of the life of the people. Nor did he consider the study of battles and treaties a waste of time. He thought in 1884 that the opportunities for specialization were greatest for the gildsman who worked in the fields of English and American political, constitutional, and social history. But he made it clear that he opposed one of the views that Herbert Spencer had expressed in his essay on "What Knowledge Is of Most Worth?", the view that the study of battles was essentially worthless, that knowledge of military history would not make for a wiser electorate.[1] What Spencer

1 Herbert Spencer, *Education: Intellectual, Moral, and Physical* (New York, 1860), pp. 64-67.

forgot, said White, was that there were battles and battles: great ones of little importance and little ones of great importance. The seemingly minor affair at Saratoga White viewed as a turning point in world history; the seemingly major affair at Austerlitz he viewed as of relatively little significance.

While he agreed with Spencer that the details of battles did not deserve all the attention which the historian had often given them, he made sure to add that there were details of battles and details of battles. The details of how, in the early stages of the Revolutionary Wars, French armies broke and fled, these were well worth knowing when Northern armies were suffering defeats in the Civil War. The details of the behavior of Dillon's troops in 1792 offered the kind of message that the Northerner needed to hear in the days after the first Battle of Bull Run. Recalling the requests for readings that he had received in Civil War days from his students at the University of Michigan, White was happy in retrospect to have been able to suggest morale-lifting pieces like Motley's account of the siege of Leyden and Macaulay's account of the siege of Londonderry. Spencer might deny that even a diligent study of all historical battles would make for wiser voting at an approaching election, but the experience of early French Revolutionary armies worked effectively in American Civil War days. It served to inform voters of their obligations as voters and to convince them not to support defeatists who would compromise on the issues of either disunion or slavery, said White, whose own anti-slavery ideas had been strong at least from his undergraduate days at Yale.[2]

Nor was it only details of French Revolutionary military experience that proved valuable in American Civil War years. Details of English military experience came in handy, too, for they were "so perfectly paralleled in our own history." Attributing the failures of parliamentary forces in the early days of the Great Rebellion to the inability of generals like Manchester and

2 *Autobiography of Andrew Dickson White* (2 vols., New York, 1905), I, 66-69.

Essex to appreciate the issues at stake, White emphasized that it was only when generals "of sterner purpose" were placed in positions of command that success attended the efforts of parliamentary forces. Details of this sort, said White, were well worth remembering; they showed the inadequacies of Spencer's view of military history.

As for Spencer's opposition to the study of palace intrigues,[3] White granted that knowledge of these intrigues often did not make for an understanding of "the causes of national progress." Yet White knew his Buckle well. He remembered how, in his *History of Civilization in England,* Buckle had derived moral and political lessons from the growth of French absolutism; so that, personally, White believed that the history of the French monarchy, with all its palace intrigues, was a wonderful subject for useful thought, one which he himself had often exploited in his lectures to undergraduates at the University of Michigan and at Cornell.[4] Thus, though White's own historical writings were in the fields of economic and cultural history, he defended the study of political and military history. In truth, he valued any type of history that contributed to an understanding of "the great lines of historical evolution.."

White was especially drawn to the investigation of the history of civilization, the kind of history that would take account of

> Aristotle in the apothecary shop, Plato in the grove, Erigena and Thomas Aquinas in the schools, Copernicus in his cell, Newton in the orchard, Cardinal D'Ailly writing his *Imago Mundi,* Grotius writing his De Jure Belli ac Pacis, Comenius writing his little *Orbis Pictus,* Volta in his university, Watt in his work-room, Descartes turning from natural science to philosophy, Paolo Sarpi advising the Venetian Republic how to meet an interdict, and writing his History of the Council of Trent, Thomasius publishing his treatise against witchcraft

3 Spencer, *op. cit.,* p. 65.

4 *Outlines of a Course of Lectures on History, Addressed to the Senior Class, in the Cornell University* (Ithaca, 1870), pp. 50-60.

in the name of a student, Beccaria writing his little book on
Crimes and Punishments, Adam Smith writing his Wealth
of Nations, Kant writing his Critiques of the Pure and Practical Reason, Beaumarchais writing his *Mariage de Figaro*,
Harriet Beecher Stowe writing her *Uncle Tom's Cabin*, Darwin on the Beagle . . . .

The important thing was that the historian should concern
himself with individuals who had significance and occurrences
which had significance. There was no such thing as being too
greatly occupied with royalty and military heroes, no such thing
as being too little occupied with "the people". The persons
studied by the historian could be "saints or miscreants, popes
or monks, kings or peasants, conquerors or conspirators, build-
ers of cathedrals or weavers of verse, railway kings or day la-
borers, publicists or satirists, philanthropists or demagogues,
statesmen or mob orators, philosophers or phrase mongers."
And the events studied by the historian could be no less diverse
than the persons. Whether the event happened to be "a poem
or a constitution, a battle or a debate, a treaty or a drama, a picture or a railway, a voyage or a book, a law or an invention, the
rise of a nation or the fall of a clique," the essential point was
that it should "signify something."

To find out the significance of an historical event White suggested that it would be helpful to use, whenever possible, such
sources as *belles-lettres* and memoirs. Drawing on his own considerable knowledge of literary history, he explained that ancient
Roman corruption, for instance, could well be traced in the
writings of Lucretius, Cicero, Lucian, Juvenal, and Tacitus,
writings which presented "moral statistics" that enabled the
historian "to see far into the spirit of the time and the causes
of that imperial decline." So, too, the memoirs of people like
St. Simon and Bourrienne enabled the historian to grasp the
inner life of a period, so much so, that White had his doubts
that even "the most elaborate collection of statistics would com-

pensate for their loss." [5] According to White, then, it was a simple thing to determine the subject-matter of history, for everything that had a bearing on "the great lines of historical evolution" deserved to be studied. It is to be regretted, however, that because of his activities as a university president and as a politician and diplomat White found so little time to engage in research and publish works that would embody his broad view of the past.

Though White's successor, George Bancroft, had also served his country as a politician and diplomat, he had managed to complete, among numerous other writings, one of the monuments of nineteenth-century scholarship, his ten-volume *History of the United States from the Discovery of the American Continent* (1834-1875). Yet while Bancroft's political involvements did not perhaps detract seriously from the length and quality of his list of publications, they did perhaps work to confirm him in his emphasis on the political aspects of the past. History, said Bancroft in his brief presidential message of 1886, dealt with "the movement of states over the scene of ever-succeeding action"; and this movement resembled "the march of so many armies with their various civilizations for their banners," he declared, showing that even at the age of eighty-six he had a command of rhetorical flourishes. Bancroft did not believe, however, that it was only the careers of states that fell within the range of history. He pointed out that history was also concerned with the "enduring contributions to the sum of human knowledge" which the people of those states made. Plainly, however, these comments were only incidental to what Bancroft had to say in 1886 about his favorite theme, his theme of themes, American self-government.

Though Bancroft had no specific changes to suggest in the traditional make-up of history, William F. Poole went out of his way to suggest such changes in "The Early Northwest." Perhaps Poole should have felt self-conscious about the suggestions he had to make. He was, after all, a librarian; and though he had contributed to Winsor's *Narrative and Critical History,* his historical writings were relatively few. Yet Poole was a mid-Westerner by adoption—and one who took the mid-West seriously. So that, when he addressed the Association in 1888, he spoke with pride of the growing interest in the study of the American West. Poole, however, spoke in the era before Turner, and it was understandable that he had a major complaint to make. For, though increasing numbers of monographs were taking into account the role of the West in American history, general histories were failing to embody the results of specialized research. As a rule, they continued to ignore the West even though it had "a varied, romantic, and entertaining record of its own, quite unlike that of the Eastern States." Hence Poole cautioned the Easterner that, if he wished to write correctly about the general history of the United States, he must grow "tall enough to look over the Appalachian range and see what has happened on the other side." He could no longer handle the Ordinance of 1787, if at all, in five lines, said Poole, singling out the historical subject on which he himself had written most notably.[6]

When Poole turned to some specific aspects of the history of the early West that required investigation, he showed his interest in political, constitutional, and military matters, in subjects like the legislative origins of the Northwest Ordinance and the campaigns of George Rogers Clark. At the same time, he showed his interest in social and economic history, urging the study of the activities of the French Company of the West, its opening of lead mines and its introduction of European agricultural methods; and he urged the study of social conditions among the early settlers of the Illinois country. Poole, in short, took a broad view of the content of history.

6 "Dr. Cutler and the Ordinance of 1787," *North American Review,* CXXII (1876), 229-65.

Nor did William Wirt Henry take any less broad a view. One of the leading local historians of his time, Henry sought in his message of 1891 to trace "The Causes Which Produced the Virginia of the Revolutionary Period." Taking for his starting-point the idea that every effect resulted from a variety of antecedents, he devoted much space to the discussion of political, constitutional, administrative, and legal factors; but he also included in his treatment of Virginia history other factors; ethnical, personal, geographic, climatic, military, economic, religious, educational, psychological, and social. Local historian though he was, Henry held no narrow view of the past; on the contrary, he showed his awareness of the richness of the content of history.

His successor, James Burrill Angell, had that awareness, too. Although he was less a historian than a college president and diplomat, he had continued to offer courses in international law and the history of treaties at the University of Michigan;[7] and he had been one of the contributors to Justin Winsor's *Narrative and Critical History*. Doubtless these facts emboldened him to venture the suggestions that he did venture when he addressed the Association in 1893 on "The Inadequate Recognition of Diplomatists by Historians." First, however, Angell had some compliments to extend. It was not without cause, he said, that the present-day historian often considered his studies superior to those of earlier writers; for he described vividly and accurately the many forces which went into the making of the modern nation. Going beyond battles, palace plots, and royal genealogies, he managed to make room for the literary, artistic, scientific, economic, and religious developments that went into the making of civilization.

Even so, Angell thought that the present-day gildsman deserved to be chided for one failing in particular, his defective handling of diplomatic history, the type of history in which

7 *The Reminiscences of James Burrill Angell* (New York, 1911), p. 242.

Angell, as a former minister to China and a member of the recent Anglo-American Northeastern Fisheries Commission, was above all interested. Thus at the same meeting at which Frederick Jackson Turner read his paper on the frontier, Angell made an appeal for a revitalized diplomatic history, the kind that would treat fully of the origins, processes, and results of negotiations, the kind that would treat no less fully of the character and influence of the negotiators. Having himself served on several diplomatic missions, Angell came to the defense of his predecessors in the profession. He complained that

> the work of international congresses, which have remade the map of Europe or the maps of other continents, which have extinguished the life of proud and ancient states or have created new states, which have given larger freedom to commerce and wider liberty in the use of the high seas, which have mitigated the cruelties of war and have swept the slave trade from the ocean; this work, so wide and far-reaching in its influence, of the diplomatic representatives of powerful states has been often passed over altogether by historians of renown or dismissed with the most succinct summary which was possible.

According to Angell, the discussions at Münster and Osnabrück deserved at least as much attention as the military events of the Thirty Years' War; and the discussions which preceded the Treaty of Paris of 1783 deserved as much attention as the battles of Trenton, Saratoga, and Yorktown. If, however, the general reader did not think so, if, in fact, he continued to prefer battles to diplomatic negotiations, it was the obligation of the historian "to correct his bad taste or to disregard it by setting forth in due proportions what is really important." Angell granted that writers like Henry Adams and Rhodes showed an appreciation of the importance of diplomatic transactions; but he insisted in 1893 that in "this age of arbitration" a full-fledged history of American diplomacy was "still a desideratum." The historian could make a most useful contribution to society if he emphasized the peaceful settlement of international disputes and accorded to diplomats and council chambers at least some of the space usually reserved for generals, admirals, and battlefields.

In the presidential messages of Angell's immediate successors, the content of history did not count for much. Henry Adams failed to discuss the subject. Having dealt with social, cultural, political, military, and diplomatic developments in his recently published *History* (1889-1891), he doubtless took it for granted that the gildsman's view of the past should be broad. As for Adams' successors, George F. Hoar, the Senator from Massachusetts, Richard S. Storrs, the Brooklyn clergyman, and James Schouler, the author of the multivolume *History of the United States of America, under the Constitution,* they weighted political history heavily in their messages. Storrs, however, was a student of religious history above all. And Schouler, though he was preeminently a political and constitutional historian, had sought in his *History* "to furnish in the true sense a history of the people of the United States, their virtues, their errors, and their wonderful development."[8] In fact, a few years after his presidential message he was to bring out a gem of a social history in his *Americans of 1776* (1906), a study of "life and manners, social, industrial and political."

Even when George Park Fisher, the church historian and author of a widely-used college textbook, discussed the content of history, it was only in an incidental way. He simply urged the study of the growth of society and its institutions. Years before his message of 1898, however, Fisher had indicated that the historian should take account of "the history of science, literature, art, and of moral and material decline or improvement"; that he should take stock not only of politics but of "manners, customs, and phases of intellectual progress."[9]

8 *History of the United States of America, under the Constitution* (7 vols., New York, 1880-1913), III, iii.

9 *Outlines of Universal History, Designed as a Text-Book and for Private Reading* (New York, 1885), p. vi; *The Colonial Era* (New York, 1892), p. viii.

Though Fisher's successor, James Ford Rhodes, also dealt with the content of history in an incidental way, he did take time out to urge the American gildsman not to confine his discussion of the past to a simple level. Often, to be sure, Rhodes's own study of *The History of the United States from the Compromise of 1850,* four volumes of which had appeared before his message of 1899, have been criticized for their narrowness, for their emphasis on political and military events. In his message, however, Rhodes extolled the richness of the American past. This richness, he said, compelled the gildsman to speak, for example, of "the broad acres and their products [and] the splendid industrial development due to the capacity and energy of the captains of industry." This richness, moreover, compelled the gildsman to dwell on American universities and colleges, "on the great numbers seeking a higher education, on the morality of the people, their purity of life, their domestic happiness." In this way Rhodes commended to the historian subjects which he had chosen largely to ignore in his own writings.

The first really large-scale presidential attack on the political and military content of history came in 1900 from Edward Eggleston, Rhodes' successor. Eggleston, it will be remembered, had turned historian at a late stage in his career; and it was perhaps his previous experience as a literary man and his relative inexperience as a historian that went to account for much of the freedom from restraint that figured in his message on "The New History." Eggleston said little in 1900 that he had not said before. What he did essentially was to restate ideas that he had already expressed in articles in the *Century Magazine* and in books like *A History of the United States and Its People for the Use of Schools* (1888) and *The Beginners of a Nation* (1896), articles and books in which he dealt with the "domestic and social life of the people, their dress, their food, their modes of thought and feeling, and their ways of making a livelihood."[10]

10 *A History of the United States and Its People for the Use of Schools* (New York, 1888), p. iv; *The Beginners of a Nation: A History of the Source and Rise of the Earliest English Settlements in America, with Special Reference to the Life and Character of the People* (New York, 1896), p. viii.

Eggleston had little of the passion for antiquity that dominated many of his contemporaries; he complained that "no other superstition has held so long as the classic." *Toujours eux, eux partout,* he said, in effect, of Thucydides and Herodotus. For he believed that the honors heaped on them were largely undeserved. He granted that their works were admirably written; for the rest, they left much to be desired. Thucydides, for example, committed what from Eggleston's standpoint was an unforgivable blunder; he ignored the literary, artistic, and social aspects of the period with which he dealt. Anyone who read his *Peloponnesian War* would not have the slightest idea that he was writing of an age which numbered such luminaries as Aeschylus, Sophocles, Euripides, Aristophanes, Phidias, Hippocrates, and Socrates, said Eggleston, raising the unreasonable objection frequently raised by those who would deny Thucydides' right to write about the things he knew best.[11] Eggleston might just as well have criticized Moltke for not writing about the ballet. However that may be, his point was this, that the mere fact that Thucydides meant to write only about the history of the Peloponnesian War meant that he considered art and literature less important than war; indeed, he considered war "the most important thing in the world," and this was condemnation enough. Accordingly, Eggleston insisted that for the writing of history in the "modern sense" Thucydides could hardly serve as a model. Yet if he would not do, Herodotus and Tacitus would do even less. Once and for all, then, the dominion of the classics must be broken. The modern gildsman must stop acting as if nothing had been learned about historical writing in a "cycle of nearly twenty-four hundred years."

Thus it was not in antiquity but elsewhere that Eggleston searched for models of what—years before James Harvey Robinson—he had been calling the "New History," the kind of history that paid attention to the small details of daily living; and

11 See, for example, James T. Shotwell, *An Introduction to the History of History* (New York, 1922), pp. 164-65; and Harry Elmer Barnes, *A History of Historical Writing* (Norman, Oklahoma, 1937), pp. 31-32.

these details he found admirably presented in a work like Sir Walter Raleigh's *History of the World,* whose neglect he denounced as much as he condemned the overrating of the *Peloponnesian War.* Voicing his opposition to those who viewed the past in the light of Edward A. Freeman's dictum, Eggleston declared: "Never was a falser thing said than that history is dead politics and politics living history. Some things are false and some things are perniciously false. This is one of the latter kind." Eggleston, to be sure, quoted Freeman out of context, ignoring the fact that what he had in mind was not the content of history but its continuity. Yet the essential point that Eggleston wished to make was that the contemporary gildsman continued to give too much space to politics; and politics Eggleston had long hated. Having lived "right at the door of Congress," he had complained about "the howl of the congressman"; and he had boasted that he was "constitutionally not interested in politics living or dead."[12] This point of view he repeated in his message, stating that politics was little more than a "superficial struggle of human ambitions crossed occasionally, but rarely, by a sincere desire to do good." Eggleston conceded that the historian should take politics into account; but the emphasis on this single aspect of the past had unhappily dominated too many a historical study.

Just as Eggleston believed that the historian should take some account of politics—as he himself had done in his *Beginners of a Nation* and in his recently published *Transit of Civilization*—so, too, he believed that he should take some account of military affairs. There was no denying that war was sensational and exciting: "Bodies of men are seen in violent movement. Life and death hang upon a hair trigger; they are in the quick decision and the prompt action. The world looks on and applauds. It is a cockfight. It is a bullfight. It is the death struggle of the gladiator. It is all of these raised to the hundreth power." Still, wars had

12 W. Stull Holt, ed., *Historical Scholarship in the United States, 1876-1901: As Revealed in the Correspondence of Herbert B. Adams* (Baltimore, 1938), p. 253.

occurred so frequently that they were commonplaces, said Eggleston, writing in the period of the Boer War. More than that, they were out of harmony with "that great world benevolence that is to be the mark of coming ages," a benevolence in which Eggleston, a former clergyman, had profound confidence. So it was that he counseled the gildsman to stop covering his pages with gore, insisting, like Angell before him, that it was the purpose of history to weed the savagery and brutality out of man and "to teach him the wisdom of diplomacy, the wisdom of avoidance—in short, the fine wisdom of arbitration, that last fruit of human experience."

Himself the author of several widely-used schoolbooks which embodied his point of view, Eggleston hoped that other schoolbooks would be rid of much that went by the name of history. For it was only so long as a narrow view of the purpose of historical instruction prevailed, it was only so long as the making of citizens and voters represented the goal of this instruction, it was only that long that the accent on military and political affairs could continue to hold sway. Once a broader view gained adherents, once it was understood that the chief object of teaching history was the making of "good men and women, cultivated and broad men and women," Eggleston was confident that his "New History," with its emphasis on the manners and customs of the people, would gain ground.

Sadly, however, he noted that the English-speaking peoples were perhaps the slowest to write about the history of the people. No doubt a splendid model for this kind of history could be found in Macaulay's famous third chapter, which was so admirable that Eggleston predicted the coming of the time when "we shall date from Macaulay." But few English and American historians had been noticeably influenced by Macaulay's approach. Ignoring John Bach McMaster, five of whose volumes in the monumental *History of the People of the United States* had appeared by 1900, ignoring Henry Adams, whose big *History* began and ended with a brilliant treatment of American society, ignoring Henry Traill, whose *Social England* (1894-1898) was "a record of the progress of the people in religion, laws, learning, arts, industry, commerce, science, literature, and manners from the earliest times to the present day," Eggleston complained that historians like John Richard Green and William Lecky were few and that the George Bancrofts were numerous, too numerous.

Writing almost a decade after Bancroft's death, Eggleston did not refrain from commenting on his inadequacies. He had personal reasons for remembering Bancroft kindly;[13] nevertheless, he believed that Bancroft had repelled more young people from the study of history than "all other influences in America," remarking that no less a dignitary than Francis Parkman had confessed to him his inability to read Bancroft. Eggleston admitted the vastness of Bancroft's knowledge; he granted that he "knew nearly everything a historian ought to know except culture history." This, however, was a major gap in his knowledge. Nor could the fact be overlooked that Bancroft was "a politician, or, if you please, a statesman. He was a diplomatist. He could not speak candidly." The upshot was that he eliminated certain unpleasant features from his account of the American past, believing that the American people could not stand a discussion of such aspects of their history. "He knew, for instance," said Eggleston, "that a majority of the pre-Revolutionary ancestors of the post-Revolutionary Americans—Colonial Dames, as like as not—came to this country in an unfree condition and were sold off the ship to pay their passage. But he left all that on one side as contemned culture history." The result of this lack of candor and this scorn for cultural history, Eggleston declared, was that Bancroft's volumes stood undisturbed along with other books which "no gentleman's library is complete without"; and a similar fate awaited any other historian whose interest was confined to political and military subjects.

13 William Pierce Randel, *Edward Eggleston: Author of The Hoosier School-Master* (New York, 1946), p. 177.

Eggleston was convinced in 1900 that the historiography of the twentieth century would prove that the gildsman had had his fill of politics and military affairs. "History," he predicted confidently, "will be better written in the ages to come. The soldier will not take the place he has taken. I do not say that the drum and trumpet history will have gone out; but when the American Historical Association shall assemble in the closing week a hundred years hence, there will be, do not doubt it, gifted writers of the history of the people. . . . We shall have the history of culture, the real history of men and women."

Eggleston condemned Freeman's statement about history and politics, but this did not prevent his successor, Charles Francis Adams, from using it to serve as one of the texts of his message of 1901. Adams, unlike Eggleston, understood the context in which the statement had originally appeared. He knew that Freeman had in mind not the content of history but its continuity; and it was the continuity of history, Adams emphasized, that made it possible for the present to draw lessons from the past.

Unlike Eggleston, Adams was not one to criticize the political and military content of history. He was, after all, the descendant of a distinguished line of statesmen, a civic leader in his own right, a friend of some of the leading political figures of his time, and the author of studies in American political, diplomatic, and military history. The important thing, according to Adams, was to bring to bear on present issues of all sorts—whether political, military, moral, economic, or intellectual—the lessons that could be drawn from the past. Immersed in the problems of his own time, he endorsed the study of any kind of history that would throw light on present difficulties. By and large, however, he preferred to leave economics to the economist. Doubtless the historian could deal with monetary questions and the problems of monopoly, said Adams, himself one of the leading railroad experts in the United States. Tariffs, however, he found unappealing; somehow, he said, "the historic spirit" failed to "kindle over tariff schedules." He preferred, accordingly, that the followers of Adam Smith rather than those of Gibbon draw the appropiate lessons from the revenue tables of the past.

Though Adams did not take to Eggleston's brand of "New History," Goldwin Smith very definitely did—at least in one major respect. Addressing the Association in 1904, the Anglo-Canadian octogenarian showed that he continued to cling to one of the basic tenets of the Manchester School, of whose early leaders he was the last to survive;[14] he made it clear that he was still what he had often been called, a Manchester peacemonger. Like Angell and Eggleston before him, he deplored the gildsman's study of the military aspects of the past. Unfortunately, war was still the most exciting of all subjects and the one that lent itself most readily to lively description, said Smith, suggesting much the same idea that Thomas Hardy was soon to present in *The Dynasts,* that war made for "rattling good history" and peace for "poor reading." But it was Smith's hope that the time would come when the gildsman would succeed in working up the interest—even of boys—in the "annals of peaceful and beneficent achievement."

While Smith was hostile to the study of military history, he had nothing to say in criticism of the political emphasis that Eggleston had deplored. Nor was this hard to understand, for Smith had engaged actively in English and Canadian politics; and his major historical writings, *Three English Statesmen* (1867), *The United States: An Outline of Political History, 1492-1871* (1893), and *The United Kingdom: A Political History* (1899), dealt largely with the theme that had called forth Eggleston's disapproval.

Smith's successor was John Bach McMaster, the one-time engineer who, having explored the American social past, had

---

14 *Reminiscences* (New York, 1910), p. 215.

been trying to lead American historians to it for upwards of two decades; and he, too, had no criticism to make of the emphasis on political developments as such. His own *History*, five volumes of which had already been published, treated not only of the people but "of presidents, of congresses, of embassies, of treaties, of the ambitions of political leaders in the senate-house, and of the rise of great parties in the nation."[15] In fact, his biographer has estimated that almost three-fourths of *A History of the People of the United States, from the Revolution to the Civil War* (1883-1913) concerned politics, diplomacy, and war.[16] It is therefore understandable that what McMaster criticized in his message on "Old Standards of Public Morals" was not the historian's emphasis on politics but the inertia that kept him from exploring the "broad domain of the past."

As McMaster thought in 1905 of the great number of historical works that had been published in the preceding decade, he imagined that almost every aspect of United States history would have been carefully investigated. Unhappily, he found that this was not at all true; after sifting the decade's historiographical output, he was convinced that "pure commercialism" lay behind much of it. It was bad enough that some of the volumes were only rehashes of older works; worse still, few had been inspired by any real desire to improve on what had previously been done. In the circumstances, McMaster, tremendous worker that he was, bewept the outcast state of the unexplored aspects of the past; and he troubled the historian with cries that he hoped would not prove bootless.

No doubt McMaster exaggerated, for purposes of effect, the inadequacies of American historical writing in the years between 1895 and 1905, years which saw the publication of such works as Philip A. Bruce's *Economic History of Virginia in the*

15 *A History of the People of the United States, from the Revolution to the Civil War* (8 vols., New York, 1883-1913), I, 1.

16 Eric F. Goldman, *John Bach McMaster: American Historian* (Philadelphia, 1943), p. 129.

Seventeenth Century, Channing and Hart's *Guide to the Study of American History,* Eggleston's *Beginners of a Nation* and *The Transit of Civilization,* John Fiske's *Old Virginia and Her Neighbors,* Moses Coit Tyler's *Literary History of the American Revolution,* Justin Winsor's *Westward Movement,* Wiliam A. Dunning's *Essays on the Civil War and Reconstruction,* Evarts B. Greene's *Provincial Governor* and his *Provincial America,* Sidney George Fisher's *True History of the American Revolution,* Claude Van Tyne's *Loyalists in the American Revolution,* Davis R. Dewey's *Financial History of the United States,* Ellen C. Semple's *American History and Its Geographic Conditions,* Edward P. Cheyney's *European Background of American History,* Andrew C. McLaughlin's *Confederation and the Constitution,* and Alice Morse Earle's studies of American social history. The same decade also saw the appearance of individual volumes in the multi-volume works of Rhodes, Schouler, Roosevelt, Osgood, and McMaster himself.

For all that, McMaster insisted in 1905 that the field of political history needed to be enriched by scholarly accounts of the Continental Congress and of the evolution of American political parties, the latter a need to which he had previously called attention in *With the Fathers,* (1896).[17] The field of social history likewise needed to be more widely investigated, he said, turning to the subject which he himself had been enriching ever since his abandonment of *Bridge and Tunnel Centres* and of *High Masonry Dams* had helped to make possible the appearance of the first volume of the *History.* Though there were, for instance, numerous accounts of the political and military aspects of the American Revolution, there was still no adequate treatment of the life of the people in Revolutionary times, McMaster complained in 1905, shortly before the appearance of Schouler's *Americans of 1776* (1906) and long before the appearance of Jameson's *The American Revolution Considered as a Social*

17 *With the Fathers: Studies in the History of the United States* (New York, 1896), p. 87.

Movement. (1926). Even so basic a feature of American history as the westward movement had inspired no satisfactory study, he said, ignoring the studies of Turner, Winsor, and Roosevelt. Then, too, there was a crying need for single-volume studies of the history of American national life and of American economic and industrial growth.

The deficiency in American historical literature that impressed McMaster the most in 1905 was of another sort. Almost forty years had passed since the appearance of the first edition of Lecky's *History of European Morals from Augustus to Charlemagne,* but no gildsman had yet seen fit to do for American morals what Lecky had done for European morals. And this, he thought, was most unfortunate, for a study of morals, especially of public morals, was sure to clarify many other aspects of history. As McMaster put it:

> The code of public morality which has at any time really been lived up to, in our country, is a great help to the understanding of the social and political conditions of that time. The sort of men who find their way into public life; the kind of government which prevails at any time or in any place; the acts done by Congresses, legislatures, city councils, municipal bodies of any sort, are just such as the mass of the people are content to have and often insist on having. What has been the conduct of the people when called on to meet great issues, where expediency, profit, prosperity stood on the one hand, and some principle of public morality on the other hand, is therefore very properly a part of our history, and sheds a flood of light on the phases of life which it is the duty of the historian to record.

Of particular interest to McMaster were the changes that public morals had undergone in the course of United States history, and to these changes he had often called attention in the past, starting, indeed, with the first page of his *History.* Once more, then, in his message he pointed out that old moral standards concerning religion, economics, and the punishment of crime had been basically transformed with the passage of time. Some practices which early Americans considered subversive of morality later generations came to tolerate. Later Americans, on the other hand, went so far, at times, as to prohibit by law some of the practices that preceding generations had accepted and even applauded, practices like the raising of funds by lotteries, imprisonment for debt, the execution of criminals in public, and slavery. Accordingly, McMaster was convinced that the historian would satisfy a real need if he studied standards of public morality and the factors that worked to change them.

While McMaster urged the study of the history of morals, his successor, Simeon E. Baldwin, urged the study of the history of religion. This is not to say that Baldwin himself had written scholarly treatises on the subject. His writings were mainly on legal subjects—as would be expected from one who taught at the Yale Law School and served as a justice on the Supreme Court of Connecticut. Yet Baldwin was a man who "lived constantly in the mood of high religious conviction"; and he was plainly disturbed in 1906 by the gildsman's insufficient recognition of religion as a subject for historical investigation. He seemed to forget that in the ten years preceding his presidency the Association had been headed by two clergymen, Storrs and Fisher, and one former clergyman, Eggleston. He seemed also to forget that among his recent predecessors were scholars like Lea, the leading authority on Roman Catholic ecclesiastical institutions, and McMaster, one of the leading authorities on the social history of religion in the United States.

Baldwin quoted the statement that history was essentially only applied psychology, the statement of Karl Lamprecht, whose *Moderne Geschichtswissenschaft* had recently been translated under the title, *What Is History?* (1905). Baldwin wished to emphasize, in other words, that the gildsman should consider the psychological forces that affected the behavior of people, and, among these forces, religion was of overwhelming importance.

Therefore, the historian should deal not only with all men but with all religions. It was not for him to determine whether any particular religion or all religions originated in "mere illusions"; that was the task of the theologian or the psychologist. The historian had enough with which to occupy himself simply in the study of religion as a motivating force in history.

Baldwin was especially interested in the investigation of the changes that religion had undergone since the eighteenth century. After all, the separation of church and state was a novelty in history; but even this separation diminished only superficially the importance of religion as an influence in historical evolution. Indeed, if the gildsman wished to understand mankind, he must realize that religion was here to stay. The church might cease to exercise power; it would never cease to exercise a controlling influence. For the ideas spread by clergymen permeated society and became a part of it; and so, the historian could hardly afford to neglect religion as the "main foundation of public opinion."

The religious mood that pervaded Baldwin's presidential message did not pervade that of his successor, J. Franklin Jameson, "the dean of the historical gild in America."[18] Though Jameson repeated Baldwin's plea for the study of religious history—and this, coming from the editor of the *American Historical Review,* was important—he based his plea on different considerations. For Jameson, who had recently taught the course in historiography at the University of Chicago,[19] was much impressed by the uses to which the modern medievalist had put the mass of religious literature known as the *acta sanctorum;* and, showing the same enthusiasm for fresh approaches that he had shown in his thoughtful lectures on *The History of His-*

18 William Archibald Dunning, "Truth in History," *A.H.R.,* XIX (1914), 218; Robert Livingston Schuyler, "John Franklin Jameson," *ibid.,* XLIII (1938), 252.

19 James Westfall Thompson and Bernard J. Holm, *A History of Historical Writing* (2 vols., New York, 1942), I, viii.

torical Writing in America (1891), he called attention in 1907 to "The American Acta Sanctorum" and to the possibility of using religious sources for the study of American social history.

Jameson tried to make clear the benefits that the modern medievalist had derived from the *acta sanctorum*. In the lives of St. Francis and St. Dominic, for example, the gildsman often found important material about religious movements; in the lives of St. Louis and St. Thomas of Canterbury, he often found important material about political developments; and in the lives of roaming saints, he often found important material about medieval conceptions of geography. But it was not what the hagiographer had to contribute in matters of religion, politics, and geography that concerned Jameson primarily; he was interested in other contributions of the hagiographer, contributions of an indirect and unintended kind. Of course, the hagiographer was actuated above all by spiritual and didactic aims, but these did not keep him from reflecting in his writings the manners, customs, and conditions of his time. Nor did these aims prevent him from furnishing valuable data for the modern medievalist who sought to reconstruct some of the lesser known aspects of the medieval scene. Jameson was impressed with the way the hagiographer often threw light on aspects of everyday living, on the life of the heathen, the Jews, and the lower and inarticulate elements of society, on disease, medicine, hygiene, domestic life, university hazing, and the use of everyday language. What many a chronicler took for granted, and therefore neglected to mention, could often be found in religious writings.

Such was the impression that the medievalist's exploitation of the *acta sanctorum* made on Jameson that he urged the American gildsman to follow the medievalist's example. In all other recorded ages, the study of religion threw valuable light on other aspects of history. Surely, then, the study of religion would light up the course of American history, too. Obviously, the American gildsman was by no means so dependent on religious sources as the medievalist, who, in many instances, had no other

materials to use. It was, in fact, the availability of great quantities of other materials that accounted for the gildsman's neglect
of American religious literature, said Jameson, himself the chairman of the Historical Manuscripts Commission and the editor
of that useful collection of documents, the *Original Narratives
of Early American History.*

So it was that Jameson—almost twenty-five years before
William Warren Sweet published the first volume of his collection of source materials, *Religion on the American Frontier*
(1931)—offered the assurance that in the Protestant hagio-
graphy of the United States much valuable data of a non-
religious sort waited to be exploited. By way of the lives of
American churchmen, the scholar could learn a great deal not
only about religious movements, politics, and geography, but
also about the social background of American history. He could
explore neglected aspects of colonial and frontier times; he could
gain rewarding information about Indian life, backwoods existence, the processes of Americanization, educational conditions,
slavery, and social life. Above all, Jameson emphasized that the
study of religious sources afforded an insight into the lives of the
poor, inarticulate, "obscure, unreading, unprinting majority,"
the kind of insight that even *belles-lettres* did not make possible.
As a source for the social history of the "toiling millions" and
as a key to American national character, Jameson rated the *acta
sanctorum* much more highly than *belles-lettres,* arguing with
considerable cogency that

> he who would understand the American of past and present
> times, and to that end would provide himself with data repre-
> senting all classes, all periods, and all religions, may find in
> the history of American religion the closest approach to the
> continuous record he desires. Not that all or even most Amer-
> icans have been religious, but there have been religious men
> and women in every class, every period, every subdivision
> of America, and multitudes of them have left individual or
> collective records of their thoughts and ways and feelings.

Millions have felt an interest in religion where thousands have felt an interest in literature or philosophy, in music or art.

Jameson did not wish to exaggerate the role of religion in the life of the American people. He admitted readily that Americans, through the years, were mainly concerned with meeting the needs of daily living. Even so, he insisted that, if an account of United States history was to be truthful, it could ignore neither the ideals of plain Americans nor their ideas of the universe and of man, and these ideals and ideas were best revealed in the history of religion, which reflected so admirably the beliefs and feelings "not of a priestly class, but of the mass of laymen."

Jameson, in seeking to further the use of religious sources, did not mean to favor a departure from the statistical approach to social history; he viewed statistics as a guarantee against the vagueness to which social history might otherwise fall heir. Similarly, he did not wish to exaggerate the elements of interest in the research project he was attempting to further. Perhaps because he himself had undertaken many a dull historical investigation, he did not hesitate to admit that the American *acta sanctorum* would involve long and barren stretches. Still, he argued, addressing his remarks chiefly and most optimistically to the young gildsman, the project was well worth undertaking. For the study of social history, as revealed in American religious literature, could provide an escape from "the well-worn grooves" of American constitutional and political history, said Jameson, who had taken his doctorate under political-minded Herbert Baxter Adams at Johns Hopkins and who had edited in the early part of his career such volumes as *Essays in the Constitutional History of the United States in the Formative Period, 1775-1789* (1889) and the heavily political *Dictionary of United States History* (1894). The Great Awakening, the religious revivals of the early nineteenth century, Mormonism, and the growth of Christian Science, these were subjects that the young historian could study with profit, and they would help him to overcome the narrowness of the traditional approach to the American past. No question about it, the historian should emancipate himself from any rigid adherence to political and constitutional matters, Jameson declared in 1907, reissuing an appeal that he had made years before in his remarkable lectures on *The History of Historical Writing in America* (1891).[20] Otherwise, "sciences less cautious than history" were bound to take over "the broad story of American culture."

Jameson's plea for less emphasis on political and constitutional history was not repeated by his successor, George Burton Adams, "the master of us all in the field of English constitutional history"[21] as well as the only American who had been invited to prepare a volume in one of the most distinguished of all European cooperative series, Hunt and Poole's *Political History of England*. Yet while Adams was mainly interested in political and constitutional affairs, he had made sure to take account of economic factors in his writings. In his widely-used textbook, *Civilization during the Middle Ages* (1894), he had suggested that "if there is one line of advance in civilization which is a necessary condition of progress in all other directions it would seem to be economic advance."[22] In his *Growth of the French Nation* (1896), he had apologized for not having paid more attention to economic history.[23] The study of political and constitutional developments had convinced Adams, as he said in his message of 1908, that economic influences were "among the most profound which have shaped human affairs." He insisted that the political historian could have "no more valuable ally than the economic historian." Specialist though Adams was in political and con-

20 *The History of Historical Writing in America* (Boston, 1891), pp. 141-43, 146-47.

21 Edward Potts Cheyney, "Law in History," *A.H.R.*, XXIX (1924), 232-33.

22 *Civilization during the Middle Ages Especially in Relation to Modern Civilization* (New York, 1894), p. 278.

23 *The Growth of the French Nation* (New York, 1896), p. iii.

stitutional matters, he took no narrow view of the content of history.

Adams' successor, Albert Bushnell Hart, the editor of the *American Nation* series and the chairman of Harvard's department of government, also defended the cause of economic history in his presidential message. Nor was there anything extraordinary about this, for Hart had often pointed up the broadness of his view of the past. In his important multi-volume source book, *American History Told by Contemporaries* (1897-1929), he had stated that in order to understand the American past it was necessary to understand "the actual conditions of common life: of country, town, and city; of farmer, artisan, merchant, and slaveholder; of church, school, and convention."[24] Similarly, Hart had declared in his "Editor's Introduction" that the *American Nation* series was "not intended to be simply a political or constitutional history: it must include the social life of the people, their religion, their literature, and their schools. It must include their economic life, occupations, labor systems, and organizations of capital. It must include their wars and their diplomacy, the relations of community with community and of the nation with other nations."[25]

It was, then, no surprise that Hart, in his presidential message of 1909, urged the historian not to confine his attention to political events but to investigate the commonplace aspects of man's past, his social and economic experiences. Hart, in fact, reminded the gildsman of what Wordsworth had written about the broad reaches of history in his tract, *Concerning the Convention of Cintra* (1809):

> The history of all ages; tumults after tumults; wars, foreign or civil, with short or no breathing spaces, from generation to generation; wars—why and wherefore? yet with courage,

24 *American History Told by Contemporaries* (5 vols., New York 1897-1929), III, viii.

25 "Editor's Introduction to the Series," in Edward Potts Cheyney, *European Background of American History, 1300-1600* (New York, 1904), p. xvii.

with perseverance, with self-sacrifice, with enthusiasm....
The visible and familiar occurrences of daily life in every
town and village; the patient curiosity and contagious ac-
clamations of the multitude in the streets of the city and
within the walls of the theatre; a procession, or a rural dance;
a hunting, or a horse-race; a flood, or a fire; rejoicing and
ringing of bells for an unexpected gift of good fortune; or
the coming of a foolish heir to his estate.

According to Hart, every aspect of history was worth studying
—whether it happened to be the fall of the Roman Empire or
the use of wampum in the American colonies. And he rejoiced
that fresh historical fields kept opening. He himself, however,
was more an organizer than a researcher; and, despite the length
of his list of publications, he had done little to open fresh fields.

His successor, Frederick Jackson Turner, on the other hand,
had done much as a pioneer, though he had relatively few publications to his credit. Indeed, one of Hart's great achievements,
as Samuel E. Morison has written, was that he managed to com-
pel Turner to finish his volume in the *American Nation* series.[26]
And it was four years after the publication of this volume on the
Rise of the New West (1906)—one of the two volumes that
Turner was to publish in his lifetime—that he delivered his
presidential message, whose relative neglect, Avery Craven has
said, explains "much of the misunderstanding" of his work.[27]
Addressing the Association at a time when Progressivism
was running high, Turner turned to the discussion of "Social
Forces in American History." Years before, in his essay of 1891
on "The Significance of History,"[28] he had called attention to

26 Samuel E. Morison, "Albert Bushnell Hart, 1889-1939," in Massachusetts Historical Society, *Proceedings, 1936-1941* (Boston, 1942), LXVI, 438.

27 Avery Craven, "Frederick Jackson Turner," in William T. Hutchinson,
ed., *The Marcus W. Jernegan Essays in American Historiography* (Chicago,
1937), p. 263.

28 *The Early Writings of Frederick Jackson Turner* (Madison, 1938), pp.
45-46, 51-54.

the need for more emphasis on American economic and industrial development. Once again, in 1910, he emphasized the need to study industrial development; nevertheless, as he surveyed some of the main social, economic, and political currents in recent United States history, he emphasized that "a complex of forces" went into its making.

> We must deal [he said] with the connections of geography, industrial growth, politics, and government. With these we must take into consideration the changing social composition, the inherited beliefs and habitual attitude of the masses of the people, the psychology of the nation and of the separate sections, as well as of the leaders.... We cannot neglect the moral tendencies and the ideals. All are related parts of the same subject and can no more be properly understood in isolation than the movement as a whole can be understood by neglecting some of these important factors, or by the use of a single method of investigation.

So it was that Turner emerged as the first president of the Association to back wholeheartedly cooperation with allied investigators. This need, he insisted, was increased by the pace of recent American economic growth; for, without the cooperation of all students of the past, recent changes in the social and economic structure of the United States could not be understood and the broad reaches of history itself could not be appreciated. Though Turner had taught courses on primitive society and on medieval and French Revolutionary history,[29] he hesitated to discuss fields in which he did not consider himself firmly grounded. Confining his comments, therefore, to the United States, he contended that the content of American history dealt mainly with "social forces" which were shaped and reshaped as a changing nation adapted itself to an environment that disclosed new phases, exercised new influences, and called forth "new social organs and functions."

Pointing to the success with which the scientist was combining old studies and forming new ones like physical chemistry,

29 W. Stull Holt, ed., *op. cit.*, p. 123.

electro-chemistry, geo-physics, and astro-physics, Turner noted
that the new-type geologist used the methods and findings of
chemistry, physics, mathematics, botany, and zoology in his
effort to understand the dynamics of the inorganic earth; and
he came to appreciate that the complexity of a geological area
made necessary the abandonment of "the single hypothesis for
the multiple hypothesis." Having learned to avoid oversimplifications, he came to emphasize not a single explanation but
a whole string of explanations, said Turner, whose own researches in frontier history had led him to a remarkable familiarity with geological literature.

The experience of the geologist offered a cue to action that
the historian could not afford to ignore. He should recognize
the variety, the complexity, and the interaction of the factors
that operated in human society; and he should incorporate in
his writings his awareness of these varied, complex, and inter-
acting factors, said Turner, whose own writings have often
been criticized for their oversimplifications. Whether the gildsman specialized in political, economic, or any other kind of history, he should make sure not to handle his major interest in
isolation. His approach should be synthetic and he should take
advantage of the findings and methods of allied scholars. The
specialist in economics, political science, psychology, sociology,
geography, literature, art, and religion, the specialist in these
and other subjects could do much to enrich the content of history. He could make capital contributions to the historian in the
way of materials, tools, viewpoints, hypotheses, and hints about
relationships, causes, and emphases. As long as each specialist
worked and groped alone, he ran the risk of being blinded by his
particular slant; he was likely to see what he was mainly interested in seeing. Once he learned the advantage of cooperation
with other specialists, he was likely to overcome that singleness of view that hindered the search for truth. Plainly, then, the
historian ought to acquaint himself with the work and training
of allied investigators, availing himself of their findings and
their methods. For their part, too, allied investigators ought

o familiarize themselves with the work and methods of the historian. For, under the conditions of modern scholorship, no specialist could wisely seek to remain independent. Only the' cooperation of all those interested in the past could make possible an understanding of the multiple and complex forces whose interplay made society what it was.

Turner's successor, William M. Sloane, also viewed the past broadly; but he made it clear that he did not go all out in his support of cooperation with allied investigators. This, as has been indicated, was doubtless due in part to his attitude towards James Harvey Robinson, his colleague at Columbia, whose enthusiasm for "The New Allies of History" was unbounded. Whatever the reason, Sloane, who had written on antiquity, eighteenth-century America, and the French Revolutionary and Napoleonic era, took the stand that history had narrow boundaries: it was limited to the ten thousand years for which records, if imperfect ones, existed. Sloane was suspicious of those who considered the whole past historical; unlike Robinson, he distrus ed the prehistoric archaeologist, the anthropologist, the geologic palaeontologist, the animal psychologist, and the social psychologist,

Chronologically, then, he took a narrow view of the boundaries of history, but in another respect his view was far from narrow. For Sloane, who had started his academic career as a teacher of Latin, believed that the historian should deal with all aspects of human life: social, economic, governmental, military, diplomatic, linguistic, scientific, numismatic, medical, religious, and literary. The historian should not confine himself to past politics, especially since politics was frequently the "resultant" of religious, social, economic, personal, or intellectual forces, said Sloane, who for a time had served as secretary to George Bancroft, minister to the German Empire.

Nor did Sloane's successor, Theodore Roosevelt, disapprove of the broad view of the past. As a matter of fact, he criticized the attempt to fix the boundaries of history, declaring that it was not "necessary rigidly to mark the limits of the province of history, nor to treat of all that is within that province, nor to exclude any subject within that province from treatment, nor yet to treat different methods of dealing with the same subject as mutually exclusive." Roosevelt insisted that it was the business of each individual gildsman to decide what really interested him personally; and even more than authority he should value his freedom to write about anything he wanted to write about, Roosevelt declared, showing wisdom of which some historians doubtless did not think him capable.

Because one gildsman was attracted by financial history, it did not follow that another should be ashamed of his interest in military history, said Roosevelt, whose first historical study had been *The Naval War of 1812* (1882). Because one gildsman was drawn to statistical tables, it failed to follow that another should not be drawn to the study of the influence of orators and poets in times of crisis. Just as the functioning of representative government ought to be examined, so the economic effects of the factory system ought to be examined. Just as Thorold Rogers' price studies deserved to be read, so Mahan's naval studies deserved to be read, said Roosevelt, putting in a good word for one of his favorite American historians.[30] To enjoy Thayer's Cavour did not mean to scorn Trevelyan's works on Garibaldi. To delight in Joinville, Villehardouin, and Froissart did not mean to scorn volumes that traced the changes in the economic status of commoners in the later Middle Ages. The effects of the spread of malaria in the Aegean region, the impact of the Black Death on the medieval labor supply, the influence of insect-borne diseases on African development, all these were subjects worthy of study.

Having indicated to a society of academicians his familiarity with historical bibliography, Roosevelt, himself the author of the multi-volume *Winning of the West* (1889-1896), empha-

30 A. B. Hart and H. R. Ferleger, eds., *Theodore Roosevelt Cyclopedia* (New York, 1941), pp. 326-27.

sized that the gildsman should deal with ordinary people, how they worked and how they played. He should ignore nothing that threw light on their life. He should examine the tools they used, the weapons with which they fought, the wills and contracts they left, the songs they sang, and the literature they wrote and read. Always, however, the historian should make sure to use his imaginative powers, remembering that a statistical table no more recreated the past than a tariff report on hides and woolens recreated the actual living conditions of cowboys and factory-workers.

Even the overwhelming importance of the living conditions of ordinary people did not rule out the need for an "especial portrayal" of extraordinary times. It was regrettable, Roosevelt pointed out—and quite correctly—that in the reaction against the old-style historian, with his stress on the heroic and the extraordinary, on war and politics, the new-style historian often went to the other extreme, ignoring the role of crises and cataclysms. Doubtless it was commonplace, everyday affairs that mattered most in the life of the ordinary citizen, but the historian should remember that critical times determined the conditions under which the ordinary life of the citizen could be resumed.

The gildsman should remember, moreover, not to view history "as something set off by itself." Like Turner, that other student of the frontier, Roosevelt took the position that history "must welcome the entrance upon its domain of every science." Quoting from Robinson's recently published *New History,* he insisted that the boundaries between departments of learning were fundamentally artificial and unreal, that it was interdependence, not independence, which made for intellectual advances. Accordingly, he urged the historian to extend a hearty welcome to the archaeologist, the anthropologist, and the palaeoethnologist, from all of whom he could gather material with which to enrich the subject-matter of historical writing.

Just as Roosevelt's remarks about the content of history were incidental to his discussion of "History as Literature," so the remarks of his successor, Wiliam A. Dunning, were incidental to his discussion of "Truth in History." Dunning, whose own researches dealt largely with the growth of European political thought and the history of the American Civil War and Reconstruction, ventured in his message to determine the limits of the historian's sphere of activity. So many events went into the making of the past that there was no escape from the conclusion that "not all truth, but certain aspects or classes of truth" concerned the historian. Dunning found it unthinkable that anyone would seriously contend that all past developments fell within the historian's realm, but he recognized that to draw the boundaries of the field was to provoke a heated controversy over what fell within it and what fell outside. For all that, Dunning took his stand in 1913, arguing that the historian's function was to determine and arrange causally those influences which had undeniably affected the "development of men in social and political life." And those influences were not only material in character, said Dunning, who had been one of the defenders of Beard's recently published *An Economic Interpretation of the Constitution;* they were also spiritual, psychic, and intellectual in character.

In this way Dunning joined many another president of the Association in stressing the richness of the subject-matter of history. Certainly no early president—even in what has often been considered the heyday of the political and military emphasis —was so rash as to argue that the gildsman's sole concerns were politics, constitutions, and wars. An awareness of the varied content of history was so basic to the thinking of the early leaders of the Association, to say nothing of their European contemporaries, that it is difficult to understand how some of the disciples of James Harvey Robinson, not to mention Robinson himself, could have succeeded in spreading the idea that the "New History" originated an essentially new conception of the content of history. In fact, it is significant that already in the early decades of the Association's life White and Roosevelt complained that the content of history was being restricted by those who would keep politics and war out of their treatments of the past.

CHAPTER X
THE CONTENT OF HISTORY:
RECENT YEARS

EVEN the coming of the first World War did not encourage the presidents to recommend the study of military and diplomatic history. Indeed, for almost a decade after 1914, they had relatively little or nothing to say about what the content of history should be, whether military, diplomatic, synthetic, or what have you. In part, perhaps, this was because a broad view of the past had come to be taken for granted in gild circles. Why, then, belabor the obvious? Since social, economic, and intellectual developments were being more and more stressed in historical writings, there was perhaps little need to urge the historian to pry himself loose from political, constitutional, and military studies.

Andrew C. McLaughlin, for instance, was preeminently a political and constitutional historian. Like his predecessor, Dunning, however, he indicated in his message of 1914 on "American History and American Democracy" that to study the past was to study not only events and the external behavior of men but ideals, goals, and matters of the spirit. The historian who dealt with democracy, for example, should consider it not only as a form of government but as a spirit that pervaded the American past. Nor should he view the history of democracy—and constitutional history in general—merely as branches of economic history, McLaughlin declared, thinking perhaps of the conclusions drawn from *An Economic Interpretation of the Constitution of the United States* by some left-wingers, whose indiscriminate praise Beard himself was to deplore.

McLaughlin was convinced that in order to understand the American past the historian should learn the art of "feeling character and divining living spirit." He should study the ideas of purpose and of destiny and the hopes for human betterment that animated the American people; and he should determine how their development was affected by "war, expansion, factories and machinery, constitutions and courts, food and physical environment, the city and the frontier, all working together. . ." By all means, moreover, he should overcome his distrust of historical intangibles—the very things which McLaughlin thought most warranted examination, though he himself had paid little attention to them in *A History of the American Nation* (1899), *The Confederation and the Constitution, 1783-1789* (1905), and *The Courts, the Constitution, and Parties* (1912). Indeed, McLaughlin suggested that what made his friend Turner so admirable an historian was that he had an appreciation of the spiritual content of history. He was aware of the role of nature in American development, but he was also aware of the spiritual significance of the frontier.

George L. Burr, addressing the Association in 1916, concerned himself even less with the content of history. An enormously well-read scholar, whose historical knowledge went far beyond the medieval period in which he specialized, Burr interrupted his discussion of "The Freedom of History" to credit Bayle, Montesquieu, and Voltaire with having broadened the scope of history to include the growth of civilization. He also took time out to comment on the deeper understanding of the past that would result from the cooperation of the historian with allied investigators. For the rest, Burr did not deal with the content of history in his message. An authority on witchcraft, tolerance, and the warfare of science with theology, he had long since made it clear that history was more than past politics.[1]

Nor did William R. Thayer deal at any length with the content of history in either of the messages that he prepared as president of the Association. He was disturbed in 1919 by the drift toward specialization in historical study—and understandably so. For his own writings on the Italian past had been conscious

1 L. O. Gibbons, ed., *George Lincoln Burr: Selections from His Writings* (Ithaca, 1943), p. 332.

attempts to achieve a synthesis of political, social, and cultural factors. But despite the growth of specialized studies of political, social, religious, financial, and industrial developments, Thayer was convinced that synthetic history would continue to thrive. Surely the study of some narrow aspect of the past did not rule out the need for the investigation of entities. "If you lop off all branches of a tree," he said, "and, after studying each branch, you study each twig, should you really know the whole tree, having failed to examine its trunk"? Thayer asserted the altogetherness of history, voicing his opposition to those who would have history "lost in its elements," whether political, social, financial, industrial, or religious.

If Thayer had little to say about the subject matter of history, his successor, Edward Channing, had nothing at all to say about it. Undertaking in 1920 an "Historical Retrospect" based on material which was shortly to appear in the fifth volume of his *History of the United States,* Channing did not talk about what the content of history should be. Instead, he showed, by using political, economic, social, and cultural data, how broad his view of the past was, or, better still, how much broader it had become in the period since he had started to work on his *magnum opus.*[2]

Even Charles H. Haskins paid only slight attention to the content of history in his message of 1922. At the time, indeed, Haskins' only important published books were those on the Normans and Norman institutions.[3] He had not yet brought out his volumes on intellectual and cultural history: *The Rise of Universities* (1923), *Studies in the History of Mediaeval Science* (1924), *The Renaissance of the Twelfth Century*

2 Cf. Ralph Ray Fahrney, "Edward Channing," in William T. Hutchinson, ed., *The Marcus W. Jernegan Essays in American Historiography* (Chicago, 1937), p. 301.

3 See the bibliography in *Anniversary Essays in Mediaeval History by Students of Charles Homer Haskins Presented on His Completion of Forty Years of Teaching* (Boston, 1929), pp. 389-98.

(1927), and *Studies in Mediaeval Culture* (1929). Parts of these volumes had, however, already been published in various periodicals, and they had done much to win for him the widespread recognition that he enjoyed in European historical circles.[4]

Discussing "European History and American Scholarship," Haskins sketched the accomplishments of American gildsmen in the various fields of European history. He took pride in the achievements of such writers of intellectual history as White, Dunning, Burr, Taylor, Robinson, and Thorndike. He also took pride in the achievements of an art historian of the Henry Adams variety. Just the same, he thought that the "best" products of American historical scholarship were those dealing with institutions, political, legal, ecclesiastical, and economic. And when he named the two Americans who had contributed the most in recent times to the study of European history, he did not single out "new" historians; he chose Lea and Mahan. As a medievalist, he was certainly qualified to pass judgment on Lea; but Charles Beard would doubtless have included Haskins among the American historians whom he referred to as being "ill-prepared to analyze and scrutinize Mahan's documentation, methods, and intellectual maneuvers."[5]

Haskins suggested that the American historian had on the whole not met with much success in studies requiring imaginative gifts. Social history he saw fit to characterize as "a new *genre,* stronger as yet in its programme than in its achievements." But if anything took him by surprise it was the neglect in the United States of the history of science and invention— this in a country whose world renown rested so largely on its scientific and technological feats. To Haskins, whose *Studies in the History of Mediaeval Science* (1924) was quickly to become a favorite among specialists, a volume to be kept "with-

4 James T. Shotwell, *At the Paris Peace Conference* (New York, 1937), p. 8.

5 Charles Austin Beard, *A Foreign Policy for America* (New York, 1940), p. 44.

in arm's reach,"[6] it seemed unthinkable that the American gildsman should have been so little moved to dig into so rich a field.

Haskins' comments of 1922 about the content of history were
only incidental to his discussion of "European History and
American Scholarship"; but the comments that Charles M.
Andrews had to make two years later formed an integral part
of his sketch of some of the main currents in American historical writing in "These Forty Years" since the founding of the
Association. Andrews, who had done his graduate work at
Johns Hopkins, attributed much of the former American emphasis on political history to the influence of German scholarship. The young American, he said, thinking perhaps of his own
teacher, Herbert Baxter Adams, acquired from his German
professors an accent on the constitutional, legal, and political
sides of history. Not only that; he also acquired from his German professors an accent on specialization, so that for a while
it appeared that history might even cease to exist as a separate
study. "Clio stood aghast, seemingly stripped of her attributes,
as one by one government, administration, economics, law,
sociology, and finance were torn from her grasp," declared
Andrews, using dramatic effects of a sort that he rarely used
in his writings. Happily, history was not reduced to the status
of a mere remainder; on the contrary, she rightly claimed recognition as "the one universal interest embracing all the rest."

Happily, too, the German worship of specialization never
had much of a chance in the United States, for the American
gildsman was generally called upon to teach in a number of
fields, said Andrews, whose own "Bryn Mawr period" was spent
mainly on English and general European history.[7] And there

6 Lynn Thorndike, "Charles Homer Haskins (1870-1937)," *Isis*, XXVIII
(1938), 55.

7 J. Franklin Jameson, "Preface," in *Essays in Colonial History Presented to Charles McLean Andrews by His Students* (New Haven, 1931),
p. xi.

was every reason to rejoice that the historian failed to take to specialization, for there was no point in fragmenting a subject whose goals were synthetic. Andrews' enthusiasm for synthesis even led him to suggest that in recent decades the tendency to think in terms of types of history—political, religious, economic, agricultural, military—had gradually given way to a tendency to think of the past in its altogetherness. Doubtless he was more optimistic than the state of historiography warranted; at any rate he made it clear that

> the historian claims the right to concern himself with any subject needed to explain the situation that he has set himself to understand and expound. He realizes, as never before, that no event or aspect or quality of the past can be understood without seeing it in connection with the entire life of the times. He may need to know something about religious creeds, socialistic theories, systems of land distribution and agronomy, the working of the common law, the influence of money and banking and international exchange, the literature, art, architecture, and philosophy of an age, and even of the laws of nature in the fields of physics, chemistry, biology, and psychology—indeed the whole historical complex in peace and war. Any part of the whole record of civilization is the legitimate object of his quest.

Nor did Andrews have any doubts about the strength of the foothold that the broad view of the content of history had gained. It would never again be possible for a Seeley or a Freeman to proclaim the preeminently political character of history; all of man's activities, not just politics, diplomacy, and war, were the historian's concern. Naturally, different scholars would place different stresses on the different activities of man, but there was no question that forms of government and the ups and downs of political parties had lost their privileged position. Andrews himself, to be sure, had long been helping the non-political tendency along. At a time when James Harvey Robinson was writing on the American Constitution and the German Bundesrath, he was making a study of Anglo-Saxon economic life that developed into *The Old English Manor* (1892). Moreover, several years before Robinson emerged as a textbook writer, he brought out his two-volume *Historical Development of Modern Europe from the Congress of Vienna to the Present Time* (1896-1898), a work in which he dealt above all with politics but also with social, intellectual, and economic subjects; and he dealt with these same subjects in *A History of England* (1903), a volume that showed the influence of John Richard Green and of the elder Arnold Toynbee, of *Industrial Revolution* fame.[8] It was therefore without self-consciousness that he could state in his message of 1924 that the growth and interplay of conditions and ideas, of institutions and thought, and the influence of economic circumstances on society and politics, these formed the main objects of present-day research.

Andrews had an opportunity in his second presidential message to discuss more concretely the variety of factors that went into the making of history. Addressing the Association in 1925, shortly after the publication of his four essays on *The Colonial Background of the American Revolution* (1924), he took for his theme one of the subjects with which he had been concerned in his book. While he considered the Revolution primarily a political and constitutional struggle, he emphasized that in order to understand it the historian must take into account not only political and constitutional factors but intellectual, financial, commercial, and social factors. He thought, for instance, that the "impact of convictions" had been too often neglected as a cause. Stressing, therefore, the need to study the Revolution in its intellectual origins, he set forth an interpretation that highlighted the rigid mental outlook of the governing elements of mid-eighteenth-century England.

8 *The Historical Development of Modern Europe from the Congress of Vienna to the Present Time* (2 vols., New York, 1896-98), I, iv; *A History of England* (Boston, 1903), pp. iii-iv.

The broad view of the content of history that Andrews backed also had the backing of Dana C. Munro, his successor. Much more than Andrews, Munro sought to get at the why of the broader content of history, and he found part of the explanation in the relationship between "War and History." Turning to the subject he knew best, the Crusades, Munro deplored the fact that recent treatments almost always overlooked the broadening influence that the Crusades had had on the writing of history. He granted that some broadening of scope had already been reflected in some of the writings on the lay investiture conflict and the Norman wars of conquest; but much more important, he thought, was the broadening that came with the age of the Crusades, when both Christian and Moslem historians made room in their works for new lands and peoples.

Nor did the Crusades stand alone among wars in fostering a broadening of historical scope. True, the post-crusading era saw the resurgence of localism as a dominant characteristic of historical writing; and history was frequently used to serve propagandist ends. Humanism itself, Munro noted, reenforced the emphasis on local and partisan history; and it was only after the French invasion of the Italies in 1494 that the "return to the larger canvas" took place. But even though the Renaissance saw some growth of interest in universal history, the historian continued to concentrate on military and political matters to the neglect of things cultural.

During the French Revolutionary and Napoleonic Age, on the other hand, there took place a marked growth of interest in the affairs of other countries and peoples; and the coming to power of erstwhile nobodies helped to bring about in historical writing a shift of focus from kings and noblemen to commoners. Generally, however, this basic expansion of the content of historical writing did not become clear until the post-Waterloo generation set to work.

Munro did not argue that all wars stimulated interest in the past and produced outstanding historians. If that had been so, he suggested in 1926, the last four centuries, war-ridden as they were, would have produced a most impressive galaxy of historians. Which, then, were the wars that exerted the most considerable influence on historiography? "They were wars," he said, "which excited the popular imagination; wars in which men were conscious of common interests; wars which were due to or caused a change in the social polity; wars by which men's interests were broadened or directed into new channels." Here, from Munro's point of view, lay the explanation of the impact of the Crusades and the French Revolution on the writing of history, for both events had worked on a large scale to speed up changes in ideas. Munro did not wish to push his evidence too much. There could be no overlooking the influence that Montesquieu, Voltaire, Robertson, Hume, and Gibbon exerted on subsequent historical writing. Similarly, there could be no ignoring the fact that the eighteenth century showed some of the emphases which the nineteenth century considered particularly its own: the secularization and democratization of the content of history, for instance, and the investigation of national character and the *Zeitgeist*.

Munro did not sidetrack the discussion of the probable impact of the first World War on historical writing. Already in pre-war days, he said, history was viewed as embracing all of man's acts and thoughts from the time he first appeared on earth; and already there were the Robinsons who favored a new type of history that would concentrate on institutions, customs, and the more normal aspects of life, said Munro, whose own *History of the Middle Ages* (1902) had emphasized topics like the civilizing work of the Church, the influence of Byzantine and Arabic civilization, and the life of the times.[9] To such an extent did the New History become "a name to conjure with" that politics, diplomacy, and war fell increasingly into disfavor. In a real sense, then, said Munro, himself a former colleague of Robinson at the University of Pennsylvania, the war had the effect of enlarging the content of history, for

9 *A History of the Middle Ages* (New York, 1902), p. v.

it helped to restore military and diplomatic history to something of their once-favored position. In the period of the Peace Conference, moreover, many peoples formerly neglected came increasingly into their own: Moslems, Asiatics, and Russians attracted greater attention—even in American textbooks. In the future, too, Munro anticipated that the scope of history would continue to broaden. The future gildsman, he was convinced, would view the past in the largest way possible, realizing always that complexity was the lifeblood of history; and the varied sources he would use would indicate the broadness of his conception of the content of history.

Munro's views were strikingly concrete—something that those of his successor, Henry Osborn Taylor, were not. One of the vaguest of the men who have headed the Association, Taylor had long delighted in elusive subjects, subjects that lacked definiteness;[10] otherwise, he might not have become a historian of ideas. However that may be, Taylor, who had taught for only two years, considered himself in a position to present "A Layman's View of History"; and he made it a point to explain how it was that he had come to be a layman-historian and how it was that his view of the content of history had developed. Lacking by his own statement originality and creativity, he had turned to what others considered "best." The study and practice of law he abandoned at an early stage because he found the field too narrow; and he turned to the humanities, for there he could investigate "the most humanly interesting elements in the aim and the endeavor—the forming an ideal, and the struggle through the man's years, or perhaps through the longer life of a people, to accomplish it." Whether or not an historical person or people reached the particular goal was a minor matter; "the true human story," according to Taylor, was the account of the effort to achieve the goal. Armed with this "first conviction as to the central human interest of the endeavor and the aim," he

10 *Freedom of the Mind in History* (London, 1923), p. vii.

had prepared his studies in intellectual history: *Ancient Ideals* (1896), *The Classical Heritage of the Middle Ages* (1901), *The Mediaeval Mind* (1911), *Thought and Expression in the Sixteenth Century* (1920), and *Freedom of the Mind in History* (1923), works that could not have been completed, he was sure, if, during his forty years of study and writing, he had also been preoccupied with teaching and administrative functions.

Suggesting that history had two meanings which needed to be distinguished, Taylor pointed out that at times it meant merely a "descriptive narrative"; other times it meant "the very life and actuality of the past, out of which the present has arisen." History, in other words, was either an account of events or the events themselves. Obviously, if history, viewed as narrative, was to be life-like and truthful, it should be the same as the past itself, the same as the past and present it sought to describe. The fact, however, remained that any historical narrative was itself an event; it was a portion of the stuff of its own age, of the intellectual milieu in which it was composed. For instance, said Taylor, the life and work of Thucydides formed a part of the age of the Peloponnesian War; and the works of Gibbon and Mommsen were events of their times, events which linked the eighteenth and the nineteenth centuries with the past. Even more striking examples of events that were at the same time narratives could be found in literature and art. The *Iliad* and the *Divine Comedy*, the Parthenon and the Cathedral of Chartres, the *Republic* and the *Summa*, all expressed the qualities of their respective ages: all were records and important pieces of historical evidence.

As a historian of ideas, Taylor was naturally attracted by the scientific and philosophic views of a period. Twentieth-century physics, psychology, and psychoanalysis, he thought, expressed the restless spirit of the times, but a future period with another outlook and temper might perhaps find much to criticize in this science. What mattered, in any case, was that the historian was a humanist, and, unlike the scientist, he found men in the center of his universe. Taylor saw no reason for the historian to be concerned with the validity of scientific data. He should view science from the humanist angle—as an aspect of the growth of the mind. And he should treat it as " a unity and a whole, made of its present and its past." As with science, so, too, with philosophy, religion, literature, art, and human institutions, political, social, and military. All these reflections of the human spirit the historian should view in their totality and unity, in the oneness of their past and present.

It was in a much more direct manner that Taylor's successor, James Henry Breasted, proclaimed the broadness of his view of the past. But the leading American Egyptologist had little to say about the content of history that he had not said before. In his *History of the Ancient Egyptians* (1908), he had tried to deal as much as possible with the people; in his *Development of Religion and Thought in Ancient Egypt* (1912), he had tried to emphasize the importance of intellectual and cultural currents; and in the several editions of the high-school textbook on which he collaborated with James Harvey Robinson he had tried to concentrate on the study of conditions and institutions, exploring the life of ancient man in its social, industrial, commercial, religious, artistic, and literary manifestations.[11] Understandably, then, Breasted rejoiced in his presidential message of 1928 on "The New Crusade" that of all views of history that which recognized it as "a record of human experience" had perhaps gained the widest acceptance. Nor did he lament the decline of political history. On the contrary, Breasted, repeating the attack that he had made in his essay on "The New Past,"[12] declared that the stress on politics and affairs of state merely testified to the deficiencies of the old-time historian's imagination; and for these deficiencies, he thought, there was really no

11 *A History of the Ancient Egyptians* (New York, 1908), p. viii; *Ancient Times: A History of the Early World: An Introduction to the Study of Ancient History and the Career of Early Man* (Boston, 1916), p. iii.

12 Breasted et al., *The New Past and Other Essays on the Development of Civilisation* (Oxford, 1925), p. 2.

excuse, for Voltaire, with his broad interpretation of human activities, had already pointed the way.

Slow as the European historian had been to follow Voltaire's leadership, the American historian had been even slower, Breasted noted with regret. German scholars responded somewhat to a writer like Burckhardt, the cultural historian of Greece and of Renaissance Italy, who insisted that the student of the past should deal with "the whole range of human life as a symmetrical whole." American scholars, however, generally lagged behind their European colleagues, refusing to recognize that *Kulturgeschichte* was "the very lifeblood of history." Breasted thought that American backwardness in adopting a broad view of history would be surprising in any case; but what made it all the more surprising was that to do justice to the American past it was obviously necessary to approach the subject from the standpoint of the growth of civilization. Americans, indeed, with their own relatively recent frontier experience, seemed singularly well qualified to understand the process of civilization in other regions.

There were difficulties, to be sure. For example, said Breasted, turning to the field which he had done so much to develop, it was hard for Americans to understand that in the Nile region wilderness and jungle preceded pyramids, sphinxes, and obelisks, that prehistoric Nile-dwellers had no civilized ancestry from whom they could inherit their culture. Even so, Breasted considered this "advent of civilization for the first time"—a theme on which he had often written before—a prerequisite to any understanding of the history of man. It was, therefore, with pride that he announced it possible to determine the site of the first appearance of civilization. A careful study of the available evidence, he argued, left little room for doubting that civilization was "born" in Egypt. Despite the recent discoveries made in the Tigris-Euphrates region, there was no real basis for questioning the priority of the Egyptians in "the advance toward civilization"—especially since Egyptian art by 3000 B. C.

was so far ahead of the crude Babylonian art of the same period.

The important point that Breasted wished to make was that so-called Western Civilization had its roots in ancient Egypt, "that earliest civilized world." This, of course, had become a commonplace in the twentieth century; but even when Ranke undertook his *Weltgeschichte* around 1880 he held that the origins of civilized society could not be determined; worse still, he considered the civilizations of the ancient Near East as altogether dissociated from "the main stream of history." In a matter of twenty years, Breasted was happy to record, Sir Arthur Evans found evidence in Crete that enabled him to dispel these erroneous notions of Ranke and assert the essential unity of history. It was this idea of "the unity of the human career" that Breasted viewed as perhaps the outstanding accomplishment of modern historical study. For, once the gildsman became aware of it, he could expand enormously the content of history; he could trace the study of mankind back to geological times and connect man's development with the evolution of other forms of planetary life; he could trace the later steps in "the upward course of the developing life of man," picking up the process of evolution where it was dropped by the scientist. Breasted could conceive of no "more inspiring task than to follow that tremendous transformation by which the primitive forest of the stone-age savage has at last given way to the modern forest of factory chimneys."

Unfortunately, there were few American historians who viewed man's career in its entirety; and Breasted complained that there were fewer still who knew where the largest amount of evidence about man's past continued to remain unexploited. The gildsman continued to treat the ancient Near East like an outcast; however much its monuments called for a New Crusade, he failed to heed a call that would enable him to enrich the content of history. Happily, a benefactor had appeared in the person of John D. Rockefeller, Jr., who, in the years after 1919, backed the activities of the Oriental Institute. And to these activities, which did such great credit to American scholarship and which he would later describe at length in his volume on *The Oriental Institute* (1933), Breasted devoted a major portion of his message, emphasizing the attempts to disclose "the gradual unfolding of ancient human life in all directions," to further knowledge of the sovereigns, statesmen, architects, engineers, and craftsmen of the ancient Near East, and to investigate the operation of social forces, the growth of rational and scientific thought, and the flowering of the Egyptian spirit.[13] And now that the financial status of the Institute was relatively secure, Breasted stressed the need for man-power, the need for young American students who would be willing to devote their lives to the study of the world's cultural indebtedness to the ancient Near East.

James Harvey Robinson, the next president, had also been a longtime advocate of a broad conception of history. Back in the early nineties, however, when McMaster, Eggleston, and Jameson were urging the enrichment of the content of history, Robinson was writing on *The Original and Derived Features of the Constitution of the United States of America* (1890) and *The German Bundesrath: A Study in Comparative Constitutional Law* (1891); and even in his *Introduction to the History of Western Europe* (1902-1903), though he sought to deal with economic, intellectual, and artistic developments as an "integral part of the narrative,"[14] his stress was overwhelmingly political. Nevertheless, with the publication in 1912 of *The New History,* a collection of some of his previously published articles, he came increasingly to be identified as the leader of the attack on the traditional content of history. Then, when his students undertook to publicize the contributions of their teacher, he emerged as an original thinker who discovered, among other things, that history dealt with more than politics and constitutions; and this

---

13 See the list of the publications of the Oriental Institute in Charles Breasted, *Pioneer to the Past: The Story of James Henry Breasted, Archaeologist* (New York, 1943), pp. 419-26.

14 *An Introduction to the History of Western Europe* (Boston, 1903), p. iv.

notion he did little to dispel, though he did acknowledge the influence of Voltaire, Spencer, Buckle, and Green.[15]

Robinson had succeeded during the course of his career in encouraging many a lively discussion. In his presidential message of 1929 on "The Newer Ways of Historians," however, he had only soft words to speak, words, he was sure, that would call forth none of the opposition of former times. His big concern was that he was voicing nothing more than platitudes like the need for more attention to the history of science and to world history rather than national history, needs which he and many other gildsmen had long been pointing out. Perhaps, then, it was mostly for old times' sake that Robinson referred to his own treatment of history as being "very large" and "reckless."

Long known for his hostility to what one of his students, Lynn Thorndike, has called "intellectual solemnity,"[16] Robinson laughed a little at the pedantry and haughtiness of the early twentieth-century historian. He laughed at his worship of primary sources; at his worship of the study of institutions and of Stubbs' *Constitutional History of England;* at his worship of the integrity of history and his fears of the social sciences. Nowadays, said Robinson in 1929, the historian thought differently. He considered formal and official sources less basic than before. He placed less stress on institutions in the old sense. He no longer feared the social sciences. Indeed, with a view to enriching the content of history, he abandoned his old-time aloofness and sought aid from quarters that would have been considered out of bounds at the start of the century. The present-day gildsman recognized the need to level all "circumvallations"; he doubted that he had "any legitimate sovereign rights to defend," said Robinson, who had long befriended "the new allies of history," except for sociology.[17]

15 *The Ordeal of Civilization: A Sketch of the Development and World-Wide Diffusion of Our Present-Day Institutions and Ideas* (New York, 1926), p. 3.

16 *Journal of Modern History,* IX (1937), 368.

17 Harry Elmer Barnes, "James Harvey Robinson," in Howard W. Odum, ed., *American Masters of Social Science* (New York, 1927), p. 365.

Like Breasted, his textbook collaborator, Robinson was delighted with "the vast backward extension of history" that had taken place in recent decades. What had only recently been prehistory was being rapidly turned into "honest-to-God history," and the old order of pre-history was yielding place to a new. Therefore, said Robinson, making much the same points that he had made so eloquently in *The Mind in the Making* (1921), the historian should devote more study to man's animal heritage; he should stop being ashamed of man's animal origins; he should recognize that man was a superanimal, not a degraded angel. "Since our animal equipment and tendencies deeply influence our civilization, which of course depends upon them," Robinson argued, " it becomes a matter of deep historical significance to compare our physical outfit and conduct with that of our nearest relatives who have not, for various reasons we now understand pretty well, ever achieved any civilization." Speaking at a time when the controversy over the teaching of evolution in the schools was still going strong, he urged the historian to study the writings of animal psychologists like Köhler, Pavlov, and Yerkes.

Robinson granted that it was easy to proclaim the superficiality of much that went by the name of history but that it was hard to find the means by which to overcome this superficiality. In studying much of the past, the historian was compelled to content himself with the outwardness of things; all too frequently he was unaware of what was taking place beneath the surface. But if he was really intent on getting to the bottom of things historical, Robinson was convinced that he should learn to exploit the belletristic survivals of different ages. He should surely thank Clio for a Jane Austen, a Richardson, a Fielding, and an Ibsen; and he could only regret that no Dickens was wandering in Jerusalem at the time of the codification of Deuteronomy, and that no H. G. Wells was called to the court of Charlemagne, said Robinson, putting in a good word for the man who had put in so many good words for him. All in all, then,

Robinson, who held the works of Chaucer and Shakespeare in greater favor as sources than the documents of Stubbs and of Gee and Hardy, suggested that the historian should use not only the traditional kinds of sources but *belles-lettres* as well, for they could often give him insight into the past of those "superanimals" known as men.

Just as Robinson viewed history in broad terms, so, too, did Carl L. Becker, Turner's most distinguished student. President of the Association in 1931, Becker had published less than many of his predecessors, but he was widely regarded as the most thoughtful of American gildsmen. Although his historical interests were many, his main interest was probably in the growth of ideas.[18] This he had shown in many of his articles and book-reviews, and in such volumes as *The United States: An Experiment in Democracy* (1920) and *The Declaration of Independence* (1922). And he showed it in the definition of history that he suggested in his message on "Everyman His Own Historian."

To start with, Becker had some distinctions to introduce. By history, for example, he meant knowledge of history—not what actually took place, but rather what was known of what took place. In other words, like Taylor before him and Beard after him, Becker distinguished between several histories: "the actual series of events that once occurred; and the ideal series that we affirm and hold in memory." While the first was absolute and unchanging, the second was relative and ever-changing; and the historian's function was to make the two histories as nearly identical as possible. As a rule, however, when the historian used the word *history* he meant knowledge of history—what he knew the past to be.

Having made his distinctions, Becker sought to work up a definition of history that would rid it of all superfluities. Immediately he disposed of *knowledge* because of its formidability;

18 Cf. George H. Sabine, "Carl Lotus Becker," in Becker, *Freedom and Responsibility in the American Way of Life* (New York, 1945), pp. xvi-xviii.

it was something "stored up in the *Encyclopaedia Britannica* or the *Summa Theologica.*" In its place he preferred a word like memory. As for *events,* another word that frequently cropped up in attempts to define history, Becker raised the objection that it smacked of the grand and the spectacular; it suggested an occurrence like the fall of the Bastille. The truth was, however, that "anything done, said, or thought" was an event. Finally, Becker saw little reason for using the word *past* in definitions of history; it was both misleading and redundant. Having eliminated words like knowledge, events, and past, he emerged with the broad definition of history that he had already set forth in his high-school textbook on *Modern History* (1931): "the memory of things said and done."[19]

If the history of historical writing betrayed at one time an emphasis on the memory of things political said and done and at another time an emphasis on the memory of things economic said and done, Becker thought the explanation not hard to find. Old history was always giving way to new history in keeping with the demands of the public. In a word, it was not the historian who determined the content of history; it was really the layman who did. For Mr. Everyman compelled the historian in times of political crisis to regard history as past politics and in times of social crisis to look for economic interpretations. Becker did not condemn the political history which the nineteenth-century historian wrote; himself the author of a doctoral dissertation on *The History of Political Parties in the Province of New York, 1760-1776* (1909), he considered this type of history a response to the needs of the time.

The next president, Herbert E. Bolton, also took a broad view of the past. A longtime advocate of the study of the Western Hemisphere, he emphasized the need to examine the "larger historical unities and interrelations" in Greater American his-

19 *Modern History: The Rise of a Democratic, Scientific, and Industrialized Civilization* (New York, 1931), pp. v-vi.

tory—intellectual and cultural no less than political and economic. So much work remained to be done on "The Epic of Greater America" that Bolton could only deplore the concentration of many a doctoral candidate on provincial, if national, subjects that had long since failed to yield sufficient returns.[20] Indicating the richness of his conception of the subject-matter of history, Bolton, who had been trained by McMaster and Turner, had these questions to ask:

> Who has written the history of the introduction of European plants and animals into the Western Hemisphere as a whole, or of the spread of cattle and horse raising from Patagonia to Labrador? Who has written on a Western Hemisphere scale the history of shipbuilding and commerce, mining, Christian missions, Indian policies, slavery and emancipation, constitutional development, arbitration, the effects of the Indian on European cultures, the rise of the common man, art, architecture, literature, or science? Who has tried to state the significance of the frontier in terms of the Americas?

Plainly, Greater America had a vast and virtually untapped past, the exploration of which would do much to enlarge historical frontiers.

By Bolton's standards, the next president, Charles A. Beard, was merely a provincial. But while Beard had ignored the possibilities of Greater America, he had succeeded in his recently published *Rise of American Civilization* (1927) in producing what has often been considered "the most brilliant historical survey of the American scene ever written,"[21] a synthetic treatment that took into account the political, social, economic, and cultural aspects of the American past. It was no surprise, then, that Beard announced in his presidential message that history,

20 For a list of the topics on which his graduate students have written, see *Greater America: Essays in Honor of Herbert Eugene Bolton* (Berkeley, 1945), pp. 549-672.

21 Samuel Eliot Morison, "Did Roosevelt Start the War? History Through a Beard," *Atlantic Monthly*, CLXXXII (August, 1948), 91.

as far as he was concerned, embraced everything that man had "done, said, felt, and thought" from the time he began his career on the planet.

Beard addressed the Association in 1933—at a time when the Roosevelt Administration, with which he had not yet come to quarrel, was grappling with agricultural, banking, monetary, relief, and labor problems. In keeping, then, with the dictates of the contemporary scene, he singled out some particular topics that needed special study. Returning to a subject to which he had called attention in his first published volume, *The Industrial Revolution* (1901), he emphasized that there was need for further investigations of economic conditions and relationships. Economic and biological pressures, he said, addressing the Association twenty years after the publication of *An Economic Interpretation of the Constitution of the United States* (1913), had not been studied enough as conditioning and determining factors. Furthermore, the history of ideas had been too much neglected by the American gildsman; and this Beard considered a serious failing, possibly the more so because he himself had tried—and most successfully perhaps in one of his lesser known pieces, an article on "Individualism and Capitalism"[22]—to view the past in the light of "the unfolding of ideas and interests in time-motion."

Guy Stanton Ford had some of the same suggestions to offer as his friend Beard. One of the few American specialists in Prussian history, Ford had been diverted to university administration. The upshot was that for many years Clio could make only small demands on his time; and so the scantiness of the literature of Prussian-German history in English, about which he often complained,[23] he could do little to remedy.

22 "Individualism and Capitalism," in *Encyclopaedia of the Social Sciences*, I, 145-63.

23 *Stein and the Era of Reform in Prussia, 1807-1815* (Princeton, 1922), p. v.

Ford's message of 1937 appeared in the same number of the *American Historical Review* that carried the obituary notice of J. Franklin Jameson, who, in his address of 1907, had urged the scholar to leave the overworked field of constitutional history. In 1937, however, the year of the sesquicentennial celebration of the drafting of the Constitution, Ford could call American constitutional history a "neglected field." Nor did he recommend any measures to change this state of affairs. By and large he took his stand with those scholars who considered science and invention the dominant factors in the modern world; compared to them, he thought, mere "instruments of government" had only minor repercussions on society. Ford's contention was that if the gildsman wished to present an accurate account of United States history since 1787, he should learn to view the Constitution in the light of the advances of technology and industrialization; he should study the changes in economic and social conditions that had been proceeding since 1787 and the changes in ways of thinking that accompanied the growth of science. For scientific advances affected man not only physically but mentally. They equipped him with new ideas and ways of thinking, and they shaped "the folkways to which laws and institutions must ultimately conform." For that matter, Ford remarked, it was unfortunate that when the gildsman did deal with science he frequently exalted physical science at the expense of biology, palaeontology, and comparative anatomy, sciences which had fundamentally altered man's view of himself and of his position in time.

Since Ford believed that history should again become the "synthesis of all that men knew of mankind and of human conduct," he advised the gildsman to make more use of studies like anthropology and psychology. A former student of Turner, he pointed out that these studies could provide important data concerning the social and physical conditions surrounding human behavior. Naturally, Ford, who in his own biography of Stein, had tried to stress economic conditions in Prussia,[24] rejoiced

24 *Loc. cit.*

that the American gildsman had abandoned the notion that United States history could be told exclusively in political terms, but he regretted that the gildsman had not yet come to learn the advantages of cooperation with other social scientists. Nevertheless, the complexities and varieties of human behavior were such that he should not run the risk of neglecting any shred of evidence that could enrich the content of history. By all means, then, said Ford, himself an active member of the Social Science Research Council, the historian should keep up with what was being done by statisticians, economists, political scientists, sociologists, ethnologists, anthropologists, and psychologists.

There were, to be sure, presidents who in the thirties used their addresses to present the results of some of their recent researches; and such presidents, too, indicated in their choice and handling of themes the extent to which things political and military had lost out in historical writing and the extent to which the synthetic view had gained ground. Evarts B. Greene, for example, whose career as a historian began with a dissertation on political history, *The Provincial Governor in the English Colonies of North America* (1898), dealt in his message of 1930 with "Persistent Problems of Church and State." In his treatment, however, he took into account many factors, political, religious, cultural, and economic. The same was true of the way in which William E. Dodd, the historian of the Old South, handled "The Emergence of the First Social Order in the United States" (1934) and of the way in which Michael Rostovtzeff, the foremost authority on ancient economic history, handled "The Hellenistic World and Its Economic Development" (1935). Both Dodd and Rostovtzeff had much to say about politics, but what they stressed was the interplay in history of political, social, cultural, and economic factors. Nor was this strange, for Dodd had long been attempting to do justice to the richness of the American past;[25]

25 See "Editor's Introduction," in Carl Lotus Becker, *Beginnings of the American People* (Boston, 1915), pp. ix-x.

and Rostovtzeff had long been attempting to connect social, economic, and cultural evolution with political and constitutional evolution.[26] It was this same interplay of factors that Frederic L. Paxson emphasized when, in 1938, he presented his account of "The Great Demobilization." Using the broad approach that he had used in his *American Democracy and the World War,* two volumes of which had already appeared, Paxson discussed not only the political and military aspects of American demobilization but its economic, social, cultural, emotional, and psychological aspects as well.

Paxson's successor, William S. Ferguson, also indicated in his message the broadness of his view of history. Years before 1939, Ferguson had made it plain in his important books on *Hellenistic Athens* (1911) and *Greek Imperialism* (1913) that history was "not all past politics," that politics, indeed, could not be understood except in relation to "other manifestations of national activity";[27] and it was, in effect, these same points that he made in his message on *"Polis* and *Idia* in Periclean Athens." Seeking to explain the compatibility of the private economic interests of the Athenian and his active participation in political life, he turned to an examination of the social and economic aspects of slavery, the effects of land and climate, and the conditions of agriculture, trade, industry, seafaring, and military and naval life. Yet though Ferguson addressed the Association shortly after the outbreak of the second World War, he did not recommend a renewed study of military history; he pointed out, as he had done years before in his *Hellenistic Athens,* that in the long run the achievements of the Athenians along military and naval lines were less important than their literary and artistic achievements.

26 *The Social and Economic History of the Roman Empire* (Oxford, 1926), p. vii; *A History of the Ancient World* (2 vols., Oxford, 1926-28), I, viii.

27 *Hellenistic Athens: An Historical Essay* (London, 1911), p. ix.

It was for another reason that Ferguson's successor, Max Farrand, referred to artistic achievements. Preeminently a political historian, a scholar whose knowledge of the framing of the American Constitution was unrivalled, Farrand, nevertheless, did not discuss the subject he knew best when his turn to address the Association came in 1940. Instead, he belabored the obvious in a message on "The Quality of Distinction." History, he said, was a synthetic subject, one that embraced the conclusions of other studies. It was, however, especially important for the historian to study such phases of life as painting, sculpture, and architecture, because, like the poet, the composer, and the artist, he dealt with values; and if he studied the creative arts, he was more likely to develop that "quality of distinction" which made for the long life of a historical work.

Farrand's successor, James Westfall Thompson, also urged the historian to study the creative arts, but his emphasis was different. One of the most productive medievalists of his time, a writer on political, social, economic, and cultural subjects, Thompson viewed the past in the light of what he called "the advancement of knowledge." Obviously, he did not want the gildsman to study "all knowledge" and all ideas. How, then, to determine the kind of knowledge that was worth studying? On the basis of the causal relationship that existed between knowledge and conduct, Thompson answered, explaining that knowledge that influenced behavior was the knowledge whose growth the historian would do well to trace. Thus, when Thompson recommended specific subjects for study, he singled out such "prime movers of human affairs" as law, government, religion, literature, and art.

Though Thompson was perhaps above all an economic historian, he saw no need in 1941 to issue a call for more attention to the study of economic history. Nor did his immediate successors, Arthur M. Schlesinger, Nellie Neilson, and William L. Westermann—all of whom had perhaps made their chief contributions in the field of economic history—recognize any need to press for more study of the subject. The truth was that by the forties the investigation of economic history in the United States had come into its own; so much so, that in 1945 Carlton J. H. Hayes, one of Robinson's earliest Ph. D.'s, announced that the time had come to stress cultural and social history no less than political and economic history. Hayes, whose own writings were heavily political but increasingly cultural in their emphasis, was impressed with the need to struggle against American intellectual isolationism; and he suggested that the historian had an important part to play in the struggle. Now that American frontiers lay on Pacific Islands, in the Azores, and on the Rhine and the Danube, the scholar should explore those subjects which were likely to help Americans to become aware of the "historic setting and current responsibilities" of their country. He should accent much more heavily than before linguistic and literary history, religious and church history, the history of art and science, and the history of ideas and their transmission. It was more than time to qualify and supplement the economic approach with a cultural one, for it was things cultural which in the past had had the profoundest effect on American relationships with the rest of the world; and since the same was likely to be true in the future, the gildsman would do well to champion the cause of cultural history. So it was that Hayes repeated an appeal that many a president had made in the years since Andrew D. White headed the Association.

CONCLUSION

It would be tempting to conclude this book with a number of startling generalizations. Yet while the presidential messages have provided little material with which to startle, they have provided enough perhaps from which to generalize. For one thing, few presidents valued historical study mainly for what it might do to develop understanding and overcome temporal provincialism. Still fewer valued it above all for the sake of the past and only incidentally for the sake of the present. Many valued it above all for the sake of the present and only incidentally for the sake of the past. Contemptuous of antiquarianism, these presidents considered it the main business of history to throw light on contemporary problems, to provide a background for current events. Preoccupied with the search for antecedents that would have immediate social utility, they seemed to forget that the past was once foreground. Determined to make use of history, they seemed to forget that to search for the present in the past has often been to put it there and to make what matters now matter then.

It is true that concern with the contemporary scene was not nearly so widespread in American historical writing in general as it was in the presidential messages. It is true, too, that individual presidents concentrated on the didactic possibilities of history in order to attract the attention of their audience. Certainly many a European would point to the presidential preoccupation with the practical value of historical study as just a further reflection of the practical cast of the American mind; but an examination of the writings of many of the leading European historians of recent times—Ashley, Churchill, Rowse, Hanotaux, Lavisse, Schmoller, Delbrück, Altamira, and Miliukov, to mention only a few—would reveal much the same preoccupation. In Europe as well as in the United States, many historians, feeling compelled to justify their existence, insisted that they were satisfying current social needs. Fearful of being treated as inmates of an ivory tower, they sought to demonstrate that like economists, political scientists, sociologists, and psychologists, they, too, had solutions to contemporary problems.

Some of the presidents who sought to take advantage of the immediate usefulness of history made sure to stress the need for readable historical prose, arguing that lack of literary merit would hinder the popularization of the lessons of the past. Other presidents advocated literary history above all for esthetic reasons, insisting that history had been literature in the past, and that it should continue to be so in the future. Few presidents took the stand that style was essentially unimportant or irrelevant to the gildsman. Surprisingly, however, no one bothered to note that just as there were competent historians who wrote poorly, so there were competent novelists, journalists, and literary critics who lacked the gift of style.

Some presidents accompanied their plea for well-written history with a criticism of the gildsman's obsession with facts. Such an obsession, they pointed out, was more than likely to guarantee dull reading. Other presidents, dealing with the problem of the selection of facts, set up standards that reflected their present-mindedness. Facts, they thought, should be chosen with an eye on the contemporary scene, with a view to establishing connections with the present. Few presidents favored their selection on the basis of what was important in the past. And few called attention to the need to discover additional facts.

Although there were frequent insistences that the gildsman should try to draw meaning from the stores of facts already available, there was not so much enthusiasm for the study of the philosophy and science of history as might have been anticipated. Individual presidents asserted their faith in the existence and discoverability of historical laws; in historical continuity and unity; in the active presence of God in history. But there can be no question that the discussion of the philosophy and science of history suffered by reason of the gildsman's fear of adventures in prophecy.

What ruled out the possibility of accurate predictions, according to some presidents, was the frequent appearance of extraordinary individuals. This is not to say, however, that the great man approach to history had any serious support in the messages. Though particular presidents ascribed varying degrees of creative and causal influence to the personal factor in history, no one denied that historical figures should be considered products of their times. And when it was a question of the standards by which such figures should be judged, it was the relativistic, rather than the Actonite, position that dominated. Few presidents opposed the notion that historical persons should be judged in the light of the standards of their own age.

Finally, views of the content of history were broad long before James Harvey Robinson loomed as a major figure on the American historiographical scene. Starting with Andrew D. White, many presidents emphasized the richness of the past. Influenced often by the examples of Voltaire, Macaulay, and Green, they insisted that the historian should deal not only with politics and war but with social, economic, and cultural developments. The drum and trumpet tradition had no drummer or trumpeter in the person of a president of the Association.

It is significant that several major topics were seriously neglected in the addresses. Consider, above all, the classroom teaching of history. Although most of the presidents were campus historians, it would be almost impossible to gather from many of their messages that they had spent a large part of their lives teaching undergraduate and graduate students. There are other neglected topics, too, which deserve to be considered in future presidential pronouncements. Historical craftsmanship, the techniques of historical criticism, the editing of documents, new methods of research, the contributions of archaeology to history, life in a papyrological seminar, imaginative literature as history, the study of historical causation, social class approaches to the past, statistics as a historical tool, the impact of fascism and communism on historiography, television in relation to the popularization of historical knowledge—these are some of the more important subjects that await their spokesmen among the future leaders of the Association. And if these presidents prepare addresses which can meet the standards set by such of their predecessors as Lea, Dunning, Andrews, Becker, and McIlwain, to mention only a few, the Association will more than have justified its continued existence.

BIBLIOGRAPHY

I

THE PRESIDENTIAL ADDRESSES

Adams, Charles Francis. "An Undeveloped Function," American Historical Association, *Annual Report, 1901*, I, 49-93. Washington, 1902.

Adams, Charles Kendall. "Recent Historical Work in the Colleges and Universities of Europe and America" [1889], American Historical Association, *Papers*, IV, 39-65. New York, 1890.

Adams, George Burton. "History and the Philosophy of History," *American Historical Review*, XIV (1909), 221-36.

Adams, Henry. "The Tendency of History," American Historical Association, *Annual Report, 1894*, pp. 17-23. Washington, 1895.

Andrews, Charles McLean. "The American Revolution: An Interpretation," *American Historical Review*, XXXI (1926), 219-32.

——. "These Forty Years," *American Historical Review*, XXX (1925), 225-50.

Angell, James Burrill. "The Inadequate Recognition of Diplomatists by Historians," American Historical Association, *Annual Report, 1893*, pp. 15-24. Washington, 1894.

Baldwin, Simeon Eben. "Religion Still the Key to History," *American Historical Review*, XII (1907), 219-43.

Bancroft, George. "On Self-government: Address of Welcome to the American Historical Association" [1886], American Historical Association, *Papers*, II, 7-13. New York, 1888.

Beard, Charles Austin. "Written History as an Act of Faith," *American Historical Review*, XXXIX (1934), 219-31.

Becker, Carl Lotus. "Everyman His Own Historian," *American Historical Review*, XXXVII (1932), 221-36.

Bolton, Herbert Eugene. "The Epic of Greater America," *American Historical Review*, XXXVIII (1933), 448-74.

Breasted, James Henry. "The New Crusade," *American Historical Review*, XXXIV (1929), 215-36.

Burr, George Lincoln. "The Freedom of History," *American Historical Review*, XXII (1917), 253-71.

Channing, Edward. "An Historical Retrospect," *American Historical Review*, XXVI (1921), 191-202.

Cheyney, Edward Potts. "Law in History," *American Historical Review*, XXIX (1924), 231-48.

Dodd, William Edward. "The Emergence of the First Social Order in the United States," *American Historical Review*, XL (1935), 217-31.

Dunning, William Archibald. "Truth in History," *American Historical Review*, XIX (1914), 217-29.

Eggleston, Edward. "The New History," American Historical Association, *Annual Report, 1900*, I, 37-47. Washington, 1901.

364 BIBLIOGRAPHY

Farrand, Max. "The Quality of Distinction," *American Historical Review,* XLVI (1941), 509-22.

Ferguson, William Scott. "*Polis* and *Idia* in Periclean Athens: The Relation between Public Service and Private Activities," *American Historical Review,* XLV (1940), 269-78.

Fisher, George Park. "The Function of the Historian as a Judge of Historic Persons," American Historical Association, *Annual Report, 1898,* pp. 15-33. Washington, 1899.

Ford, Guy Stanton. "Some Suggestions to American Historians," *American Historical Review,* XLIII (1938), 253-69.

Ford, Worthington Chauncey. "The Editorial Function in United States History," *American Historical Review,* XXIII (1918), 273-86.

Greene, Evarts Boutell. "Persistent Problems of Church and State," *American Historical Review,* XXXVI (1931), 257-73.

Hart, Albert Bushnell. "Imagination in History," *American Historical Review,* XV (1910), 227-51.

Haskins, Charles Homer. "European History and American Scholarship," *American Historical Review,* XXVIII (1923), 215-27.

Hayes, Carlton Joseph Huntley. "The American Frontier—Frontier of What?", *American Historical Review,* LI (1946), 199-216.

Henry, William Wirt. "The Causes Which Produced the Virginia of the Revolutionary Period," American Historical Association, *Annual Report, 1891,* pp. 15-29. Washington, 1892.

Hoar, George Frisbie. "Popular Discontent with Representative Government," American Historical Association, *Annual Report, 1895,* pp. 21-43. Washington, 1896.

Jameson, John Franklin. "The American *Acta Sanctorum,*" *American Historical Review,* XIII (1908), 286-302.

Jay, John. "The Demand for Education in American History" [1890], American Historical Association, *Papers,* V, 19-43. New York, 1891.

Jusserand, Jean Jules. "The School for Ambassadors," *American Historical Review,* XXVII (1922), 426-64.

Lea, Henry Charles. "Ethical Values in History," *American Historical Review,* IX (1904), 233-46.

McIlwain, Charles Howard. "The Historian's Part in a Changing World," *American Historical Review,* XLII (1937), 207-24.

McLaughlin, Andrew Cunningham. "American History and American Democracy," *American Historical Review,* XX (1915), 255-76.

McMaster, John Bach. "Old Standards of Public Morals," *American Historical Review,* XI (1906), 515-28.

Mahan, Alfred Thayer. "Subordination in Historical Treatment," American Historical Association, *Annual Report, 1902,* I, 49-63. Washington, 1903.

Munro, Dana Carleton. "War and History," *American Historical Review,* XXXII (1927), 219-31.

Neilson, Nellie. "The Early Pattern of the Common Law," *American Historical Review,* XLIX (1944), 199-212.

Paxson, Frederic Logan. "The Great Demobilization," *American Historical Review*, XLIV (1939), 237-51.

Poole, William Frederick. "The Early Northwest" [1888], American Historical Association, *Papers*, III, 277-300. New York, 1889.

Rhodes, James Ford. "History," American Historical Association, *Annual Report, 1899*, I, 45-63. Washington, 1900.

Robinson, James Harvey. "The Newer Ways of Historians," *American Historical Review*, XXXV (1930), 245-55.

Roosevelt, Theodore. "History as Literature," *American Historical Review*, XVIII (1913), 473-89.

Rostovtzeff, Michael Ivanovich. "The Hellenistic World and Its Economic Development," *American Historical Review*, XLI (1936), 231-52.

Schlesinger Arthur Meier. "What Then Is the American, This New Man?", *American Historical Review*, XLVIII (1943), 225-44.

Schouler, James. "A New Federal Convention," American Historical Association, *Annual Report, 1897*, pp. 21-34. Washington, 1898.

Sloane, William Milligan. "The Substance and Vision of History," *American Historical Review*, XVII (1912), 235-51.

Smith, Goldwin. "The Treatment of History," *American Historical Review*, X (1905), 511-20.

Stephens, Henry Morse. "Nationality and History," *American Historical Review*, XXI (1916), 225-36.

Storrs, Richard Salter. "Contributions Made to Our National Development by Plain Men," American Historical Association, *Annual Report, 1896*, I, 37-63. Washington, 1897.

Taylor, Henry Osborn. "A Layman's View of History," *American Historical Review*, XXXIII (1928), 247-56.

Thayer, William Roscoe. "Fallacies in History," *American Historical Review*, XXV (1920), 179-90.

——. "Vagaries of Historians," *American Historical Review*, XXIV (1919), 183-95.

Thompson, James Westfall. "The Age of Mabillon and Montfaucon," *American Historical Review*, XLVII (1942), 225-44.

Turner, Frederick Jackson. "Social Forces in American History," *American Historical Review*, XVI (1911), 217-33.

Westermann, William Linn. "Between Slavery and Freedom," *American Historical Review*, L (1945), 213-27.

White, Andrew Dickson. "The Influence of American Ideas upon the French Revolution" [1885], American Historical Association, *Papers*, I, 429-33. New York, 1886.

——. "On Studies in General History and the History of Civilization" [1884], American Historical Association, *Papers*, I, 49-72. New York, 1886.

Winsor, Justin. "Manuscript Sources of American History—The Conspicuous Collections Extant" [1887], American Historical Association, *Papers*, III, 9-27. New York, 1889.

366

BIBLIOGRAPHY

II
SELECTED WRITINGS ABOUT THE PRESIDENTS

Owing to the high cost of publication, it has been necessary to restrict this bibliography to a fragment of its original size.

Adams, James Truslow. *Henry Adams.* New York, 1933.

Anniversary Essays in Mediaeval History by Students of Charles Homer Haskins Presented on His Completion of Forty Years of Teaching. Boston, 1929.

Athenian Studies Presented to William Scott Ferguson. Cambridge, 1940.

Bainton, Roland H. *George Lincoln Burr: His Life.* Ithaca, 1943.

Bean, Walton E. "Revolt Among Historians," *Sewanee Review,* XLVII (1939), 330-341.

Beard, Charles Austin. "Retrospect and Recollection." William E. Dodd, Jr., and Martha Dodd, eds. *Ambassador Dodd's Diary, 1933-1938.* New York, 1941.

——. "Turner's 'The Frontier in American History'." Malcolm Cowley and Bernard Smith, eds. *Books That Changed Our Minds.* New York, 1939.

Becker, Carl Lotus. *Cornell University: Founders and the Founding.* Ithaca, 1943.

——. *Everyman His Own Historian: Essays on History and Politics.* New York, 1935. Contains essays on Henry Adams, Bancroft, and Turner.

Bellot, H. Hale. "Some Aspects of the Recent History of American Historiography," Royal Historical Society, *Transactions,* Fourth Series, XXVIII, 121-48. London, 1946.

Billington, Ray A. "The Historians of the Northwest Ordinance," Illinois State Historical Society, *Journal,* XL (1947), 397-413.

Bishop, Joseph Bucklin. *Theodore Roosevelt and His Time Shown in His Own Letters.* 2 vols. New York, 1920.

Bradley, Edward Sculley. *Henry Charles Lea: A Biography.* Philadelphia, 1931.

Breasted, Charles. *Pioneer to the Past: The Story of James Henry Breasted, Archaeologist.* New York, 1943.

Burr, George Lincoln. "Andrew Dickson White." Lois O. Gibbons, ed. *George Lincoln Burr: Selections from His Writings.* Ithaca, 1943.

Casey, P. H. *Notes on A History of Auricular Confession: H. C. Lea's Account of the Power of the Keys in the Early Church.* Philadelphia, 1899.

Channing, Edward. "Justin Winsor," *American Historical Review,* III (1898), 197-202.

Church of the Pilgrims. *The Fiftieth Anniversary of the Installation of Richard Salter Storrs as Pastor of the Church of the Pilgrims.* Brooklyn, 1897.

Columbia University. *A Bibliography of the Faculty of Political Science of Columbia University, 1880-1930.* New York, 1931. Contains lists of the writings of Beard, Dunning, Greene, Hayes, Robinson, Sloane, and Westermann.

Coulton, G. G. *Sectarian History*. Taunton, England, 1937.

Craven, Avery, ed. *Essays in Honor of William E. Dodd by His Former Students at the University of Chicago*. Chicago, 1935.

Curti, Merle. "A Great Teacher's Teacher," *Social Education*, XIII (1949), 263-66, 274.

Dunning, William Archibald. *Truth in History and Other Essays*. New York, 1937. Contains essays on Henry Adams, Hoar, Rhodes, and Schouler.

Earle, Edward Mead, ed. *Nationalism and Internationalism: Essays Inscribed to Carlton J. H. Hayes*. New York, 1950.

Essays in Colonial History Presented to Charles McLean Andrews by His Students. New Haven, 1931. Contains essays by J. Franklin Jameson and Nellie Neilson.

Essays in History and Political Theory in Honor of Charles Howard McIlwain. Cambridge, 1936.

Essays in Intellectual History Dedicated to James Harvey Robinson by His Former Seminar Students. New York, 1929.

Farrand, Max. "Frederick Jackson Turner: A Memoir," Massachusetts Historical Society, *Proceedings*, 1932-1936, LXV, 432-440. Boston, 1940.

Garner, James W., ed. *Studies in Southern History and Politics Inscribed to William Archibald Dunning by His Former Pupils the Authors*. New York, 1914.

Gershoy, Leo. "Carl Becker on Progress and Power," *American Historical Review*, LV (1949), 22-35.

Gillett, Frederick H. *George Frisbie Hoar*. Boston, 1934.

Goldman, Eric F. *John Bach McMaster: American Historian*. Philadelphia, 1943.

———, ed. *Historiography and Urbanization: Essays in American History in Honor of W. Stull Holt*. Baltimore, 1941.

Grattan, C. Hartley. "The Historians Cut Loose." Harry Elmer Barnes. *In Quest of Truth and Justice: De-Bunking the War Guilt Myth*. Chicago, 1928.

Greater America: Essays in Honor of Herbert Eugene Bolton. Berkeley, 1945.

Hale, Edward Everett. "George F. Hoar," American Antiquarian Society, *Proceedings*, New Series, XVII (1905), 150-66.

Hamilton, J. G. de Roulhac. "Introduction," William A. Dunning, *Truth in History and Other Essays*. New York, 1937.

Haskins, Charles Homer. "Henry Charles Lea." *Studies in Mediaeval Culture*. Oxford, 1929.

Hayes, Carlton J. H. "Evarts Boutell Greene (1870-1947)," American Philosophical Society, *Year Book, 1947*. Philadelphia, 1948.

Hendricks, Luther Virgil. *James Harvey Robinson: Teacher of History*. New York, 1946.

Hofstadter, Richard. "Turner and the Frontier Myth," *American Scholar*, XVIII (1949), 433-43.

Howe, Mark Antony DeWolfe. *James Ford Rhodes, American Historian.* New York, 1929.
——. *The Life and Letters of George Bancroft.* 2 vols. New York, 1908.
Hutchinson, William T., ed. *The Marcus W. Jernegan Essays in American Historiography.* Chicago, 1937. Contains essays on Henry Adams, Bancroft, Channing, McMaster, Mahan, Rhodes, Roosevelt, Schouler, Turner, and Wilson.
Johnson Allen, Dumas Malone, and Harris E. Starr, eds. *Dictionary of American Biography.* 21 vols. New York, 1929-1944. Contains articles on C. F. Adams, C. K. Adams, G. B. Adams, Henry Adams, Angell, Baldwin, Bancroft, Breasted, Channing, Dunning, Eggleston, Fisher, Henry, Hoar, Jay, Lea, McMaster, Mahan, Munro, Poole, Rhodes, Roosevelt, Schouler, Sloane, Stephens, Storrs, Thayer, Turner, White, and Winsor.
Kraus, Michael. *A History of American History.* New York, 1937.
Lingelbach, William E. "Edward Potts Cheyney (1860-1947)," American Philosophical Society, *Year Book, 1947.* Philadelphia, 1948.
Livezey, William E. *Mahan on Sea Power.* Norman, Oklahoma, 1947.
MacMahon, Arthur W. "Charles Austin Beard as a Teacher," *Political Science Quarterly,* LXV (1950), 1-19.
Mood, Fulmer. "Turner's Formative Period." *The Early Writings of Frederick Jackson Turner.* Madison, 1938.
Morison, Samuel Eliot. "Albert Bushnell Hart, 1889-1939," Massachusetts Historical Society, *Proceedings,* 1936-1941, LXVI, 434-438. Boston, 1942.
——. "Did Roosevelt Start the War? History Through a Beard," *Atlantic Monthly,* CLXXXII (August 1948), 91-97.
——. "Edward Channing: A Memoir," Massachusetts Historical Society, *Proceedings,* 1930-1932, LXIV, 250-284. Boston, 1932.
Morris, Richard Brandon, ed. *The Era of the American Revolution: Studies Inscribed to Evarts Boutell Greene.* New York, 1939.
New Spain and the Anglo-American West: Historical Contributions Presented to Herbert Eugene Bolton. 2 vols. Los Angeles, 1932.
Newberry Library. *Memorial Sketch of Dr. William Frederick Poole.* Chicago, 1895.
Nye, Russel B. *George Bancroft: Brahmin Rebel.* New York, 1944.
Odum, Howard W., ed. *American Masters of Social Science: An Approach to the Study of the Social Sciences through a Neglected Field of Biography.* New York, 1927. Contains essays on Dunning, Robinson, and Turner.
Paetow, Louis J., ed. *The Crusades and Other Historical Essays Presented to Dana C. Munro by His Former Students.* New York, 1928.
Pease, Theodore C. "Evarts Boutell Greene, 1870-1947," Illinois State Historical Society, *Journal,* XLI (1948), 7-15.
Persecution and Liberty: Essays in Honor of George Lincoln Burr. New York, 1931.
Pringle, Henry F. *Theodore Roosevelt: A Biography.* New York, 1931.

Puleston, William D. *Mahan: The Life and Work of Captain Alfred Thayer Mahan, U.S.N.* New Haven, 1939.

Randel, William Peirce. *Edward Eggleston: Author of The Hoosier School-Master.* New York, 1946.

Records and Addresses in Memory of Simeon E. Baldwin, 1840-1927. New Haven, 1928.

Reinhold, Meyer. "Historian of the Classic World: A Critique of Rostovtzeff," *Science and Society,* X (1946), 361-391.

Rogers, Walter P. *Andrew D. White and the Modern University.* Ithaca, 1942.

Sabine, George H. "Carl Lotus Becker." Carl L. Becker, *Freedom and Responsibility in the American Way of Life.* New York, 1945.

Saveth, Edward N. *American Historians and European Immigrants, 1875-1925.* New York, 1948.

Schuyler, Robert Livingston. "John Franklin Jameson," *American Historical Review,* XLIII (1938), 243-252.

Seligman, Edwin R. A., ed. *Encyclopaedia of the Social Sciences.* 15 vols. New York, 1930-1935. Contains articles on C. F. Adams, G. B. Adams, Henry Adams, Angell, Bancroft, Dunning, Eggleston, Lea, McMaster, Mahan, Rhodes, Roosevelt, Schouler, Smith, Stephens, Thayer, Turner, and White.

Sloane, William M. "George Bancroft—in Society, in Politics, in Letters," *Century Illustrated Monthly Magazine,* New Series, XI (1887), 473-487.

Smith, Charles Forster. *Charles Kendall Adams: A Life-Sketch.* Madison, 1925.

Thorndike, Lynn. "Charles Homer Haskins (1870-1937)," *Isis,* XXVIII (1938), 53-56.

Vincent, George E. "Guy Stanton Ford: An Appreciation." G. S. Ford. *On and Off the Campus.* Minneapolis, 1938.

Wallace, Elisabeth. "Goldwin Smith and Social Reform," *Canadian Historical Review, XXIX* (1948), 363-69.

White, Morton G. *Social Thought in America: The Revolt against Formalism.* New York, 1949.

INDEX